The Children
of
Château de la Hille

by

Sebastian Steiger

Translated into English by Jocelyn Hoy
With a Preface by Henry Massie

The Children of Château de la Hille

Sebastian Steiger

Translated from the French and German by Jocelyn Hoy
Preface © 2017 Henry Massie

Lexographic Press
33 W Huron St, Unit 305
Chicago, Illinois 60654, US

ISBN: 978-0-9847142-5-4

Cover design and production: James Sparling, Lexographic
Text design and production: Lexographic, Chicago

Set in Quixo Light 9.5/12pt

Printed in the United States of America

Wonderful stories—some in the children's own words--of endurance, overcoming, and tragically for a few, surrendering.

It is not easy to capture the essence of childhood, especially when children live in constant danger and under the hardship of cold, hunger and disease. Yet Sebastian Steiger writes, in this translation by Jocelyn Hoy, about a group of youngsters and teenagers, most Jewish orphans sheltered during World War II in southern France, with such liveliness, humor, and energy that I was transfixed. They made me laugh, cry and pray for the children who now--those alive--are in their 80s and 90s. These are wonderful stories of endurance, overcoming, and tragically for a few, surrendering--some told in the children's own words from their diaries.

Lenore Terr, MD, Clinical Professor of Psychiatry,
University of California, School of Medicine, San Francisco;
author of Too Scared to Cry, Unchained Memories,
and Magical Moments of Change.

Under the threat of death one hundred children were hidden at an abandoned château in Vichy France, it's gate painted with the Swiss Red Cross. The cross was not enough to protect them from the SS nor the French *melice*. You can see the children's faces in the photographs, hear their voices in their diaries, and feel the guiding voice of Sebastian Steiger who came from Switzerland as a young man to teach and try to keep them alive. Reading this book was like watching Stalag 17, with children just out of reach of death. Some escaped over mountains to Switzerland guided through snow by young Swiss women who worked at the château; some were guided by *passeurs* over the Pyrenees into Spain; some were betrayed by their *passeurs* and lost their lives; many endured hoping in vain for visas to America and elsewhere.

In the pages of this book you can listen breathlessly as the police invade the chateau to try to find the teenagers' (always fair game to the Nazis) hiding place and turn them over to the SS. At first Steiger himself couldn't find the hiding place until he was shown. Though comparisons to Anne Frank's diary are apt, a better comparison is to Margo Minco's *Bitter Herbs*, for her father had prepared an emergency exit and practiced her escape. She survived.

Nathan Szajnberg, MD
San Francisco Center for Psychoanalysis;
Former Freud Professor, Hebrew University, Israel.

Contents

Contents

About the Author

Sebastian Steiger was born on October 14, 1918 in Oltingen, a small village in the Swiss canton Basel-Campagne. His father, Walter Steiger, was a Reformed pastor in the parishes of Oltingen, Wenslingen and Anwil. Sebastian lived in Oltingen with his four brothers and sisters while attending primary school. When his father was appointed pastor in Binningen, a suburb of Basel, Sebastian attended lycée there. In Schiers, he completed his higher education in teaching. In 1940 he received his teaching certificate and worked as a substitute teacher until 1943 while he was continuing course work for a semester at the University of Zürich.

From 1943 to 1945 Sebastian Steiger served in the Children's Aid program of the Swiss Red Cross in occupied France. In 1946 he completed his studies at the University of Zürich earning an advanced degree in health education. In the same year he was appointed instructor at the primary school in Arlesheim, and in 1947 at a girls' school in Basel. He married in 1956 and was the father of three children.

From 1958 to 1990 Sebastian Steiger organized the "Day of the Jewish Child," an annual event in May dedicated to the memory of the million-and-a-half Jewish children killed by the Nazis. He often visited and lectured in Israel. When he retired in 1982 he spent nearly six years compiling *Die Kinder von Schloß La Hille (The Children of Château de La Hille)*, a book recounting his daily life under the German occupation in France.

Sebastian Steiger was a member of the Association for Jewish-Christian Alliance and of the Swiss-Israeli Society. He was a central figure on the Committee of the Friends of the Swiss Children's Village Kirjath Jearim in Israel. For more than 40 years he was engaged in promoting Israel.

Forty-one years after their shared experience at the Château de La Hille in France, Ruth Schütz and Peter Salz, two of the surviving children from the Château, organized a reunion of all the "Children of the Château de La Hille" whom they were able to contact in Europe, Australia and the United States. The reunion took place in 1985 at the kibbutz Lehavor Habasham in Israel. Sebastian Steiger described this reunion as one of the most meaningful experiences in his life.

Sebastian Steiger died in July 2012 in Basel.

Preface to the English Edition
Dr. Henry Massie

The Château de La Hille is a stolid, forbidding manor that sits on a hillside shelf (*hilla* in old Norse) above the Lèze River in the foothills of the Pyrenees mountains in the south of France. In the early 20th century it was abandoned. Then came World War II and it rang with the laughter of barefoot children in the summer and the clatter of their wooden clogs on cold, bare floors in winter. One hundred Jewish children found shelter there from the Nazis after their parents were sent to death camps.

The story of how young volunteers from the Swiss Red Cross— Aid to Children (*Croix Rouge Suisse—Secours aux Enfants*) took over the abandoned Château and gave a refuge to the children during the German occupation of France is not unknown. A few of the survivors have written their story as adults, as have some of the adults who protected the children. However the most detailed account of the children's time at the Château de La Hille, by their school teacher Sebastian Steiger, *The Children of Château de La Hille*, has not been available in English until now.

Moved by a desire to help children during the time of horrors, Steiger joined neutral Switzerland's Red Cross and was posted to the Château in 1943. It was a year into the Occupation, he was 25, and had just received his teacher's certificate.

His memoir first appeared in his native German in 1992, and was translated into French in 1999. It is a unique document of the times because of how astutely it describes the children, and how compellingly it shows Steiger and the other volunteers, mostly young, inventing ways to meet the children's needs. The children rallied to him for support, and sometimes even supported him in his novice efforts.

Ranging in age from mid-childhood to mid-teens, the children largely came from German, Austrian, and Polish Jewish families, and with few exceptions had already lost both parents. In some instances the parents had found temporary shelter for their children before they were wrenched away by the Gestapo; some of the children escaped Nazi detention on their own. Then sympathetic citizens and volunteer organizations helped them along many different paths to the south of France where they were safe until 1942. Then they had to go into hiding.

The Château de La Hille lies in the remote Ariège region of France many kilometers from the nearest gendarme and Gestapo posts of the time in Pamiers. When the Swiss Red Cross arrived there was no plumbing, heating, or electricity. But it had a watchtower where lookouts could see approaching authorities, and a secret cellar where the children could hide when necessary.

Telling his story in a teacher's clear, direct voice, Steiger's memoir conveys his sense of wonder as he gets to know each child, as he discovers their resilience and bravery, and discovers his own creativity in helping them. In fact it is a story of children and teacher working together to create a semblance of a normal life in the face of ever-present danger—to continue their education, keep warm, swim in local streams in summer, grow and forage for food, and raise the alert when the enemy approached.

Each chapter of the memoir narrates different episodes of life at the Château during the war and shows the roles, mishaps and successes of all of the volunteer caregivers with their children. The stories show the adults to have been bold, brave, and indefatigable; photographs of them and the children, often smiling, belie the tragedy in the youngsters' lives.

Steiger himself was selfless: He put his life in jeopardy by giving his identity card, marked Protestant, to one of the Jewish teenagers; under the nose of the Gestapo and collaborationist gendarmes he scoured villages for chalk for the slate boards and readers so he could conduct classes; he figured out how to help children overcome enuresis; and he treated their injuries and illness with what little was at hand. In the eyes of the children he was their doctor, their father or older brother, their recreational director, and the teacher who helped them believe that all was not lost because they could go to class in the Château to learn math, reading, writing, and French every day. In 1993 Israel honored Sebastian Steiger as one of the "Just Among Nations."

In the spring of 2016, my friend, Martine Robin, who grew up in the village of Bonnac near the Château, gave me the French edition of Sebastian Steiger's memoir and asked if I could arrange an English translation. Though living in Paris, Martine remains connected to her childhood home and is on the board of the one-room memorial museum to the wartime Château in the village of Montégut. When I read Steiger's memoir I was transfixed. I am a child psychiatrist in Berkeley, California, formerly on the faculty of the University of California School of Medicine in San Francisco, and have done research on childhood trauma. Steiger's memoir is far more vivid than any work I have done. He makes personal what I tried to show academically—that the presence of strong, kindly adults for children to identify with and to lean on can work miracles in sheltering them against the ravages of losing parents and confronting cruelty.

To translate Steiger's memoir into English, I enlisted Jocelyn Hoy, Ph.D., a recently-retired member of the philosophy faculty at the University of California in Santa Cruz, California. She worked from both the German original and the French translation. In addition I visited the Château de La Hille and the surrounding area, including the not distant site of the Le Vernet camp. There the French Vichy Government, in collaboration with the Nazis, kept thousands of political prisoners, Jews, and other "undesirables" before loading many onto boxcars to ship to death camps in Germany and Poland. The Swiss Red Cross managed to separate 48 Jewish children from this camp and get them to the Château in time. I also deepened my understanding of the Château by meeting with the local board members of the museum. They are the grown children of local French men and women who were enemies of the occupiers, partisans of the free French, and gave clandestine help to the Château.

I also arranged with the Holocaust Museum and Learning Center in St. Louis, Missouri, directed by Jean Cavender, where I grew up, to sponsor the translation project. One of the children of La Hille, Addi Nussbaum, came to America after the war and became a professor of mathematics at Washington University in St. Louis, where my father was also on the faculty. Addi's son, Karl Nussbaum, is a video artist who recently created a surrealistic video memorial to his father and the Château de La Hille titled *Days on End*.

In addition I had the opportunity to meet with two of the grown children from the Château. Rosa Moreau (in childhood Rosa Marimon), in her mid-80s, drove from her home several hours away, for my visit. She remembers her time at the Château as like "an endless summer camp." She added, "But I had my parents." She and her parents had crossed the Pyrenees from Spain to France to escape the fascist forces during the Spanish Civil War in the late 1930s. Her mother managed the laundry at the Château and her father cultivated the vegetable garden, with help from the children.

Another still very active survivor of the château in his mid-80s is Isy Veleris (Isi Bravermann as a child) whom I met with in Paris where he lives. He became a highly successful photographer of the cultural scene and fashion in America and France. He and his parents fled Belgium during the war for the south of France, but he shortly lost his father to illness. When he was nine, he and his mother were hiding from the collaborationist French gendarmes in a barn. He went out to look for food, and his mother was discovered and sent to her death. Isy found refuge at La Hille, and remains bonded to it to this day. Not long ago he helped design the memorial stone and plaque that sits outside the Château. When he told me of losing his mother 73 years earlier he began to cry. "I still feel it. I still feel guilty as if I were responsible in some way for her death, of abandoning her."

I know personally how the tragedy of the Holocaust endures in the survivors. My mother, from Poland, was a university student in France in the late 1930s. When the Nazis came to power she used a "white marriage" (paper marriage) to go to Palestine, and later to get a visa to emigrate to America. Her mother died at Treblinka and her younger brother was killed fighting with the Polish partisans in the forests near Bialystock, Poland. When my mother was 97, she would look at the photograph of her brother on her bedroom wall and still cry 62 years later.

Amazingly 89 of the 100 children at the Château de La Hille survived the war.

Of the eleven who did not, several were caught trying to cross the border from France into Switzerland and Spain; a few of the older boys joined the *Maquis*, the underground French resistance, and died fighting; one child was caught near the Château, and one child died of grief in a psychiatric hospital. The 89 survivors have come together from many parts of the world for reunions with each other and their wartime caregivers at La Hille and in Israel. This is one of the few relatively happy stories to come out of the Holocaust. It is also a message about the importance of offering human kindness and support to the hundreds of thousands of refugees from war in our day.

Henry Massie
Berkeley, California, 2016

References

1. *Die Kinder von Schloss La Hille,* Sebastian Steiger, Brunnen Verlag, Basel 1992.

2. *Les Enfants du Château de La Hille*, Sebastian Steiger, Translated by Joséphine Mikorey and Lydie Smagghe, Brunnen, Verlag, Basel, 1999.

3. *La Filière—En France Occupée 1942-1944* (The Path—In Occupied France 1942-1944), Anne-Marie Im Hof-Piguet, Parcours, Editions De La Thiele, 1985. This is the memoir of one of the young Swiss volunteers who grew up near the Swiss— French border. She personally guided children from La Hille on mountain trails in harrowing conditions from France into neutral Switzerland.

4. *The Children of La Hille: Eluding Nazi Capture During World War II,* Walter Reed, Syracuse University Press, Syracuse, 2015. One of the children looks back from adulthood.

5. *Inge—A Girl's Journey Across Nazi Europe,* Inge Joseph Bleier and David E. Gumpert, William Eerdman Publishing, Grand Rapids and Cambridge, U.K., 2004. One of the children looks back from adulthood.

6. *Days on End,* a video by Karl Nussbaum memorializing his father and the Château de La Hille, available at: https://video.com/143603123.

7. *Lives Across Time/Growing Up—Paths to Emotional Health and Emotional Illness in 76 People from Birth to Age 30*, Henry Massie and Nathan Szajnberg, Karnac Books, London, 2008.

8. *Art of a Jewish Woman—From the Holocaust to the Halls of Modern Art* [original title, *Felice's Worlds*], Henry Massie, an ebook, BooksBnimble, New Orleans, 2012, and Amazon. This is the biography of my mother, Felice Ozerovicz Massie, whose peregrinations led from her home in a village on the Polish-Russian border, to France and to Palestine, and ultimately to America and a life in abstract expressionist art.

Translator's Preface

Sebastian Steiger's book *The Children of Château de La Hille* was first published in German in 1992 and translated into French in 1999. While German was the original language of Steiger's text, French was the official language of the Château de La Hille. The original one hundred Jewish children who found refuge at the Château de La Hille were almost all native German speakers, while the children who subsequently took their places were mostly native French speakers, with some Spanish as well. Of the five teachers and director, four were native Swiss-German speakers, while only one was a native French speaker. One can imagine, then, that the conversations among the children themselves, among the teachers, and between the children and teachers were a mixture or alternation of German and French.

Sebastian Steiger was born, raised and spent his career working in the area of Basel, the geographic and linguistic confluence of Switzerland, Germany and France. Since French was the official language of the Château, Mr. Steiger, a native Swiss German speaker, was teaching his younger students to read and write in French. He was probably speaking French with them both in the classroom and out on their many excursions into the countryside. When he compiles their stories for publication over forty years later, one can well imagine that the young French voices from the past are reverberating in the background as the stories take shape in the German words on the pages. Given the intertwining of French and German at the Château de La Hille, it seems appropriate that my work translating this text was a constant back-and-forth from the German to the French, and from the French to the German.

While my English translation is a particular rendition of the German and French texts, English too entered the life-world of the Château de La Hille at that time. The staff, consisting of three Spanish couples who were refugees from the Spanish Civil War as well as the teachers and director, would gather in their salon to listen to "the English"—how they referred to the BBC news broadcasts. While listening to English in this way risked severe Nazi retribution, when they finally hear the news of the long anticipated Allied invasion, English becomes the language of their liberation.

When Mr. Steiger revisits the Château de La Hille after many, many years, he sadly reflects on how the Château has died: "It is dead without the children." Metaphorically, the "language of the Château" consisted of the high-pitched voices of the children, their clear laughter and shrieks of joy at play—the sounds from any children's playground during recess. What you hear is not for the most part specifically German, French or English, but some more universal sounds of excitement, joy, and laughter, and also perhaps cries of fear, pain, anger, or loneliness. In his moving stories Mr. Steiger shares with us the underlying emotions of these particular children caught in this particular war-torn space and time.

Uncovering these emotions and experiences from the standpoint of children and teachers lends his history insight and impact usually forgotten or neglected.

Jocelyn Hoy
Santa Cruz, California, 2016

The Children
of
Château de la Hille

Foreword to the German Edition (1992) by Professor Ernst Ludwig Ehrlich

I am deeply pleased that Sebastian Steiger's valuable book has finally been published, for this book greatly contributes to our knowledge of the war in France. The many episodes recounted by the author as if they had taken place only yesterday constitute historical documents of great importance.

Today we must live with the fact that the German Nazis organized and carried out the Holocaust. But the success of these Nazi criminals was possible only thanks to the collaboration of others, in other countries. The Vichy government, unfortunately, played a considerable role in this tragedy. Switzerland also has her "skeletons in the closet"—the untold numbers of Jews, young and old, refused entry at the Swiss borders only to be deported later on to Auschwitz. It is therefore all the more important to become acquainted through these pages with those people who were motivated only by the dictates of their conscience to willingly leave behind their relative security in Switzerland to aid the Jewish children in occupied France. This book witnesses to the fact that many of these children were saved, while some were not able to escape the police: the police were stronger.

In these stories of real experiences we learn more than in many history books that devote only a few lines or no more than a page to the events of the Nazi period in France. Sebastian Steiger has succeeded in making his activities among the Jewish children come to life. He represents "another" Switzerland, different from the one that denied entry to the Jews on the grounds that "the boat was too full."

Let us remember not only those many people who followed the convictions of Dr. Heinrich Rothmund and his collaborationist officers, but also those Swiss people who risked their lives to oppose them. Sebastian Steiger is one of the latter. As a young teacher at the time, he did everything he could to save the Jewish children from the fate allotted to them by the Nazi executioners and their accomplices in various countries.

We have high expectations for the readers of this book: that they

3

identify with the victims and not their persecutors. With these pages, the deeds of Sebastian Steiger and others devoted to the Château de La Hille become part of history.

Professor Ernst Ludwig Ehrlich
Secretary General of the Association for the Judeo-Christian Alliance

Author's Prologue

How I Came to Set Out for Occupied France

After I obtained by teaching certificate in 1940, I worked as a substitute teacher, for many of the other teachers were already mobilized to the front. As a substitute teacher I had students of all ages in various schools. I had vaguely heard about "homes" in France, directed by some Swiss, devoted to helping children afflicted by the war. "That's what I'd like to do," I thought to myself, before mentioning this to my family. Unfortunately, I didn't know where these children's homes were located and couldn't recall the name of the person who had told me about them. So I continued to teach, pretty much forgetting about this intriguing prospect of working for a year or two in France aiding young war victims. Two years later, my mother said to me: "You talked about going to work in a children's refuge home in France. I know where to find one!" I was flabbergasted! She explained how she had met a woman at the grocery store whose son directs one of these children's "colonies" in France. She had already approached him to ask for the address. "There you are!" she added, and simply handed me a scrap of paper:

Auguste Bohny, Colony of the Swiss Red Cross
Le Chambon-sur-Lignon, Haute-Loire

I couldn't get over it! This address would allow me to realize my dream! I said to my mother: "It's incredible that you met up with this woman by chance! Perhaps that will decide my future!"

That's how I came to set out for occupied France. My book *The Children of Château de La Hille* bears witness to my rich and varied experiences while I was there. But for now, what happened next? I wrote to Mr. Bohny who directed me to the Red Cross in Berne. In the return mail I was thanked for having applied and told it would take a few months for me to obtain the necessary German and French visas. At that point I moved to Zürich to enroll in a year-long seminar in health education at the University. I received no news for months. In June, I finally received a letter stating that my request for a visa had been transferred to the German Consulate in Basel.

I was just finishing my first semester in Zürich before beginning an apprenticeship in a local children's shelter called "Gotthelf" in Biberist. In mid- August I had a call from my parents saying that the visas had arrived and that I had to depart immediately! I packed my bags as quickly as possible and returned to Basel. My preparations had to be extremely rushed, but since I was headed to Vichy France, I had to think about so many things: not only the usual underwear, shirts, pants, and sweaters, but also chocolate, coffee, powdered cocoa, condensed milk, and so on. In three days I filled two large suitcases. In addition, a pharmacist offered me a well-stocked medical bag that proved invaluable during my stay in France.

Finally, on August 21, 1943, at seven o'clock in the morning my train left the Basel railway station for Geneva. Upon arrival, I left my bags at the checked baggage counter while I went to find the office of the Swiss Red Cross Children's Aid where I was warmly welcomed. Since there were no more trains for Lyon that day, I had to spend the night in town. The next morning, a worker for the Red Cross wearing an armband saying "Children's Aid" accompanied me to the railroad station. She helped me as best she could to carry my two very heavy bags and purchased my ticket for Lyon. On the platform my train was ready for departure. She helped me arrange my bags across two benches facing each other in a compartment I had all to myself.

When the bags were stowed, she warned me: "I hope you don't have anything written or printed in those suitcases. The Germans are very strict with their inspections." She gave me her armband with a picture on it of two children's faces beneath the rays of the Red Cross. "Maybe this will be useful," she added as she got off the train. When the train started up, I began to worry. It felt unsettling to be in a compartment completely empty. What was I getting myself into? Everything around me seemed suddenly menacing. Lost in thought, I stood at the window gazing absently at the passing countryside. But then I remembered my suitcases. Maybe the Germans would find something incriminating in them! Maybe there was something printed I hadn't thought about. I rummaged through each of them in turn. Luckily, at home I had already replaced the newspaper I had used to wrap my shoes with some blank paper. But in flipping through a totally new notebook lying in my second suitcase, a letter fell out. Actually it was only one page very carefully handwritten, a letter from a child. How did it get there? I had no idea, but I read it over. The letter concluded by saying: "Don't go to France, you will die of hunger. Best wishes, Daniela."

Much later, when I did experience great hunger, I remembered this warning. But what should I do with the letter right now? I had it in my hands when the train stopped. Some German soldiers passed by beneath my window. Suddenly I was in a panic. When the Germans got on the train, I tore the letter into a thousand pieces before throwing them into the toilet at the end of the corridor. Later on I regretted my action, for that letter was my last souvenir of Switzerland, a souvenir from a child's hand.

Chapter 1

Montluel

Château de La Hille
Swiss Colony
MONTÉGUT, Ariège
Train from Lyon to Toulouse
From Toulouse take the bus in the direction of Mas-d'Azil
Get off in Pailhès

Mr. Kempf had written down these instructions for my trip in the notebook that still sits on my bureau today. The word 'train' was stressed, and Pailhès was underlined twice. It seems that Mr. Kempf wrote this note just yesterday, but in fact it was over forty-nine years ago. Just a few months after my brief visit with him, he was shot down by the Germans.

On August 26, 1943, I got off the overcrowded bus at the village center in Montluel, situated twenty-one kilometers from Lyon. When I tried to get off, a man whom I had already noticed in Lyon, blocked my way. Short, stocky and very unpleasant, he shouted: "Whose fat bags are these?" Then he repeated the question even louder and more threateningly. I realized that they couldn't belong to anyone else but me, so I said:

"They're mine."

"Yours? Good," said the man, letting me get off but following close on my heels. The driver had retrieved my truly over-stuffed bags from the luggage compartment and stood them in front of me and "my shadow," a French SS-agent and collaborator. "Open this suitcase!" he gruffly ordered. I opened one of the suitcases and he pounced on it like a famished lion on a piece of meat. He rifled through all my clothes, throwing some of them on the ground. From time to time he bellowed: "Why do you have so many shirts? Why do you have so many clothes?" He became more and more agitated as a hostile group of bystanders surrounded us. More passengers from the bus got off to see what was going to happen.

"Open the other suitcase," the hateful guy yelled. I followed his orders, and again he rifled through that one even more thoroughly. He was becoming even angrier, but he didn't find what he was looking for. Was he looking for weapons? With the hostile spectators curiously looking on, he finally gave it up and asked:

"What are you doing here?"

"I came to work for the Children's Aid of the Swiss Red Cross."

"Your passport," he ordered abruptly. I complied. Angrily he made his way through the crowd of onlookers and disappeared into a restaurant not far from where we were standing.

Feeling utterly distressed and unsure of myself, I stood there with the silent crowd encircling me and waited for him to return.

It didn't take long. The Gestapo-man came back waving my passport and yelled, "You'll hear from me soon!" Then he got back on the bus that had waited for him, followed by all those who had gotten off out of pure curiosity. Several people stayed behind to watch me repack my belongings. In the restaurant I called the Swiss Colony and a half-hour later a member of the Children's Aid came to get me. Luckily, she had a cart.

We crossed a splendid park before arriving at a building that looked like a castle. I was immediately taken to see the director, a woman, who showed me a map of France hanging in the corridor. "You are here in Montluel, but this is not where you are supposed to be." She glided her index finger over the map to Lyon, then toward Toulouse and the Pyrénées. "It's roughly here," she said, tapping the map with her finger. "Here is the Château La Hille, another Swiss colony, and that's where you need to go."

"Today, you mean?" I asked anxiously. I was still wearing my raincoat. She smiled. "No, not today. Perhaps in two or three days."

They put me up with Mr. Kempf, a lively, kind little Alsatian man. He asked if I was going to stay in Montluel, and I answered that I needed to continue my trip to another Swiss colony situated in a Château in the Pyrénées. Delighted, he exclaimed:

"Ah! That's the Château de La Hille! I know it well! I lived very close by in Gabre, only nine kilometers from the Château."

"Is it a real Château, this Château de La Hille?"

"Indeed! There are grand ramparts with look-outs, four corner towers, an entrance tower, and another one which is truly magnificent!"

"You said you were from Alsace. How is it that you came to such a desolate place?"

Mr. Kempf began his story. "I fled Alsace with my wife and son when the Germans occupied it. We found a little house in Gabre, quite near the Château. It was a very primitive house, really, with rough stone walls and floor, no lighting and no running water, with only an open fireplace for cooking. We had virtually nothing except three chairs and a table. We had to sleep on the stone floor. What made it worse was that we had left such a pretty house in Alsace!"

"But you didn't stay in Gabre?" I asked.

"Well, that is a very sad story. My wife became more and more depressed.

She just couldn't get used to living such a primitive life filled with so many hardships. We had been living comfortably in Oltingen in Alsace. Our house had wallpaper, parquet floors, carpets. The house in Gabre was built out of roughly hewn stones that felt like they were crushing us. We couldn't even drive a nail into the wall to hang a picture. The worst was the cooking situation. My wife bitterly missed her electric stove, her Alsatian dishes—in short, everything. She sank into a deep depression, and I couldn't do anything about it. I felt helpless. All I could do was hope that over time she would get used to our new living conditions. Our son François was ten years old, and I took him along to work all day on a scrap of land we had been given for our own use. Luckily for us, our plantings were doing well.

We already had some peas, beans, carrots and lettuce. I had even planted some potatoes, but we never got to harvest them.

"We had fled Alsace in the spring, and the horrible event happened in mid- summer. One evening when my son and I returned from the fields, I found my wife hanging from the crossbars of the window. She was dead."

After a long silence, Mr. Kempf continued telling his story in a monotone: "My wife's death was a trauma for François and me. We weren't able to cope. I tried to make an effort for my son's sake, but he would just sit totally mute, pale as a ghost, under a tree in front of the house, staring straight ahead, not budging from his place all day long.

The villagers were kind to us, brought us food and gave us some good advice. The village doctor, Dr. Pic, told me about the Château de La Hille near Montégut, a neighboring village. He said that about a hundred children at the Château were being cared for by the Swiss, and he advised me to go there to find work and a place to live.

"I decided instantly. I packed up our meager belongings, took François by the hand, and hiked to the so-called Château. It was a beautiful, warm summer day. To make a long story short, the director Miss Tännler welcomed us warm...ly. François was happy to find himself among so many young comrades, a situation that helped ease his pain

"So that's where I need to be," I said. Mr. Kempf agreed and wrote down in my notebook the directions I already mentioned.

"The Château is very isolated," he added. "By foot it's about four kilometers from Pailhès. The county road skirts along a little stream hidden by bushes and trees. At a certain point, you will suddenly see beyond some trees the high walls of what looks like a monastery. There a path branches off to the right. You will come to a little dilapidated wooden bridge, and the Château will appear about another hundred meters further on. You'll see: it's like a vision from a fairytale—the ramparts, the crenellations, the towers..." Mr. Kempf had become dreamy-eyed.

"I'm certainly curious to see it," I said. "I will set out from here in two or three days. But why didn't you stay there?"

"They didn't really need us at La Hille. Anyway, they sent us to another Swiss colony, here in Montluel. I love this place. I'm the jack-of-all-trades and believe me, there's plenty to do here. In fact, it's ten o'clock. Let's listen to 'the English' on the BBC."

He turned on an old-fashioned little radio. We hit it just right. The famous English signal, quite disturbing, reverberated: Boom! Boom! Boom!

"Isn't it forbidden to listen to the BBC?" I asked.

"And how! It's the death sentence!" he exclaimed. The voice coming from the radio announced: "This is England, with the news. The Germans continue to retreat on all the Russian borders."

I was shaken upon hearing this news for the first time in France. What if the Germans were eavesdropping on us? Mr. Kempf himself was visibly nervous. He had lowered the volume to the minimum. "The worse it gets for the Germans there, they will become all the more dangerous here!"

Little did he know that he himself would be shot and killed in less than a year.

I stayed three days in Montluel helping out a little here and there.

At the time there were many Spanish children, rather wild-looking with their black hair and sparkling dark eyes. They wanted to tease me by speaking Spanish, knowing full well that I didn't understand a word they were saying. So I had the brilliant idea of speaking Swiss-German to them. "Tüend doch nid so saublöd. [Don't be so silly.] If you speak Spanish, then I'll speak Swiss-German!" They quickly fell silent, perplexed. When I continued to speak Swiss-German, again they were astonished! "I don't understand a thing!" one charming little girl with sparkling dark eyes said to me.

"What's your name?" I asked her. "Dolores," she said.

"You see," I said. "If you speak to me in Spanish, I will speak to you in Swiss- German!" From then on they stopped that game.

That same evening after dinner the children put on a play. In the dining-hall they had built a make-shift platform for a stage. When the gong sounded, the little ones as well as the bigger ones came in to enjoy the performance.

A man laden down with two very large suitcases came on stage. I thought I was dreaming: that's me, I thought! The guy was dressed in my pants, my raincoat and my shoes! He put down his bags, and a heavy-set character showed up shouting: "What do you have in those suitcases? Open 'em up!" I knew what happened next. It was pretty amusing for everyone, the children as well as their teachers, the gardeners and the cooks.

The second skit was a dance with mechanical dolls. The curtain—and there was a real curtain—opened on the "dolls" standing frozen in their long colorful skirts. Dolores, Rafaela and the other dolls began to come to life. One of the teachers accompanied them on the piano with some popular Spanish songs. The dolls began to dance, and then, after a while, gradually moved more and more slowly until they were completely still. The little girls were utterly charming and completely won over the audience, taking many bows to acknowledge the applause.

Later that evening Mr. Kempf and I again listened to "the English." Above us, in the night sky, we could hear the rumbling of airplanes heading toward Germany.

My last night there, I visited the teacher who had come to pick me up at the bus stop. Her kindergarten was located in an annex in the park. She said to me: "The children would like to say goodbye to you, but they are already in bed."

She took me into a large room so dimly lighted by a night-light that I could barely make out the little beds lined up in rows. I sat down, and then all the little ones got up from their beds and came over to me, some climbing on my lap, others embracing me. Their spontaneous trust and affection were profoundly moving. They made me realize the heavy responsibility that lay ahead.

Chapter 2

On the Way to the Château de La Hille

I had to say my goodbyes rather quickly. Dolores, Rafaela, the gardener Ortiz, Mr. Kempf and François accompanied me to the train station. I left one of my big suitcases behind, and had enough trouble traveling with just one of them plus a backpack and the medical bag. However, Mr. Ortiz added an extra burden: he handed me a giant melon through the train window!

Weighed down with all my belongings, it was not so easy to make my connection in Lyon, but I managed to catch the fast train to Toulouse just in the nick of time. The melon rolled away from me twice, luckily without bursting. It's funny how a person with the best of intentions can add to a poor traveler's distress with a last minute gift at the train station!

I spent the night in the corridor sitting on my suitcase, constantly being jostled by other passengers on their way to the toilets. Every time I had to stand up to let someone get by, the melon rolled away!

The train arrived in Toulouse around 7am After such an uncomfortable, sleepless night, I was happy to reach my destination. I dragged my suitcase and the rest of my things onto the platform. When the melon made a dash for freedom and rolled under a merchant's wagon, I happily left it there! After stowing my bags at the baggage consignment, I gave a sigh of relief: I felt like a free man. I left the station and wandered around the streets of Toulouse.

The Germans were everywhere, fitted out with machine-guns

and helmets decorated with skulls. The thought of what these soldiers could do with their terrifying weapons filled me with dread. On every street corner there was a veritable forest of street signs and directions to orient the occupying soldiers. "It's incredible," I thought to myself, "that the Germans have advanced deep into Russia, just outside Moscow and Leningrad, and into Norway, Poland, Belgium, Holland, France, Yugoslavia and Greece, and still have enough soldiers left over to occupy a town like Toulouse. What organization!"

Outside the food stores I saw long lines. I was famished so I went into a simple café to get some breakfast. Without any coupons, however, I had to settle for some bad coffee.

I needed to check the bus schedule at the train station, so I retraced my steps.

When I purchased my bus ticket for Pailhès, I was advised to show up an hour before departure time in order to get a seat. Then I set out for the office of the Swiss Red Cross, Children's Aid, on Taur Street in order to alert the director, Mr. Gilg that I had arrived. As it happened, I had to drop off a letter to a Mrs. Petitpierre who also lived on the same street. She was so happy to receive the letter from Montluel that she invited me to stay for lunch. I was very hungry and gladly accepted the invitation. While this kind woman was busy in the kitchen, I fell asleep in my chair. When I awoke, I saw that she had beautifully laid the table with a delicious meal. As I generously served myself, I wondered how long she had had to stand in line to procure this meat and these vegetables. When the meal was over, I thanked her and took my leave.

I showed up at the office of the Children's Aid Society, but no one paid much attention to me. Not until much later did I meet my superiors, Mr. Gilg and Mr. Parera. So I simply announced my arrival and headed back to the train station where I would catch my bus. Encountering more and more German soldiers along the way made me feel terribly uncomfortable. I collected my bags at the train station and dragged them to the bus stop where the bus was already waiting. Luckily my big bag was stowed on the roof. Meanwhile, with my fully outfitted medical bag and heavy backpack I stood in line a long time— in the end to secure only a standing place wedged between several other passengers. Unbelievably, another large group of people were still waiting at the door. With much pushing and shoving, everyone somehow managed to get on, and the bus finally took off just as my legs began to buckle. The sleepless night spent on the train had definitely caught up with me. But at least we were on our way.

At every station along the way, people got off the bus, leaving me a bit more room to maneuver. After two hours, however, I was on the verge of collapse. Finally a tiny seat opened up next to an enormously fat man. If he hadn't squeezed me like a lemon on every curve, things would have been perfect. Luckily, he got off before I did, leaving me some time to recuperate.

In the evening, we arrived in Pailhès. Surprisingly, the bus pulled up right next to the National Police Headquarters. The driver climbed up on the bus roof and handed down my suitcase. "Four kilometers from Pailhès, by the county road," Mr. Kempf had said. But how was I going to make that with my heavy luggage? The bus departed, leaving me standing alone in the countryside.

Just then, out of the dusky evening, I saw a boy approaching with a huge grin that reminded me of the Cheshire cat in Alice in Wonderland. He asked me if I was named Steiger and if I was going to the Château de La Hille. When I said yes, he happily shook my hand, still smiling from ear to ear, and introduced himself: "My name is Onze. I'm here to pick you up. I have an old bicycle, and I'll try laying your suitcase on top of it."

He grabbed hold of my suitcase and dragged it to a nearby wall where he had parked his bicycle. With tremendous strength he lifted the suitcase in the air and perched it on the seat and handlebars. The bike wobbled dangerously as he tried to push it forwards. But that didn't stop him from talking! In a genial manner, he introduced himself a second time: "I'm Onze, but actually my name is Kurt Klein. I belong..." The suitcase fell to the ground with a crash, breaking off a bit of a corner. While I held the bicycle, Onze picked up the suitcase and loaded it back on. As he tried once again to push off, he resumed talking from where he had been interrupted: "I belong to the older kids group at the Château de La Hille. Many other Germans like me are there too, and nonsensically we have to hide from the Germans!" The suitcase threatened to fall off again, and Onze had to work hard to reestablish the balance before he continued: "You are going to be in charge of the Middles, about fifteen boys between the ages of eleven and fourteen. What a bloody band of rascals! They don't listen to anyone! They do what they want! Even the village teacher can't get through to them. One day from an open window on the second floor they even spit on his head! They will try to get the better of you, these scamps. They. " A second time the suitcase fell off onto the street. Onze was quite annoyed. "We can't go on like this," he grumbled, but he didn't know what to do.

Luckily, help was at hand! A young man in Pailhès had spotted us. Onze knew him and introduced us. The young man was Manfred Kammerer, also one of the older ones at the Château who worked for a farmer in Pailhès. His brother Walter was a pianist whom I had heard about in Montluel. Very obligingly, Manfred had turned up a cart for my luggage. What a relief! "You go ahead on the bicycle," Onze proposed. "I'll follow with the bags." With my heavy backpack on the handlebars, I got on the bicycle and set off toward the fabled Château de La Hille that would play such an important role in my life.

Chapter 3
Arrival at the Château

Thrown off balance by my heavy backpack, I zigzagged from one side of the pavement to the other like a drunkard. Suddenly, behind the trees that flanked the road, I spied the Château on my right. I saw high, grayish-black stone walls that looked distinctively like a prison. "H'mm, that doesn't look very attractive," I thought to myself while slowing down. Coming to the fork in the road, I could no longer see anything of the Château, hidden now by the giant pines and chestnut trees. Just past the trees I came to a little bridge over a tiny stream almost dried up. I tried to cross the bridge, but with my very best effort, I couldn't manage to keep my wheels on the thick logs spaced out over the stream, and had to get down off the bike. My heavy backpack likewise fell down from the handlebars and nearly took a bath. I wedged the backpack under my arm and steered the bike with my free hand. The path gradually went up hill—and there it was, the Château!

Fantastic! Now it looked marvelous! From this angle it was radiant and welcoming, just as I had pictured it in my dreams. A real Château, like in the fairy- tales, stood before me: a stately building surrounded by high ramparts and towers!

From the courtyard children's high-pitched shouts, cries and happy laughter greeted me.

Here it was, the Château de La Hille! I had finally arrived! I stood still for a long moment, my backpack under my arm, my hand on the bike. "The Château! I can't believe it! It's incredible how it has come to life filled with all these children whom I will soon get to know!"

Many years later I returned to the Château. Its lusterless windows and cold stone walls sent a chill down my spine. The silence weighed heavy on my heart. No more children's laughter, only my tears. "The Château is dead—it is dead without the children." I felt so sad. I could imagine again the children's high-pitched voices, their laughter. I thought back on that first day when I stood amazed, looking at the Château bursting with life. At that time, its windows sparkled like eyes looking out for us, its walls radiated brightness and warmth, and its high towers protected us with friendly greetings.

Well, that was once upon a time...

Lost in my admiration of the Château, I stood there leaning on the old, rusty bike. I took off my backpack. Some children passed me, peeking at me from the corners of their eyes. A stranger!

I finally broke off from my daydreaming and continued toward the building. I had to follow an alleyway shaded by chestnut trees and then passed under the majestic entrance tower. I parked the bicycle and entered the courtyard. I felt a little lost. There were children everywhere, playing and chasing each other—just like recess in a regular schoolyard. My sudden appearance made them stop in their tracks. Their eyes followed me as far as the entrance.

At a landing I came to a staircase. I caught a glimpse of the dining-hall through a partially opened door. A young girl in a red dress was setting the table all alone. Where were the other personnel? At the top of the stairs I finally met an adult, a woman whom I greeted in Swiss-German.

"You are Mr....?" she responded.

"Steiger."

"Ah yes, good, we have been waiting for you. My name is Anne-Marie. Welcome!" I was a little disappointed to hear her speaking French but she was very gracious. "You must be very thirsty," she noted. "Come have some tea in the kitchen."

I was in fact dying of thirst from the long trip, and the tea would do me a world of good. But first we went down to the dining-hall. "This is the most beautiful room in the Château," she said. "Look at this grand fireplace and all the fine woodwork!" I admired everything as the occasion demanded, and then asked about the little girl in the red dress. "This is Paulette," she said. "She sets the table for dinner."

There were a great number of battered tin plates lined up symmetrically on the long tables. Anne-Marie noticed my surprise. "We eat everything from these tin plates." She pointed out a table at the far end of the room and explained:

"That is where the personnel sit. We have five Swiss altogether. Three women: Miss Tännler, the director; Miss Tobler who takes care of the "Mickeys"—the little ones—and myself. I'm in charge of the "Middles," and Mr. Lyrer has the older ones†[1]. Let's go into the kitchen to meet Mrs. Schlesinger our cook from Vienna...Oh, too bad, she's not here! And I don't know where to find the tea. I'm so sorry to disappoint you!"

"Where do you do the cooking?" I asked. "Are these big steamers for the laundry?"

"No, they are used for cooking."

"Do you have to light a fire under each of these pots?" "But of course!"

Paulette came in just then to tell us that Onze was looking for us. He arrived with his wide grin—and my luggage.

The three of us left the kitchen. Onze carried my suitcase on his shoulders, Anne-Marie took the medical bag, and I dealt with the backpack.

Anne-Marie led us upstairs on a creaky staircase. Anne-Marie's room was on the left and there was another door to the right. "Watch your head," she warned. The low, heavy crossbeams required us to stoop. Onze had to shift my bag down to his hand. Along the very narrow corridor, difficult to maneuver, was a whole series of doors. My guide opened one of them and said, "Here's your room, Mr. Steiger. Go on in!"

The room was miniscule. One could take only about two steps standing upright; this was an attic room located right under the mansard roof. It didn't even have a full window, only a tiny dormer that let in some light. An iron bed and a footstool were arranged under the dormer "window." That was it! But in fact, there wasn't room for anything else anyway. We dropped off all my things in my room—that later on almost became my tomb!

I looked around for some kind of washbasin. Anne-Marie immediately guessed what I was looking for.

"That's a problem," she said. "There is no running water in the Château." "But even more importantly, what about toilets?" I inquired.

---

† As explained here, the term 'Mickeys' refers to the youngest children, from pre- school through 4th grade. The 'Middles' refers to the middle-school children, roughly 11 through 13 or 14. In French the term 'les Grands' and in German 'die Grossen' was used at the Château to refer to the older teenagers, roughly 16 to 19, although a couple of them were already in their early twenties. I did not come up with one term for them, so I typically just referred to them as "the older ones" or "the older teens." Since these "children" under the circumstances were already facing adult decisions regarding life-and-death, calling them 'the big kids' didn't seem appropriate.—Translator

"Behind the Château there are two toilets in an ugly, concrete out-house. For the children, we put pails in front of the dormitory doors for the night."

"Do we get pails too?" I wondered.

"No, for the adults there is a rather primitive little spot at the other end of the Château in the tower with all the steps. I'll show you later."

Just then a bell began to ring in the courtyard. "It's dinner time," Onze signaled me—Onze always with his Cheshire cat smile. I later learned the reason for his nickname. Because he was German, he had a hard time pronouncing the word 'onze', which is French for 'eleven, but instead said 'On-tse' so the kids nicknamed him Onze.

You couldn't miss hearing the bell. But first I got up on the footstool, opened my tiny "porthole," and wriggled my upper body through the opening out onto the gradually sloped roof. From my new vantage point, I had a magnificent view of the countryside! It resembled the Jura Mountains quite a bit, with their hills and sparsely growing forests, but here were the foothills and dales of the Pyrénées, whose rather jagged peaks stood out against the blue sky. The bell continued to sound from the courtyard, but from the roof I couldn't see down into the courtyard where the bell was located. In any case, it was time to wriggle back off the roof, down through my "window," and back into my room where Anne-Marie and Onze were waiting for me.

"What a splendid view," I said enthusiastically. We all filed into the dining hall where Anne-Marie introduced me to the director, Miss Tännler—a small, rather fragile looking person, who shook my hand, welcomed me kindly, and introduced me to the Spaniards on the staff: Mr. and Mrs. Marimon, Mr. and Mrs. Nadal, and Mr. and Mrs. Palau. They were already seated at the table when Miss Tobler and Mr. Lyrer came in a little late and also wished me a hearty welcome.

Miss Tännler took her place at the head of the table and waited for silence.

Then she said simply: "Bon appétit!" Everyone grabbed their spoons. Our meal consisted of potatoes cooked in their skins and cut into slices, served with a white sauce that smelled rather disgusting. Despite my hunger, I ate hesitantly. But I would come to know much worse!

Chapter 4
My First Day at the Château

B reakfast was at eight o'clock. Getting out of bed proved to be a problem. I was done in by my long trip, laden with all my bags and overwhelmed by mixed emotions. I was still disorientated in my tiny room, and when I went down for breakfast, only half awake, I managed to hit my head against the low beams more than once.

All the staff and the children were already at the table. I said good morning and sat down. "Bon appétit!" said Miss Tännler. For breakfast we had puréed chestnuts with a little piece of bread, and some kind of fake coffee. Rumor had it that the coffee was made from acorns. The meal revived me. But then came the big question: what was I going to do?

Miss Tännler put me in charge of the "Middles," the eleven-to-thirteen year olds. This was the "gang" Onze had told me about, and indeed they seemed ready for all kinds of mischief.

As they all gathered around me expectantly, I recognized that they certainly were going to test me. "The children don't have school right now," said the director. "They are on vacation. Keep them busy until this evening." Well, there you have it!

One of the boldest asked: "What are we going to do?"

"We'll see," I answered, not really having a clue myself. "Let's go down to the courtyard." Leading them outside under the chestnut trees, I lamely suggested we play a game. While I enthusiastically proposed one game after another, explaining the rules and how to play, I had no success. As I began to explain each game, one boy after another shouted: "I don't want to play," and flopped down on the lawn with no interest whatsoever. I ended up abandoning that idea, and opted instead for a walk.

That proved to be a disaster! Some of them formed little groups and chatted among themselves, walking as slowly as possible. Others quickly set off way ahead, where I couldn't even see them.

By noon, I was exhausted. After lunch, I had to deal with them again, so I stoically set out with my group of "rascals." Again, they started crossing the fields in various directions with no apparent purpose, leaving me not a moment to enjoy the landscape. The boys monopolized my full attention. Sometimes they got into fights, sometimes they climbed the trees to pick and eat the green apples. Some of them got way ahead, others stayed way behind. It was pointless to scold them or shout at them: I didn't even know their names! They kept calling each other by different names and were having a gay old time completely befuddling me. I was in despair.

The afternoon dragged on interminably!

That evening I was so tired I could barely stand up. I went to bed early, but just before falling into a deep sleep, I thought to myself: "What a day, my first day! And to think it will all start up again tomorrow! What a prospect!"

Chapter 5
Saved by the "Little Train" and the "New Mill"

I awoke the next morning stiff all over. The start of a new day seemed like torture. Feeling overwhelmed, I set out after breakfast with "my gang." They broke loose like a pack of little devils, running and jumping all over, climbing trees along the way, picking plums, pears and apples, gobbling down all the fruit that fell into their hands. They even pulled up some carrots and cabbages. I was utterly powerless to stop them. It couldn't go on this way! The thought of having to deal with their antics day after day, week after week made me feel sick. How much more time do they have for vacation? But then what?

Little Max Simon from Toulouse, a boy with long blond hair, came up to talk to me. Watching me wave my arms despairingly and calling out in all directions from my post beneath a tree, little Max earnestly tried to console me: "You know, it was worse with the village school teacher. The kids would throw him to the ground and wash his face with the blackboard sponge." Horror-stricken, I looked at my little confidant and asked: "Well, what can I do if they don't listen to me?"

"Take us to the New Mill. We can go swimming there, and we like that a lot."

We returned to the Château in a straggly line of rag-tag groups. My inability to control the boys depressed me. I thought I had a lot of experience with children, but now I began to doubt myself. What about this "New Mill"? Perhaps it offered a glimmer of hope.

At lunch, I confided all my worries and bad experiences to Anne-

Marie, and I asked her about the New Mill. "That's a wonderful place," she confirmed enthusiastically. "You should take them there to give them a little space and yourself a little peace. The kids can swim and relax. It will be perfect."

My suggestion to go to the New Mill after lunch was a big hit. The boys knew the way. We climbed a path overgrown with yellow broom as far as Borda Blanca, a tiny hamlet at the top of the hill, then we went down the other side along the "White Road" that led us directly to the New Mill.

The boys were transformed! We walked at a good clip, and that led me to conclude that with children it's crucial to have a goal.

Pierre Bergmann—I was slowly learning their names—was a lively little twelve-year-old who always had something to say and would launch into interminable conversations with the blond Gustav. Pierre came up to me to explain the location of the New Mill. Pointing out two downward slopes in the mountains, he said, "You see, the New Mill is right there where the two mountains meet."

I was anxious to see this reportedly magnificent swimming hole. A little further on, a fork in the path led us to a very old, broken down building that eons ago had indeed been a mill. Paradoxically it was named the New Mill. There was dead silence. Nobody moved. Then we crept quietly by the ancient building: one can never know if a vicious dog might suddenly spring out at us!

On a narrow, overgrown grassy path bordered by wild hedgerows, we arrived at the "Lord's Spring" and then went through a small woods until we came to the Lèze River, that small river with many winding detours that flows past the Château. Over thousands of years, this tiny river amazingly cut a ravine through the huge rocks where it then formed a small but very deep lake now called the "Lord's Spring."

The boys paused for a moment, and then in a flash they completely undressed and dove into the icy water. What a free-for-all! I watched them in amazement. They were in their element.

Isi, a darker-skinned boy, and Mane, a chubby little lad, climbed onto a tall rock that stretched almost at a right angle over the water—an excellent diving board! All the others followed suit. Perched on my rock, I watched the daring divers, applauding them with a loud "bravo" for their best dives. Boisterous and dripping wet, the boys scrambled around on the rocks like monkeys. A real letting go indeed!

An hour later, each of them found a comfortable place on a rock to lie down for some sunbathing. For a moment, everything calmed down. From my rock I had a magnificent view of the New Mill and the River Lèze that wound its way through the rocky countryside. Lying quietly in the sun, the children seemed part of the landscape.

On the way back, we circuited the Lord's Spring by way of the rocks in the direction of the White Road, and then climbed a wall that led us to a quarry. The boys investigated every nook and cranny and collected all kinds of things. They even came across some rails half buried in a pile of debris. Gustav called out: "Mr. Steiger, I've found something!" His friends rushed toward him. "There's a wheel buried in the debris, but I can't get it out!" I went over to take a look at the situation. Gustav and Pierre had unsuccessfully tried to dig out the wheel. But then I had an idea: "That must have been a kind of trolley-cart from the quarry that got buried here before the war so that it would not be stolen. The wheels fit the rails, so that makes sense!"

My "gang" wanted to extract it immediately, but I explained to them that they needed the proper tools. "We can come back tomorrow with some pickaxes and shovels!" I promised.

They were overjoyed!

We returned home in a very good mood. I went to bed that night feeling quite satisfied. I had won over the notorious Middles! My worries dissipated; my fear of failing with this "band of rascals" evaporated. I slept like a log.

The next morning my "gang," armed with picks and shovels, was waiting for me impatiently. Onze couldn't believe it and stood there dumbfounded. He had never seen them like this.

"What did you do with them?" he asked incredulously.

"With the gang of no-goods?" I replied. "Come on, let's get going!" I called out to them. Flabbergasted, Onze looked on as we set off, still shaking his head.

Arriving at our spot in the quarry, we divided the tasks. Some got busy with the trolley-cart, and the others with the rails. Working in shifts, we labored all morning like a chain gang. At lunchtime, we hurried back to the Château, and returned to the job as quickly as possible. Onze was still sitting in the courtyard, not believing his eyes.

We dug all we could dig around the trolley-cart, still solidly anchored in the ground. The work was hard, and we had to spell each other several times. Despite our determination, it was impossible to budge the devil! Somehow we had to get it out! We had tried clearing away the earth by every means possible. By evening, we were at the end of our rope. The cart had emerged only halfway. The next day we returned to the same spot, full of energy and good will for the job ahead. By that evening the trolley had been cleared! We shrieked with joy!

On the third day, we cleaned it off. The trolley-cart was astonishingly well preserved. Even its wheels still turned. Our next job was to set the rails in place.

Pooling all our strength, we managed to arrange the rails curving up to the top of the large pile of gravel.

Despite our best efforts with some pieces of wood, blocks, and nails, connecting the rails was very difficult. Our patience was worn thin, for we wanted so badly to actually try out the trolley. When the rails seemed stable enough, we pushed the trolley-cart to the highest point of the track. What anticipation before the first ride! Gustav had braked the wheels with a branch to let four boys get in the cart. At the signal, they were off! The trolley bolted to a start with a deafening sound. The rails gave a little on the curve and the cart ground to a halt in the gravel.

Gustav's brother Mane and Jacques were thrown out of the cart.

What a run! The boys shouted excitedly and clapped their hands. They quickly reset the rails for another ride down the hill. That evening we arrived back at the Château as hungry as wolves.

I never had another problem with the Middles. All I had to do was take them to ride "the little train" or swim at the New Mill.

Chapter 6
The Big Excursion

Two weeks after my arrival at the Château, Anne-Marie came up to me with an idea: "We'd like to take the middle group on a three-day excursion." I was a bit taken aback.

"A three-day excursion?"

"Why not? We could leave... let's say tomorrow morning!"

And that's what we did. We walked that whole day and arrived at an impressive cloister composed of four or five buildings arranged in a horseshoe with a chapel in the center. A strange silence prevailed. We proceeded cautiously with tiny steps because we thought we would stumble upon the monks at any instant.

When we finally realized there hadn't been any monks here for many years, the group came back to life. Every nook and cranny had to be explored. First we visited the buildings connected by long corridors. We wandered into several of the innumerable cells that were completely empty, and then followed the narrow corridors that led us to the refectory, the kitchen, the bedrooms, and finally the chapel. We finished by discovering the subterranean burial places, something like catacombs. The coffins were stacked on top of each other, and some of them were open. A true deathly silence pervaded the gloomy atmosphere. Thanks to my flashlight, we could see some well-preserved, blanched skeletons lying in the stacked-up coffins. The boys were visibly shaken with fear and emotion. When a bat took flight right over our heads, we flew out of that forbidding place as fast as we could! We regrouped outside in a kind of park whose past splendors we could see epitomized in an ancient basin with a small fountain. We imagined the monks walking and meditating in this garden. What had chased them away from here?

At the end of this first expedition, we rejoined Anne-Marie who had prepared a picnic for us. Comfortably settled beneath a chestnut tree, we recounted to her our thrilling adventures. Before going any further, I should cite the names of the boys who were there. First, there was Robert Weinberg, twelve years old, tall and thin, always by my side, his face expressing his loyalty. "That was amazing in the cellar," he whispered to me.

"I was afraid," confessed Isi Bravermann, twelve years old. He was still shaking and kept running his fingers through his hair. Pierre Bergmann, a big talker, always ready with a joke, tapped Isi on the shoulder and cried out:

"It was amazing! The skeletons were horrifying!"

"Everyone's here?" asked Anne-Marie. "Nobody got lost in the cloister?"

I counted them up: Pierre, Isi, Mane and Gustav Manasse, Jacques and Gilbert Detchebery—the two quarrelsome brothers—Pierre and Georges Costeseque, Henri Vos, Jacques Palau, Simon, Raoul and Bernard—everyone was here.

Night came on quickly. While we were getting settled in the hay for the night, the inseparable Gustav and Pierre, along with Isi and Mane, decided to go find a cell in the cloister. "Maybe there'll be some beds," explained Pierre, always on the lookout for adventure.

We let them go. What could happen? Raoul went with them.

The ones who stayed behind talked in a loud voice. They were still preoccupied with the dead. All of a sudden, I felt anxious. "I'm going to check on Pierre and the others. Who wants to come along?" Robert, of course, with Jacques and Bernard. "OK, let's go!"

Armed with my flashlight, I took the lead. We went through several of the buildings with the interminable corridors and innumerable cells. No one! Where did they go, then? We walked in total silence—no talking, no footsteps, for we were barefoot. I shone my light into each of the individual cells. The wind whistled down the long corridor. With the play of the air currents, the casement windows opened and shut with a bang.

We finally found our anguished adventurers in the last building near the chapel. They had noticed some light flickering behind the windows facing them and some silhouettes in the courtyard. They had no idea we had come looking for them and retreated into their cell.

When they heard some noises approaching and the doors banging, they were deeply frightened. They thought they were living their final moments when the door opened and my flashlight shone on them. We said right away who we were. Boy! Were they relieved!

"Oh, it's you, Mr. Steiger," gasped Raoul. Gustav added: "If only I had known!"

"If you had known, you wouldn't have trembled like that, you little coward!" I added, smiling. "Do you want to come with us or stay here?"

"We'll stay," asserted Pierre Bergmann.

They actually did stay, and it was with mixed feelings that we rejoined our group in the hayloft that night.

Chapter 7

Danger Threatens

O n the third day of our excursion we arrived in the delightful little town of Foix in the valley at the foot of the Pyrénées. The landmark greeting the visitor to Foix is the mighty tower of an imposing ruin set high on the rocks overlooking the entire region.

In this ruin dating from the middle ages we made ourselves comfortable to enjoy the magnificent view while we ate some peaches purchased in town at a very reasonable price. I was alone with the boys, while Anne-Marie had gone off to visit the police headquarters. "I know someone in a good position who can tell me about the situation for foreigners. I'm going to ask her if everything is alright," she said upon taking off.

She returned much sooner than expected. After looking cautiously around, she leaned toward us and confided in an anguished tone of voice: "The police are on their way to the Château. I have to get back as quickly as possible to warn the older ones. I have a bicycle." Without further ado, she left. We were paralyzed with fright as we watched her head off with her irregular gait. (She suffered from a hip deformity.) Then she disappeared around the corner of the old town wall. After studying the map, I said: "She has about twenty kilometers to go. Let's hope she arrives in time."

"But what do the police want," Raoul asked innocently. "They're looking for the older ones," I said brusquely. "But why? Did they do something stupid?"

Simon, the youngest, looked at me inquisitively. He knew absolutely nothing. I shook my head and responded: "The police are coming to look for the older ones because the Germans ordered them to."

Pierre Costeseque, a rather ill-tempered boy who usually didn't say much, asked: "Why are the Boches wanting to round up the older ones?"

"You know, don't you?" I asked Gustav. He angrily threw his peach pit over our heads, and his usually smiling face turned into a mask grimacing with anger. He looked around several times and then said through his teeth: "They want to kill all of them because they are Jews. Me too, and my little brother, and Pierre Bergmann, and Henri Vos and you..."

"That's not true," interrupted his little brother Mane, shaking with anger. "You never told me that," he cried. "You're lying, you're lying, no one wants to kill us."

"Yes, it's true, Mane," Isi intervened. "They trapped me and my mother and sent us off to Camp Vernet. It's a miracle I am still alive. My mother..."

"But that's completely crazy," Mane stammered. "They want to kill me? But I never did anything to them!" He started to cry. He was so young. I wanted to console him, but suddenly something snapped in me, and I myself was overcome with rage. "They *are* crazy! They *are* crazy! You're absolutely right!" I yelled out.

The children were stunned, petrified. I got hold of myself and carefully looked around. Luckily we were alone.

We remained silent a long time. We had forgotten the peaches.

Chapter 8
Alarm at the Château

I don't know how, but after finishing our fruit we managed to get back to the Château in less than five hours. The fear that the older group would be arrested gave us wings. Staggering with fatigue, we arrived just in time for dinner. Our first question: "Have the police arrived?"

No, the police hadn't come yet. Reassured a bit, we sat down to eat. Since we had eaten only peaches at noon, we were hungry as wolves. I was as delighted as a child by the prospect of a good meal, but I was bitterly disappointed. Once again, we had potatoes with that awful white sauce made from curdled milk. This was the third time! Gross!

Since I was sitting next to Miss Tännler, as usual, I tried to act normally and bravely eat my potatoes. Already at the beginning of the meal I noticed that the older ones were not there. Once the younger ones were allowed to leave the table, I signaled Miss Tännler:

"Where are they?"

"In the *Zwiebelkeller*," she said getting up.

"In the *Zwiebelkeller*? There's a special cellar for onions?" I asked.

"No, it's what we call our hiding place. Would you like to go look for it? You don't yet really know the Château."

"Okay, that will give me an excuse to explore. I'm going to try to find the hiding place."

Miss Tännler nodded and left. There was still daylight, and I was exhausted, but I decided to find this hiding place. I didn't know my way around the entire Château, for no one had taken me on a tour of it. I went upstairs on the wide, gnarled wooden steps that went past the giant clock standing in the corner. Our staff "salon" was on the left. The staff occasionally gathered there for tea or, more rarely, a coffee.

There were some real chairs and stools made by Mr. Nadal as well as a threadbare green couch. Near the door was a stand for our radio. We would often come here to listen to the BBC broadcast. In any case, the famous hiding place was not in there.

Next, I went into the little girls' dormitory, opposite the staff meeting room, and then into the older girls' dormitory. I very carefully examined the wallpaper for some indication of a concealed door, but I found nothing suspicious. I was going to explore the opposite wing of the Château, but just as I went back into the older girls' dorm, I saw the door open at the other end of the long room, and two policemen armed with guns came in with Miss Tännler, the director. They also were looking for the hiding place! At that point, I wanted to disappear under the floorboards. What to do? I certainly did not want to meet them. They would undoubtedly interrogate me about the older ones, and I would not make a convincing liar. Luckily they didn't even notice me. Miss Tännler led them to a tall armoire. "Look inside! Maybe they are in there!" she suggested in a provocative tone—and in poor French!

I admired her composure and ability to lie under pressure. Fortunately, when the gendarmes put their heads into the armoire in question, I was able to quietly slip away. In the hallway I felt relieved. For now, pursuing my search for the hiding place was surely out of the question. I went down to sit at a table in the courtyard where the children were playing, and my spirits began to lift a bit.

All the children were there in the courtyard: the little ones were playing tag, and the middle ones, tired out, were lounging on the grass. Pierre Bergmann and Bernard, avid marbles players, were the only ones keeping busy. They were very talented at shooting their marbles on the track marked on the ground. One had to hit the opponent's marble to capture it. I nervously kept one eye on the game and the other on the entrance. At some point or another the police would have to leave, perhaps taking the older ones with them. That would depend on the success of their search. I was literally shaking.

Since their places at table were still empty at dinnertime, I understood that all the older ones must still be in the mysterious hiding place. I regretted that I had only a fleeting acquaintance with some of them. I was thinking especially about Edith Goldapper, a young nearsighted girl, and her best friend Inge Schragenheim. In Montluel they told me about two musicians: the violonist Heinz Storosum who had long dark hair tied in back, and Walter Kammerer who wore thick glasses and had prominent facial features. I was acquainted with Addi Nussbaum, the talented mathematician who came to my gymnastics class that I organized after the construction of the "little train." Addi was astonished to see my success with the Middles—whom he called the wild savages. Of course, Onze was the most flabbergasted of them all. With his perennial smile, he kept asking me: "How did you manage that?"

But for now the older ones were all in hiding.

While I was daydreaming, the sky had darkened. Suddenly my anxiety increased again. Where were the policemen? Why hadn't they returned?

A little way off, Pierre Bergmann and Bernard were battling over the last marble. The rest of the middle ones were indifferently watching their fearsome battle. All was quiet. Miss Tobler had taken the little ones to put them to bed.

I couldn't sit still any longer, so I got up to look through the kitchen window.

Mrs. Schlesinger wasn't there. She too had disappeared!

I had turned my head away for just a moment and that's precisely when the policemen showed up. I grimaced with fright but they didn't notice. In their khaki uniforms, with their shotguns slung across their shoulders and their military caps at a jaunty angle, they crossed the courtyard and went out through the tower entrance. They were alone! Luckily they hadn't found anyone! Anne-Marie came up to me, visibly calmer.

"They've gone!"

"So I noticed," I said tersely. "That went well. But were they looking for all of them or only a select few?"

"They came for four of them: our violinist Heinz Storosum, Walter's brother Manfred Kammerer, Addi Nussbaum and Ilse's brother Henri Brünell."

"What about Walter Kammerer himself?"

"They don't know him; he's not on any list."

"But they were all hiding?"

"Of course! We never know whom they are coming for."

"Lucky for us they didn't find them. We have an excellent hiding place, I've been told!"

"Indeed! Even the Germans haven't found our Zweibelkeller!" I resolved to find it myself, this mysterious onion cellar.

"And how was your trip on the bicycle?" I followed up.

"Fine, but I was very anxious about arriving too late."

"And what happens now?"

"Walter Kammerer can stay at the Château, of course, since he's not being sought. But Heinz Storosum, Henri Brünell and Manfred can no longer stay here. It's too dangerous. Addi Nussbaum can't stay either, since he has no papers. I'm going to take them to Switzerland."

"What about the others?"

"They are in contact with 'JOINT,' a secret organization for helping Jews.

JOINT has procured identity cards for all the teenagers at the Château. At the beginning of the year, they sent someone here to take a photo of all the older ones. A little while later, they sent us the identity papers. According to these papers, they all come from Alsace—Strasbourg, Colmar or Sélestat. They have Alsatian names like Berger, Stüssi, Belin or something like that."

"Addi doesn't have papers?"

"Addi was working for a farmer when the photographer came. Apparently our photographer was shot and killed in Nice. Otherwise he would have come back. But I'm especially worried about Heinz Storosum. With his long dark hair, he gets himself noticed wherever he goes. He's risking his life. I already tried to get him to cut his hair, but he refused. He doesn't want anyone to touch his hair. The police already arrested him during a concert at the Château. Since his liberation from 'Camp Noé,' he is always fearful. What he has gone through! Walter can tell you some things."

She was ready to leave.

"And you're going to take them to Switzerland—just like that?"

"There isn't any other solution."

"But you said that Addi doesn't have papers..."

"That's why he can't stay in France. We have no other possibility but to cross the border under false identity. My father is a forest ranger in the Joux Valley. His forests I know very well. They are for the most part in France, and we have good friends along the way."

"When do you leave?"

"I'm too tired today, so we will leave tomorrow night around 1am. We will walk as far as Saint-Jean-de-Verges, a very long way. Then we'll take the train for five hours to Toulouse."

Anne-Marie was in a hurry to go back in to make sure her charges were in bed.

Night had fallen.

During our gymnastics class in the morning—for the first time without Addi—my middle ones spied the gendarmes. They were sitting behind a pile of straw near the woodshop. Taking advantage of the dark, they had quietly slipped back to keep watch on the Château the entire night!

Chapter 9
The Visitor

I had been at the Château for three weeks, and everything had gone pretty well. I had gotten used to my new life, and the gang of my eleven-to-thirteen year-olds no longer gave me any problems thanks to frequent excursions to "the little train." It was a real attraction! We had lengthened the track for the trolley-cart and that made the descent all the more thrilling. The boys were always so excited that they needed to cool off in the river before heading home.

For the middle of September, it was still rather mild.

Of the personnel, I had become acquainted with Miss Tobler (who took care of the little ones), Anne-Marie, Mrs. Schlesinger (the cook), and the Spaniards. Mr. and Mrs. Marimon had a delicate little six-year-old girl named Rosa. She had long dark hair in corkscrew curls. Mr. and Mrs. Palau had a daughter the same age named Conchita. She was blond—rather surprising to me for a Spaniard—and cheerful.

Pepito, her little two-year-old brother, was the youngest at the Château. Her older brother Jacques, one of the Middles, had put in a lot of work helping to set up the train.

There was also another person on the staff: a rather mysterious-looking man, pale and thin, with deep-set eyes. His narrow face and dark hair slicked back made him look like a gangster. We had been introduced but so far hadn't exchanged one word. Right after every meal he unobtrusively disappeared. I would soon get to know him better under rather unusual circumstances.

Anne-Marie had been gone for several days when we had a visitor—a rare occurrence. It was already late, and I had taken the middle ones to get ready for bed. I was passing through the dimly lighted dining-hall when I saw two men sitting near the kitchen. I immediately recognized the mystery man, but the other was a stranger.

I passed them and greeted them—in French, naturally, since it was the "official language" of the Château.

For the first time, the mystery man paid me a little attention. He asked me to sit down—speaking Swiss-German! Since I had always been taken for French, I was very surprised.

"This is a new one, a Swiss, who arrived here not so long ago," he explained to the stranger. Then he turned to me: "And this is Ruedi Schmutz from Tambouret, a Swiss also."

We shook hands, and I sat down.

They had a jug of tea on the table along with a plate of petit-beurre cookies—a miracle! It was a long time since I had seen sweets like these.

The visitor didn't stand on ceremony, and began addressing me with the familiar form right off the bat.

"You like it here?"

"Oh yes, of course," I responded. "I've gotten used to the place, but I haven't gotten to know all the children yet. There are so many! And you (I used the formal address), you come from...?"

"From Tambouret, a farm about sixteen kilometers from here. You can use the familiar."

"You didn't come by foot, did you?"

"No, by..." The light suddenly went out and we sat there in complete darkness.

We patiently waited and waited. The light would surely come back on—and it did after a few long minutes. Instantly our eyes turned to the plate of cookies: it was empty! All these marvelous sweets had disappeared as if by magic!

Feeling a bit uneasy, we looked at each other with surprise. Then we burst out laughing. Taking advantage of the dark, each of us had generously helped ourselves to the cookies. Keep in mind: there hadn't been any sweets at the Château or elsewhere for such a long time. That's why we were craving them so badly!

Now that the ice was broken, the "mystery man" also proposed that we use the familiar address with each other. His name was Eugen Lyrer, and he came from Zürich. We chatted amicably and, before departing for the night, Ruedi had invited me to attend the wedding of his brother in Tambouret.

Chapter 10

How Ruedi Schmutz Saved Edgar Chaim

From then on Eugen Lyrer no longer seemed full of mystery. Now and then we chatted with each other like old friends, and more frequently our discussions turned to Ruedi Schmutz.

Eugen told me all about the Schmutz family from Tambouret.

"You can't imagine the destitution in which they live on this farm. They have no electricity or running water. "

"You've been there?"

"Yes. They always serve me a good coffee with a thick piece of buttered bread. Did I tell you that one of our older ones, Edgar Chaim, is living with them right now?"

"Ah, so that's why I haven't seen him for a while. He always used to come to the gymnastics class with Addi Nussbaum. Addi should be in Switzerland by now. Let's hope that everything went well. But wasn't Edgar at the Château when the gendarmes came by?"

"No, he was already at Tambouret. Since his misadventure during his attempted escape into Spain, he never felt safe here. He lived in constant anxiety, like an animal being tracked. He was always ready to flee or hide at the drop of a hat. You probably didn't notice. For him the worst moment was in May, just after his attempted escape. Someone had betrayed him. The police were after him, and came several times to the Château. For a few weeks Edgar hid in the bushes along the Lèze River. He slept there and came out only to find food."

"Why didn't he simply go to Ruedi's?"

"He did that several times, but since he didn't have any papers, Ruedi could keep him no more than a week. But now Ruedi has bought him off for the time being."

"What do you mean, 'bought him off'?"

"Ruedi went to the police headquarters in Pamiers, where he knew everyone. He brought a big, beautiful, fat rabbit, laid it on the table, and said to the astonished gendarmes: "Prepare yourself a good meal, but leave me my Jew. I need him to work in my stable and in the fields."

"And that's what happened! Ruedi obtained a work-permit for Edgar Chaim, and the young man was saved!"

Chapter 11
We Swim and Play

According to law, the Middles, or middle-schoolers, were required to go back to school in the village of Montégut in mid-September. However, something didn't quite click. Did the village schoolteacher refuse to teach our children? Since Miss Tännler hadn't said anything more about it, the boys stayed under my supervision every day from morning to night.

Luckily the good weather allowed us to go regularly to the rocks around the New Mill to go swimming and to finish our days in the quarry working on our train. We always started with swimming because I didn't want my boys to have too much time to hurt themselves on the ever-steeper descent. We had lengthened the track, but now we had to redo the curve and make it more solid so the rails wouldn't come apart with each ride.

In the course of all this work on the train, we had become better and better organized. For the perilous descent, we delegated various jobs to different boys, for the cart was indeed very heavy despite not having its "tipper," the part that would have tipped up the trolley-cart in order to unload its cargo of rocks. We had to push the trolley up the slope step by step. At the signal, each of four boys had to slide a thick branch carefully under the wheel that he was in charge of to prevent it from rolling back too soon. This maneuver allowed those pushing the cart with all their might to stop every two or three meters for a rest. Once the cart had reached the top, it was ready to go! It was Mane Manasse, Gustav, Pierre Costeseque and Jacques Palau's turn. Raoul gave the signal: "Ready! One, two, three—go!" Each of the brakemen withdrew his branch. The trolley-cart started up with a loud rattling noise. The boys screamed with excitement. The cart approached the curve at break-neck speed! Oh my gosh! The rails so carefully laid flew apart in all directions.

With endless patience, and without any wire (because we didn't have any), we repaired the damage as best we could. The brakemen were spelled, and the ritual began again. The new passengers were Isi Bravermann, Pierre Bergmann, Bernard and Gilbert. Robert Weinberg gave the signal.

Chapter 12
Edgar's Attempted Escape into Spain

At the end of September, we suddenly found ourselves with a new director, Miss Groth. She was big and strong, but nevertheless appeared quite reserved. She arrived just in time to relieve Miss Tännler, who had fallen ill. Miss Tännler felt weak and totally worn-out, and feared she had jaundice. She asked me to accompany her to the Schmutz's at Tambouret, which I agreed to do the next morning. Having handed over my "gang" to Eugen Lyrer, Miss Tännler and I set out on this long, strenuous walk.

We walked along the Lèze River on the county road that took us to Pailhès. At the police station we had to take the road past the old ruined chapel, then ascend by way of steep switch-backs to reach the pass that allowed us to gain access to the plain. After that, we arrived at the little village of Écosse. We had already traveled sixteen kilometers on foot, and the Tambouret farm was not much farther, very close to the hill behind the village that we could already glimpse in the distance. We had made it there is less than five hours. Miss Tännler was about to collapse, but Mrs. Schmutz, who was no longer young herself, took her in to care for her until she sufficiently recovered from her illness.

I looked around for Ruedi but he was still in the fields harvesting corn with his brother Hans and his father.

I sat down on a broken-down bench in front of the stable to rest my aching feet. As if in a dream, I contemplated the marvelous countryside spread before me like a beautiful tapestry. I fantasized over the delicious bread and butter that would be served for dinner.

"Good evening, Mr. Steiger!" Edgar Chaim tore me away from my daydreaming. I was happy to see him again and invited him to sit down. We talked about this and that, but I couldn't restrain myself from asking him about his unsuccessful attempt to escape to Spain.

"I will gladly tell you about that this evening," he responded, "but I still have some work to do in the stable. Please excuse me."

Then he changed his mind.

"Well, in fact I can always do that work later. The day is long!" So he sat down again to tell me about the adventure that had nearly cost him his life.

"Kurt Moser, Edith's brother, had failed to cross the Swiss border on his first attempt and now wanted to try again, but this time in the direction of Spain. Like me at Tambouret, and others from our group, he worked for a farmer in Conteret, not far from Mazères and Saint-Girons. In Saint-Girons, he counted on locating a guide, a so-called passeur, or "smuggler" who would take him to Spain.

"He had luck—or really bad luck—in finding one. As it turned out, the guy was really a traitor who worked for the Germans. He and Kurt got together on various occasions to work out all the details for the illegal passage over the Spanish border. Unfortunately, Kurt didn't suspect a thing.

"Kurt came to see us several times at the Château to report on the progress of his plans. According to him, the smuggler was a nice guy and completely trustworthy. His passage into Spain seemed to him a sure thing. He proposed that we follow him, and we were certainly interested in doing so.

"On his third visit to the Château, Kurt confidently confirmed that the moment had come: our departure was scheduled for June 15, and the meeting place was the square in Saint-Girons. Five of us had decided to go with him: Fritz Wertheimer, Werner Eppstein, Charles Blumenfeld, Addi Nussbaum and myself."

"I'll never forget the conversation we had in that square in Saint-Girons, Mr. Steiger. After we greeted each other, Kurt said to us:

"Fritz and Werner left for La Bastide an hour ago. The five people who have joined us also left an hour ago. That makes ten of us altogether!"

"That's new!" I said.

"You want to try to cross the border with ten people?" asked Addi in an agitated tone. "That's crazy, we will be arrested, for sure! And why

La Bastide? We never talked about that before. It's quite far from the border."

"True enough, but it's isolated," Kurt responded. "We won't go into the town.

A small truck will pick us up and take us to the border."

"But that's incredible!" Addi interjected. "A small truck is even more conspicuous. They can take us directly to the Gestapo! The Germans pay quite a bit for a living Jew, you know. If there are ten of us, the smuggler makes a tidy sum. And by the way, how much did you pay him?" Addi was at the end of his rope.

"Thirty thousand francs for all ten of us," answered Kurt. "At that price, he certainly could afford to put a small truck at our disposal!"

"This is crazy!" Addi practically cried out.

"Shush! Not so loud," Kurt said. Addi went on in a lower voice: "I'm not going along with you. The smuggler has made himself a great deal with us—and with the Germans! I'm going back to the Château!" Addi turned on his heels and was gone—and that saved him!

"I let myself fall back on a bench," continued Edgar, "sick at heart at the idea that the S.S. could arrest us and take us off.

"Kurt lost his composure for a moment. Then he continued:

"We have to try something. We always run the risk of being arrested..."

"We don't know anything about this small truck," objected Charles.

"That was supposed to have been a pleasant surprise!" Kurt responded.

"Edgar, you rest here a while, and join us at La Bastide in half an hour," Kurt ordered.

"I stayed on the bench, exhausted, and fell asleep. When I awoke, it was already getting dark. I was hungry and thirsty, and by chance, found a bistro where they gave me something to eat and drink without any coupons. I looked pretty awful! Reinvigorated by my snack, I followed the same road my friends had taken in the direction of La Bastide. The route seemed pretty dangerous. In the dark it was even more difficult than in daylight to quickly hide behind a tree or in a ditch.

Several times, I found myself in the headlights of a car, as if I were in the spotlight on stage. What a nightmare! I was terrified! The Germans could nab me at any moment and that would be the end of me for sure. Then I froze. Not a sound. My fear turned to utter panic. Addi was right: something did not add up. Hesitating a moment more,

I turned back and began running like crazy toward Saint-Girons, then toward the Château. More than once I had to throw myself into the ditch below road level to avoid oncoming headlights. I ran and ran, the whole time feeling that a horde of S.S. men were on my tail. It was frightful!"

Edgar let out a sigh in recalling that terrible night.

It was fear that saved Addi and Edgar. Werner, Charles, Kurt and Fritz were lost. The five others, apart from a certain Mr. Meyer, were lost as well.

In an isolated spot in La Bastide, very close to a German checkpoint, the smuggler met with each of his victims individually. He had them fork over their cash, took their watches and everything else of value on them. Instead of leading them into Spain, as promised, he handed them over one by one to the pitiless, omnipresent Gestapo in exchange for money. A living Jew, after all, did fetch a good price. So it all came down exactly as Addi had predicted. Charles, Kurt, Fritz and Werner were first taken to Drancy. Werner somehow managed to toss a letter from the boxcar transporting them. Miraculously, the letter arrived at the Château. It was very brief and written in pencil.

"Our smuggler was a dirty traitor. After fleecing us, he delivered us to the Gestapo. We are on our way to Drancy, and from there... Our final greetings to everyone at the Château. Charles, Kurt, Werner, and Fritz"

Later on all four of them were transferred from the notorious camp in Drancy to the slaughterhouse in Auschwitz.

For quite a while Edgar and I sat silently lost in thought. The sun had set. The cows returned from the pasture, and with them Ruedi and Hans, the two brothers. It was dinnertime. The mother had set the table in the kitchen and the father matter-of-factly lighted the carbide lamp. They had neither electricity nor running water, but we had a sumptuous meal: bread, butter, cheese, lard, real coffee and milk. All of this freely at our disposal! It was like a fairy-tale!

Chapter 13

Isi Bravermann is Saved at the Last Minute

The next day I went hiking again with my middle-schoolers. They were more famished than usual because at lunch we had only some horrible, spoiled fava beans. Racked with hunger, we were always on the lookout for fruit trees. We especially favored the plum trees in Pailhès, not far from the Lèze. Isi Bravermann seemed particularly starving. He scampered up the first tree he came to, even though most of the plums had fallen to the ground. (The farmers never bothered to pick them.)

Isi was a rather calm, even withdrawn 12-year-old. He was dark skinned with very curly dark hair and a round face with Mediterranean features.

Only later on, Eugen Lyrer told me the story of how Isi escaped death at Camp Vernet several months earlier. The story took place in June. A telegram from Camp Vernet arrived at the Château: "Come quick, a boy is waiting for you."

Eugen decided immediately that he would go himself to get this child. He procured a bicycle and rode to Ecosse and then on to Pamiers, our supply village thirty kilometers from the Château. In Pamiers he took a train to Vernet, and then walked to the camp on foot. He announced his arrival with the management and showed them the telegram. The director of the camp, visibly annoyed, read the message and demanded: "Why are you already here?"

"When it's a matter of someone's life," Eugen affirmed, "there is no time to reflect. One must act. Can I have the child now?"

Five minutes later, a woman and a boy were led in. Eugen inquired: "I received a telegram... Is this your son?"

She answered with a nod of her head.

"I've come to get him." He took the boy by the hand and drew him closer. The mother threw herself on her child, clutching him tightly, crying and moaning.

"If you do not let him go, I will leave him here!" Eugen warned.

That worked. Pulling herself together, the mother was resigned and whispered: "Please, just let me say goodbye to him."

In despair, she smothered him with hugs and kisses, then let him go. Lyrer took the boy, briefly said farewell, and was off.

It was in the nick of time, for just as they were leaving the camp, German trucks arrived to take away the prisoners. Isi was saved!

Our Jewish children and teenagers never received mail. They heard nothing from their families. At the Château, their suffering the same fate eventually tied the children together and helped them cope with the loss of their homes and families.

But some of them did not manage to cope. Rosa Goldmark remained an outsider to the group. She was virtually lost. No one could help her, for she lived in her own world of suffering apart from the others. Often she would wander around the Château like a ghost, her hand over her mouth as if she had just said something foolish. When we tried to speak to her, she would run away, frightened.

Isi, in contrast, quickly became used to life in the Château, and felt at ease among his comrades. But let's return to that moment when Isi was perched on a tree limb, eating some plums. The rest of us were stretched out in the shade. All of a sudden I was racked with pain, seized with stomach cramps. I crawled to a sunnier spot, lay on my back, and hoped the cramps would go away. But the rest of the group began to feel squeamish also, with the sole exceptions of Mane and Gustav. From high up on his branch, Isi was moaning with pain, while the others were moaning on the ground.

The situation was becoming dire. What should we do? How long would we have to suffer in such a state? I gathered my troops and set out for home, moaning and groaning, doubled over in pain. Naturally we refused any dinner and went straight to bed—except Mane and Gustav.

Our painful cramps finally diminished, but were followed by a truly terrible diarrhea.

(Why Mane and Gustav were spared we never did find out.)

Chapter 14

Walter Kammerer

I spent my days with the Middles. We would go swimming near the Lèze or in the deep swimming hole near the New Mill. We lost interest in the little train but enjoyed exploring our area.

To the dismay of my group but to my great delight, the rentrée, the beginning of school, was set for September 25 at the schoolhouse in Montégut, five kilometers from the Château.

But I was rejoicing too soon. In the morning, the boys and girls dejectedly set out in silence, their heads bowed. Two hours later, they came back all excited:

"They sent us home! The schoolteacher sent us home!" they cried out in glee, somersaulting with joy. That's not what I needed to hear!

Whenever I had the opportunity, I searched out Walter Kammerer, the pianist, to talk with him. At twenty-two, he was the oldest of the group. Since his name did not appear on any list, apparently he was not being hunted.

The older ones were all Jewish, as were many of the middle ones. Originally, there were one hundred Jewish children and teenagers from Austria and Germany who came to the Château de La Hille by way of Belgium.

Walter Kammerer recounted how in Berlin in 1938 he was the sole Jew left in his high-school class. The reason was that they needed him for their concerts—but the day came when he too would be excluded.

Thanks to the border passes issued by the Belgian Consulate, he was able to rejoin his brother Manfred in Brussels.

Following Kristallnacht, or Crystal Night, there were several from the older group who had taken advantage of the border passes generously issued by the Belgian consulates in several German cities such as Berlin, Cologne, Frankfurt, Leipzig and others. At this time there was a veritable exodus of Jewish children.

Anxious about their future, the parents brought their children, each with a suitcase filled with their belongings, to the train station. According to Walter Kammerer, about a hundred Jewish children from Germany and Austria would land in two children's "homes" near Brussels.

After Germany's brutal invasion, Elka Frank, the director of a Red Cross colony for girls, organized their hurried departure into France. In Anderlecht, where Walter was holed up at the time, Mr. Gaspard, the director, rejoined his students with the other boys and girls.

Walter gave me the details of their escape, the bombing of Dieppe, and their terrible train trip through all of France. Arriving in Toulouse, they could finally get out of the overcrowded boxcar. They were taken to Seyre, a tiny village—not to a Château, as rumored, but to an old dilapidated barn that was in fact fairly close to a Château! In Seyre they all had to sleep on hay, and the conditions generally were primitive.

Some of the older teenagers, including Walter, had been arrested by the police and sent to a camp in Saint-Cyprien, close to the sea—a camp sadly well-known as a center for deportation to Germany. While he was there, Walter contracted typhus and nearly died. He as well as Werner Eppstein, Berthold Elkan and others were liberated from the camp just in time by the Swiss Aid Society, a civil-service organization that was already famous for its work in Spain. They were sent back to Seyre.

During his absence, the Belgian "management"—that is, Mr. and Mrs. Gaspard—secretly departed. That was rather lucky for the children, because Mr. Gaspard was a very strict, even sadistic teacher who ruled by terror! The Gaspards were replaced by Mr. and Mrs. Frank, who quickly ran into serious debt because Mr. Gaspard had burned through the entire budget! The Franks sought and found help from the Swiss Children's Aid Society, that in 1940 took charge of the one hundred children in Seyre. For starters, each child was given a simple sleeping bag!

It was a long story that Walter recounted in bits and pieces. I will go back to certain details later on, but for the moment I will present an overview of his account.

The winter at Seyre posed a real threat to the children's health, and many of them became ill. They suffered various epidemics, including jaundice, boils and scabies. A Mr. Dubois from the Swiss Red Cross based in Toulouse came to see them. He recognized the seriousness of their plight but couldn't help because of lack of medicines and supplies. After some negotiations in Berne, the Swiss Red Cross took over the Swiss Aid society, and thus became the "Swiss Red Cross Children's Aid Society."

Above all, for the children at Seyre it became urgent to find other accommodations. Scouring the Ariège region by car, Mrs. Dubois discovered the uninhabited Château de La Hille. She succeeded in tracking down the responsible agent in Foix , and rented the Château for a very reasonable price.

Rösli Näf, a Swiss woman, was appointed director at the Château de La Hille.

She also had worked in civil service, and for three years had worked with Albert Schweitzer in Lambaréné in Gabon, Africa.

In February 1941, all the older boys and girls were sent to the Château de La Hille. Everything needed to be done to make it inhabitable, for the Château had stood empty for the last twenty years! There was no furniture, no beds, no dishes, nothing. Mr. Nadal, a Spanish carpenter and refugee from Barcelona, arrived with his wife and children at the Château de La Hille. In one of the outbuildings of the Château originally designed for agricultural purposes, Mr. Nadal set up a simple carpenter's workshop. With little to work with, Mr. Nadal made some beautiful, solid pieces of furniture, including tables, benches and footstools.

The Red Cross provided iron beds from Toulouse, eating utensils made of tin, and whatever else was necessary. With great effort and difficulty, some of the older boys dug a well in the courtyard, but when finally completed it barely provided enough water for the weekly laundry. Electricians were summoned to install lights in the dining-hall, the dormitories, and the other individual rooms.

In April and May, the rest of the children, the younger ones at Seyre were taken to the Château, at the time when Miss Näf and Mr. and Mrs. Frank arrived as well.

For Walter, the "reign" of Director Rösli Näf was difficult. No one at the Château knew he was suffering from an advanced stage of tuberculosis. He could barely do any work, let alone chop wood or carry water. The director took an instant dislike to him and considered him to be a lazy do-nothing. Because she was so strict, many did not like her very much. But Walter himself seems to have had a patron.

Somehow or other he had been given an old piano that enabled him to practice and play, and even give some concerts from time to time, usually accompanied by Heinz Storosum and sometimes by Edith Goldapper.

At the end of his long, detailed history of the children at Château de La Hille, I asked Walter why since he was in the older group his name did not appear on any police list and thus he did not risk being arrested. That was not the case for Mr. Schlesinger or Walter Strauss.

He responded: "Oh! That's not true," he insisted. "They could have come for me at any moment. I honestly don't know why my name is not on any list."

"How do the police get these lists anyway?" I inquired further.

"Very simple. Nearly every month they show up at the Château with their guns slung over their shoulders and ask for all those girls and boys older than sixteen. First they take down their names, and then they return later on to deport them. These policemen are following orders from the Germans who demand the delivery of a certain number of Jews each month."

He was silent for a moment, and then continued:

"Ever since we established our excellent hiding place—the Zwiebelkeller—they haven't caught anyone. We have sentries who alert us that the gendarmes are coming by crying 'Short-circuit!' When the police show up and demand certain names, Mr. Lyrer, who arrived in 1941, retorts that the Château is not a prison. Even so, he says, he could not possibly round up children. It would be better if the good officers got used to that fact."

"But where is it then, this famous hiding place?" I asked.

"The chapel's attic. In the old days, they used it to store onions. The entrance is hidden and truly undiscoverable."

Chapter 15
I Fall Ill

When Eugen returned from the wedding at Tambouret, to which Ruedi had invited us both, my middle ones were swimming in the Lèze. Eugen loaned me an old, rusty bike he had fished out from somewhere or other, and I set out on my own to the family Schmutz. It was a long, tiresome way. I was surprised how quickly I became exhausted and arrived totally beat. The wedding feast was long over, but they welcomed me warmly and offered me various delicacies that strangely enough did not taste good to me. Ruedi's brother Gottfried and his wife had been fittingly celebrated. Hans played the harmonica accompanied by Edgar who kept the beat by tapping on a broomstick. The music was unusual but pleasant to listen to.

We all drank some plum *eau de vie*, and I was beginning to feel rather strange. What had I done? My heart was beating too fast. I could barely stand up and went to lie down. But lying down made me feel even worse. My heart was throbbing in my chest like a trapped bird gone berserk. I felt my final hours were upon me, but the night dragged on interminably.

I got up at seven o'clock and left on my bike without saying goodbye, and even foregoing the delicious breakfast of buttered bread and milk.

I had eight kilometers to go on foot, pushing my bicycle up to the mountain pass. It was a real nightmare! Since I was so weak, I barely made any progress. Every kilometer was like climbing an Alpine summit. I couldn't go on. I managed to rest a bit by leaning for a moment on the metal meter-markers along the road. I dragged myself from one marker to the next: from the seventh to the eighth, then another hundred meters to the ninth.... Finally I arrived at the tenth, with its yellow cap marking a kilometer—and I began again... It was hell! I struggled for hours, and at last I got to the pass. I was saved! From there on the route was all downhill as far as Pailhès. What a relief!

When I finally arrived at the Château, half-dead, the bell tolled for the midday meal, but I was in no shape to meet up with anyone. I did my best to drag myself up the stairs to my attic cubbyhole. I threw myself down on my bed and didn't budge.

Loyal Robert, who always showed up to see how I was doing, peeked into my room, but since I didn't say a word, he silently slipped away, full of worries.

Toward evening after I had slept for several hours, I gathered my strength to get up. I certainly felt better, but still was not quite there. What had happened to me?

Down in the courtyard my middle group gathered around me. They had been left alone the whole afternoon. I wondered if I should do something with them, but since it was already quite late I let them go off on their own. Robert came to sit by me, and I told him about the wedding, my terrible night, and how I was actually doing better.

We watched the Mickeys happily playing in the courtyard until dinnertime. When we heard the dinner bell, we went into the dining-hall. Miss Groth sat at the head of the table and I sat at her left. I apologized for my absence at the midday meal, and she asked me how I was doing. Obviously she could tell that something was terribly wrong with me.

She looked around at all the children who were sitting on their benches at the table, and then she laid a packet of letters next to her plate. She always went through this routine. I glanced at the pile of letters and I immediately noticed my parents' handwriting on an envelope addressed to me. I asked politely, "May I have my letter, please?" but she ignored me. In her usual loud voice, she simply said "Bon appétit!" and we all began to eat: grits with milk and applesauce served in the large tin plates. Completely famished, I ate my meal and felt much better afterwards.

Before allowing anyone to leave the table, the director informed us that a new Swiss colleague had been scheduled to arrive just before lunch. Then she said the usual "You may leave the table!" and handed me my letter. I had already been in France for six weeks, and the letter had taken three weeks to arrive.

Chapter 16
Heinrich Kägi's Arrival and My Deplorable Condition

At nine o'clock in the evening, all the staff, except Mrs. Schlesinger, were in the salon, when Miss Groth came in with our new colleague. This was quite an event. All eyes were on him: a tall, well-built young man who returned our gaze through his tortoiseshell glasses. Then he offered our director the tin of Nescafé he had been holding. He was introduced to us as "our new colleague, Professor Heinrich Kägi from Zürich." He went around and shook hands with the Swiss—Miss Tobler, Mr. Lyrer and me—and then the Spaniards—the Nadals, the Palaus and the Marimons. (Anne-Marie had not yet returned from Switzerland.)

Cilly and Gerti immediately brought in some hot water in large tin mugs, and Mrs. Schlesinger carried in some teacups on a tray. (Where did they come from? I had never seen them before, since we always drank from "glass bowls" without handles, while the children had their beat-up tin cups we called their "quarts.")

Thanks to our newcomer we all drank coffee and had a very nice time—despite the proximity of the police and the German SS troops in the process of arresting, torturing, shooting and deporting so many people not that far away from us!

As already mentioned, there was no running water in the Château. Using an old, rusty pump we had to draw the water from across the courtyard by the entrance tower. The rotation of a large wheel circulated a chain of earthenware receptacles that would be lowered into the well, get filled with water and brought to the surface. The water would then be poured into a giant pail, and when the pail was full, it would have to be hauled to Mrs. Schlesinger in the kitchen. We managed to carry the heavy pail by putting it between two wooden rods, as if the pail were a patient being carried on a stretcher!

This pump still exists today in front of the "workshop," an old out-building initially used for animal stalls, storing hay and straw, and finally housing Mr. Nadal's carpentry workshop. In the right wing of this building next to the workshop were two rooms—one occupied by the Nadals and the other for storage.

The day after Heinrich Kägi arrived, I was in this storage room with my middle ones who were unpacking crates of pears that a framer had brought us. The boys were having a good time, sitting on the ground and munching on the fruit. I ate a pear also, but was soon filled with pangs of remorse—actually, severe body pains and a splitting headache. I sat there glassy eyed, not knowing what to do. At that moment Miss Groth came along with Mr. Kägi. She had been giving him a tour of the Château and the surroundings. They arrived as if they had been summoned! I stood up, greeted them and asked Mr. Kägi to supervise the boys.

"I'm shivering, I have an incredible headache, and I think I should go lie down," I explained as I departed. I headed to my room as quickly as possible, clambered through the tiny dormer opening onto the roof, and lay down on the hot tiled roof in the dazzling midday sun. I thought the heat would do me good, but in fact—as I learned later—it could very well have killed me. Luckily someone knocked on my door. I called "Come in!" through the dormer opening. The thought that someone would enter the empty room greatly amused me for a moment, but then I thought better of it and slipped back down into my room.

It was Friedel Kriegstein from Cologne, a ten-year-old with long black corkscrew curls framing her pretty face. Her friend Peggy Weinberg from Vienna was with her. "I fell down in the courtyard," Friedel sobbed, and showed me her bloody knee.

I pointed to the footstool and tried consoling her. "Oh, it's not so bad. I'll put on a nice bandage. Come, sit down."

Friedel took her seat and Peggy, Robert's sister, stood by her. Peggy—also ten years old—had a strong, high-spirited personality. Her hair fell in long black skeins, her lips were full, and her eyes sparkling. She wore a pretty little summer skirt and floral blouse. It was still warm; autumn was late in coming.

When I went to reach for my doctors-satchel behind the door, I suddenly felt faint. Everything went black. I had to sit down again on my bed to regain my equilibrium. I opened the satchel and took out everything I needed and set it alongside me. I had to carefully clean the rather large wound and remove the countless grains of sand embedded in it. Friedel courageously clenched her teeth while Peggy held her hand. A quarter of an hour later, Friedel could proudly show off her artfully handmade bandage, while flashing her usual smile.

"Thank you. Mr. Steiger," Friedel said in parting.

I said goodbye, accompanied them to the door, and then collapsed onto my bed, completely done in. I stayed in this position for four hours. Nothing moved in the Château. Silence. I vaguely heard some children's voices. No one came by to see me. "I could croak right here, and no one would notice," I thought to myself. "Not even Robert who follows me around like a puppy dog." (Robert was the complete opposite of Pierre Bergmann who was small, dark and extremely talkative. Robert was tall, rather withdrawn and very serious for his age, very clearheaded. When his comrades got overly excited, he backed away from them. He had never left me since our three-day excursion, following me everywhere, always quiet and discreet, without ever posing any questions.)

Night began to fall. My tiny dormer "port-hole" seemed to stare at me like a Cyclops' eye. I looked at the darkening, now menacing sky. "Why had I come to France?" I wondered. "To die miserably in this hole?" I stared into the darkness, and there I saw—Death.

Somebody knocked. It was Robert. "Do you see Death over there?" I mumbled, pointing to the darkest corner of my attic room.

"I don't see anything," he responded, visibly shaken.

"You're right, it's nothing. I'm hallucinating. I'm sick. Come back tomorrow." Frightened, Robert left without saying a word.

I fell into an agonizing semi-consciousness. Around midnight I got up to make my way down the long corridor to the WC in the tower. I was weak and wobbly, and hit my head on all the attic beams. I must have had a very high fever. Once I got back to my tiny room, I undressed and slipped back into bed. Death seemed near.

After this dreadful night, I finally glimpsed the dawn. A miracle! I was still alive! Mrs. Palau brought me some soup that I couldn't manage to swallow. It tasted like water from the Dead Sea. Mrs. Schlesinger brought me some bread that turned my stomach. My senses of taste and smell were no longer functioning, signs of the beginning of the end.

My physical suffering was tortuous– but what could possibly be the cause?

Added to that came another plague: flies! They sounded like an American bombardier in the distance. Without mercy the flies walked along my lips, my nose, my forehead, tickling my neck, and parading on my hands. They were driving me crazy!

Luckily, Robert dropped in to see me again. He came in on tiptoe and stood in front of my bed.

"Hello, Mr. Steiger. How are you?"

"Very bad. Listen, would you do me a favor? Take a hand-towel from my suitcase over there and chase away these flies. They are walking all over me by the hundreds, and I can't stand it any longer! Maybe they think I'm already dead."

Robert understood immediately and got busy with the chase. He set every dead fly on the footstool. Before leaving, he gathered them into a little pile—"to make the others scared," he explained.

From then on, Robert would come to see me several times a day, killing the flies and augmenting the pile on the footstool "to scare them away." Then he would quietly disappear.

I stayed in bed gravely ill for about ten days. From time to time, Mrs. Palau would bring me some soup without salt or some potatoes, for I couldn't bring myself to eat anything else. Except for her and Robert, no one else came to see me. I guess they were afraid of catching my illness. I took to getting up in the middle of the night, around three in the morning, when my back was too sore to lie in bed any longer. I would throw on my green jogging suit and prowl along the staircases of the sleeping Château like the phantom of Canterville. All I needed to complete the role were the chains to rattle along behind me.

Chapter 17
Doctor Pic

The third or fourth night of my illness—when I was as yellow as a lemon—I was terribly uncomfortable lying in bed. Just at the moment when I tried getting up, some heartrending cries reverberated through the corridors that sent a shiver up my spine. Should I get up and try to help?

The long, shrill cries were repeated. Then all was quiet just as suddenly as when they started. Again silence enveloped the Château. What was happening?

The Marimons' and our new colleague's rooms were side-by-side. But the Palaus had a room at the far end of the corridor. Something must have happened to Mrs. Marimon, our small, dark, vivacious Spaniard with the twinkling eyes.

That night I stayed in bed. I restlessly tossed and turned without falling asleep. Everything that could hurt in my body did hurt, but that was hardly important. The cries still resonated in my head. And if it wasn't Mrs. Marimon? In any case, someone was suffering worse than I.

The next morning when Mrs. Palau brought me some soup, she explained that Mrs. Marimon had had a serious heart attack, and that they had called the doctor in Gabre seven kilometers away. The doctor, Dr. Pic, arrived fairly soon after the call. He was a rugged sort of man with a pointy nose above his handlebar mustache.

"Couldn't you have gotten here sooner?" Mr. Marimon asked agitatedly. I can still picture him clearly—a small, typically empathetic, strong Spaniard, as he stood outside my door screaming and gesticulating. "My wife could very well have died!"

I hear him say it even now, as the door was closed again. Dr. Pic also stopped by to see me. He didn't enter my room but stood in the doorway, studied me intensely, and said: "Noted!"

He wrote me a prescription, laid it on the footstool next to the pile of flies, and went away. I had a jaundice—that's why I was so yellow. Was Dr. Pic worried about catching my disease?

Later on, when Mrs. Marimon was stabilized, Mr. Marimon told me: "This Dr. Pic really got on my nerves. Do you know what he said to me in a low voice when my wife had her first attack? That the crises would return more and more often and that she was going to die. He had the nerve to talk to me like that!" Mr. Marimon was trembling all over.

After Dr. Pic's brief visit, I could put a name to my illness, which somewhat reassured me. Luckily, however, I did not know that a jaundice could be fatal.

In the evening, after an interminable, worrisome day, my fear began to lessen. Somehow I had overcome it. I hoped for a more comfortable night, but I was disappointed yet again. A new plague was waiting for me...

It began around midnight. Mice! Famished, emaciated mice! They made up a very amusing game. They scampered onto my clothes hanging above my bed and then dropped one by one onto my pillow and my face. Then they took off at top speed to hide in the sleeves of my jacket or in the legs of my pants. It was unbearable!

Dead-tired, I nevertheless managed to fall out of bed and began on my knees to chase these villainous beasties, armed with a shoe. They easily avoided my attempted smashes, and scurried under my bed and behind my trunk, disappearing momentarily to regroup for the next attack. My blows, however hard, were in vain.

Then it was quiet. Nothing moved. Just as I was catching my breath, my door opened. Our newcomer, Mr. Kägi, in a long white nightshirt, loomed in the doorway.

Embarrassed, we just looked at each other for a moment. Then he relaxed a bit and asked, in a sympathetic tone: "Tell me, have you gone completely crazy?"

Just then, a mouse squeezed by me and I struck at it...into the void. "I can't take it anymore. These horrible, hideous mice!"

Around three in the morning, Mrs. Marimon once again began to wail in pain.

Like the Nadals, the Marimons had fled Spain. On January 27, 1939, toward the end of the bloody Spanish civil war, a mass of refugees headed toward the French borders that finally had just been opened. The first day there were fifteen thousand refugees, and after that many more. Afflicted by the bitter cold and near starvation, the Marimons, with their two-year-old daughter, and the Palaus, with their eight-year-old son Remington and their two-year-old daughter Conchita, were among those escaping on foot across the snowy Pyrénées. I cannot imagine what strength it took them to carry their children and all their belongings across that snowy expanse. Many died of exhaustion or hypothermia.

Reflecting on those innumerable tragic stories, I forgot about my own pitiful state and fell into a long, deep sleep.

Chapter 18
My Slow Recovery

Thanks to the pills prescribed by Dr. Pic, my condition gradually improved. On the tenth day of my illness, October 14, I was still in bed, but the Mickeys arrived with Miss Tobler singing "Happy Birthday" to celebrate my 25th birthday. Their singing was a bit out of tune, but brought tears to my eyes. It was a prelude to my new life.

Apart from this birthday visit, and the visits by Robert and Mrs. Palau, I was left alone in my tiny room. My illness seems to have genuinely frightened the others away. Robert came by every day to deal with the flies. Mrs. Palau brought me either soup or potatoes without salt. What else could she possibly have brought me anyway, since there never was any butter, milk, meat or eggs?

I slowly began to come to life. I would get up, get dressed, and go down to the courtyard to take advantage of the warm sunshine. I was still rather weak, but I simply sat there at the wooden table, daydreaming and observing what was going on around me. Two noisy sparrows perched on the table in front of me. They glanced at me with their merrily glinting eyes, then flew away. Life! I was once again among the living!

The Mickeys came back from their walk and welcomed me in high spirits.

Among them were chubby little Josette; serious Rosa the Marimon's little girl; Raoul's brother Guy, the sturdy one; Robert's sister Peggy the tall brunette; little Percy; Friedel with the beautiful curly hair; Jojo the sensitive one; and François and André, the mischievous ones.

The Middles arrived in turn, with Heinrich Kägi at their head.

"Hello Heinrich! Hello children! I am back from the dead!" What a joy to come back from the stillness of the grave!

I was still unable to work for several more days, but I was gradually regaining my strength enough to go down to the courtyard regularly. To my great surprise, Miss Groth gave me a tin of powdered cocoa from her emergency supplies.

A whole tin of cocoa! Unbelievable! It was like the branch laden with ripe fruit approaching Tantalus rather than moving away from him!

Then another miracle happened: every day the youngest of the Mickeys—Rosa the quiet, Conchita the boisterous, Josette the plump, Jojo the sensitive, and Guy the sturdy—received a "quart" of real milk mixed with cocoa. We called their tin mugs "quarts," so it was really just a mug of milk. And now even I got to have some real milk. That way I could take full advantage of my cocoa!

The milk and cocoa helped me regain my strength. Gradually I could take short walks, then slightly longer ones, but mainly I sat in the sunshine in the courtyard. That gave me many occasions to chat with the endearing Mickeys, the rambunctious Middles, and the older ones too.

The children that interested me most were the teenaged German and Austrian Jews. They could be arrested at any moment. The jaundice thus did have its positive side, for I had time to get better acquainted with Walter Kammerer, Onze (Kurt Klein), Ruedi Oelbaum, Rosa Goldmark (still wandering), Edith Goldapper, Inge Schragenheim, Irene and Guita Kokotek, as well as others. Moreover, I had the opportunity to study the history of the Château de La Hille.

Toward the end of October, I returned to eating with the Château's large family for the first time since my illness. I took my usual place, to the left of the director; along the sides were the Nadals, then Mr. Marimon without his wife, Miss Tobler, and Mr. Lyrer. Anne-Marie was still in Switzerland, and Heinrich Kägi sat at the table with the older group. Everything went along normally, as if I had never been sick.

As usual, for breakfast we had a piece of bread with some chestnut puré. At the end of the meal, "Heiri"—that's the nickname I gave him—proposed that we go check out the middle ones behind the Château.

"They're going to have a relay race. You should come watch!" he said.

"There will be nothing to see," I retorted. "They never want to play any kind of game. Despite all my attempts and encouragement, they always say 'I'm not playing'."

"Nope, this time they really are going to race. Want to bet?" he asked.

"OK, two bonbons!" (After lunch we once in a while got bonbons for dessert, and we used these for betting.)

Heiri agreed.

The race was going to start in a quarter of an hour on the wide lawn behind the Château. There were two teams. The first had Georges Costeseque, Bernard, Isi Bravermann, Pierre Bergmann, Jacques Palau and Raoul Perry. The other had Robert Weinberg, Henri Vos, the Detchebery brothers, Gustav Manasse and Pierre Costeseque.

Contrary to my expectations, everything went off as planned. The boys took off running as if wild beasts were hot on their heels. I had never seen them move like that! I didn't understand why.

"Heiri, there's something fishy going on here. Show me what you've got hidden in that bag."

"Swiss chocolates! For a tiny square of chocolate they are ready to run as if their lives depended on it." Ah, so that was it!

Returning to the Château, I bumped into Mr. Marimon. From a distance I recognized his silhouette, bent over in the vegetable garden at the foot of the high wall. Just the way he was picking the tomatoes, one could tell he was burdened by something. As soon as he saw me, he said hello. He gave me some good news about his wife, that thankfully she had had no more attacks.

"I consulted a doctor in Toulouse, and he gave me an excellent remedy," Mr. Marimon offered. His face lined with worry lightened up a bit. Then he frowned. "May that Dr. Pic never set foot on this place again!" he added in a menacing tone.

Mrs. Schlesinger, the cook, came down to meet us. She was a tall woman with a gentle face, who wore her hair tied in a knot at the back of her neck. Two older girls were with her; they came to find out about the tomatoes for lunch.

"I filled four cases. Is that enough?" asked Mr. Marimon. The cook said yes. "I will bring them to you in the wheelbarrow."

"Thank you, Mr. Marimon."

I accompanied Mrs. Schlesinger back to the Château, and the girls took off. "I don't really know them," I said, watching them disappear.

"The tall one with the glasses is Edith Goldapper from Vienna, just like me, by the way. The little blond is Inge Schragenheim from

Cologne. Both of them are nineteen."

"You come from Vienna? How did you end up in such an isolated place?" "By a number of complicated detours. It would be too long to tell you everything. Now, I am alone with my son Pauli, whom you have met. They came looking for my husband at the Château and what is worse, it was my fault that they found him." Overwhelmed by emotion, she couldn't go on.

Lost in our own thoughts, we walked in silence back to the entrance of the old tower. Passing through the little door always left open, we arrived at the back courtyard and the kitchen.

I remember the kitchen very well. A sink without water was under the window. There was a large black stove that no longer functioned, a solid table made by Mr. Nadal (Heiri would smash twenty-seven flies at a time with one swat on this table), and the door leading to the dining-hall. On the right was a huge pail for water with its carrying poles. Higher up, beneath the hood of the chimney, were two enormous laundry pots that were used to cook the meals for a hundred people. How Mrs. Schlesinger managed all this was a mystery to me. All the eating utensils were arranged on shelves: the tin plates, mugs for the small children, the salad-bowls and plates, and the "glass bowls" for the staff.

There was a constant buzzing of thousands of flies circling in the room like bombardiers. One day Miss Groth brought in a flytrap with honey and glue. In less than five minutes it was completely full of flies and was totally useless.

Mrs. Schlesinger put on her apron to start drawing water for one of the huge cooking pots. Abruptly, she turned toward me and took up the conversation from where she had left off.

"It is my fault that my husband is dead. When the police came, he was very well hidden. They never would have found him in that hiding place. But they said to me: 'We just have to check some ration coupons for tobacco, a simple formality.' I believed them and went to get my husband. They took him, deported him, and he never returned."

She didn't say anything about the four older ones who were taken at the same time. She could think only of her husband, of her excruciating error, and wept in silence.

The flies continued to buzz, Mrs. Schlesinger had to draw the water, and I was late for dinner. Unfortunately, the meal of tomatoes and the potatoes did not satisfy my ravenous stomach. I was always hungry. But I ended up getting used to it. Besides, I was recovering more and more.

I just finished my siesta from noon to two o'clock in my "tomb," and decided to visit a charming spot I had recently discovered. From there I had a gorgeous view of the entire Château and its environs. I brought along some colored crayons and paper, and spent the entire afternoon drawing until dusk.

Chapter 19
Miss Groth Lets Me Take Over the Infirmary

That evening, I was euphoric. I impatiently awaited my meal of rice and tomato salad (again), and I ate like an ogre. But I was still hungry afterwards. One of the results of the jaundice was an insatiable appetite.

After the ritual of dismissing the children from the table, Miss Groth turned toward me and asked: "Would you like to help me take care of the children in the infirmary? You know, in the evenings I take care of the little ones who have something wrong."

Indeed, I was very interested. I had already put my trusty doctor's kit to use in taking care of some of them, and loved seeing them consoled with a nice bandage.

We left the dining-hall through the kitchen and entered the tower. There we had to climb the narrow, creaky wooden steps that went up at right-angles at every landing. The first room on the right, directly above the classroom for the little ones, was the infirmary. The only furnishings were a long table and two benches, nothing else— no decorations, not even a picture on the wall. In fact, there were no pictures anywhere in the Château. Only the old, wide fireplace no longer in use lent a bit of imaginary warmth to this cold, whitewashed room. Miss Groth put on her white doctor's coat hanging by the door, and from a satchel sitting on the edge of the fireplace she took out her supply of bandages, ointments and disinfectants. She set everything out on the table.

When the first of the children arrived, she set to work. One after the other they sat straddling the bench in front of her and showed her an oozing cut on a knee, a scratch on an arm, a festering wound on a foot, or whatever needed attention. I saw that Miss Groth had very few bandages, which made me think of my own first- aid reserves. She read my mind. "What if you took over the infirmary in the evenings? You have such a nice medical kit!"

I was both surprised and delighted.

Starting the next day I took over my new role—that lasted more than a year! Rumors circulated quickly. By first thing the next morning, little Josette and Conchita were whispering together. They looked at me with their big eyes: "Are you our doctor now?"

"Yes, every evening."

"See, Conchita, I told you so." Josette said triumphantly. After dinner, the children came to see me in groups. They wanted to "try out" the new doctor. I already had everything I needed set out on the table. I put on the doctor's white coat and was all set to go!

My supplies were ample. I was readily able to take care of the scratches, cuts, boils and infected wounds. The little ones were often content to get a little ointment on their "booboos" and went off feeling "cured" and well taken care of.

My first session was a success. The new doctor was accepted.

Just as I was putting everything away, along came three of the older ones: Onze, Ruedi Oelbaum (a young Jewish boy from Berlin) and Ilse Brünell. Onze complained of a headache, and I gave him some pain medicine and advised him to go lie down.

While I was treating Ruedi's boil, Ilse opened the cupboard next to the fireplace. "Do you know about our hiding place, Mr. Steiger?"

At first I didn't understand what she had in mind. Then I realized: "You mean the secret *Zwiebelkeller*?"

"Exactly, the undiscoverable hiding place. Are you familiar with it?"

"No. No one has shown it to me."

"I'll do it! Here," she said, pointing to the cupboard.

"I don't believe you!" I got up to go check it out. In the cupboard were nothing but shelves filled with empty jam jars. Disappointed, I shook my head and said: "Ilse, you're making fun of me."

"But it's there, the *Zwiebelkeller*! There's a passageway. Mr. Nadal disguised it with boards and shelves."

"Where does it go?"

"To the loft in the chapel. You know the chapel. It's right next to the central building of the Château, and has a cross on top."

"I know, with a little staircase in front of the entrance."

"Yes, but it's locked, and we are not allowed to go in. Old furnishings from the Château are stored in there."

"But how can one get to the loft with these shelves in the way?"

"The bottom shelf is movable. There is just enough space for a person to squeeze through."

"Have you already done that?"

"Of course. All of us older ones have. We have hidden there more than once, when the police came or we got an alert."

"You too?" I asked Ruedi Oelbaum. "It all seems so unbelievable to me."

"Sure," said Ruedi. "I've gone in there at least ten times! When the situation becomes dangerous, our look-out warns us from his post on the way to the Lèze. He calls out 'Short-circuit!' and all of us disappear."

Ilse closed the cupboard and sat down. "The *Zwiebelkeller* is our salvation," she affirmed, and Ruedi agreed. After I sent Ruedi off with a bandage, Ilse turned toward me and said: "But you knew about it, our *Zwiebelkeller*."

"Yes indeed. Walter had told me about it, but I didn't know about the entrance. Certainly the Germans will never find it."

"They won't look for too long, but simply set fire to the whole Château."

"Well, that's possible. But tell me, is it dark in there?"

"No, there's a tiny window. You can see it when you are facing the Château.

The last time we were hiding in there, you were already here, so you probably remember. Two policemen were watching the Château the whole night. They were sitting just across from us, under the old chestnut tree. We had to be careful not to show ourselves at the window and could only whisper very softly."

"That was a month ago," I recalled. "I was looking for all of you—Addi Nussbaum (who went off to Switzerland with Anne-Marie), Manfred Kammerer, Heinz Storosum and the others. Then I inadvertently ran into the police in the girls' dormitory. We were worried about Heinz, the violinist, with the long black hair. We advised him to cut it, but he refused. Do you have any news from him? You and he were very close."

"Yes, he wrote to me. The Jewish organization JOINT is trying to get him into Spain, and then Palestine, where I will join him. For starters, I am going to work for a family in Foix as of tomorrow. Miss Groth found me this position. So this is goodbye, Mr. Steiger."

"Good luck, Ilse! Perhaps we will meet again sometime!"

And indeed, thirty-three years later we met at a reunion in Haifa, Israel!

Chapter 20
The Waking Therapy

During my long convalescence, when I began to feel alive again, even to experience periods of euphoria, another sort of thing happened—not especially of great importance, but still, it upset me a bit and preoccupied me for several weeks. One day after breakfast, Miss Groth summoned a little girl and told her to bring out her wet mattress to dry in the sunshine.

At first I thought I had misunderstood. Little Aurora came out of the dining- hall in tears. Outraged, I turned to Miss Groth: "No, Miss Groth, you can't do that!

Psychologically it's a big mistake. Aurora will think she is being punished and will wet her bed all the more as a result. Wetting the bed is a psychological problem, a kind of sickness," I said bluntly. Miss Groth seemed rather embarrassed and upset by my outbreak and at first didn't know how to react. Finally, she said: "Alright, Mr. Steiger, why don't you take over the issue of bed-wetting and *do* something about it."

From then on, I was in charge of the Mickeys every day. In the mornings, I would take note of who had wet the bed—which was easy to do given the little puddle beneath. Then I had an idea and a plan.

The Russian scientist Pavlov had developed a theory of reflex conditioning. A dog salivates when shown a piece of meat. That is an unconditioned reflex. Then each time the dog eats, it is given a loud signal or sees a light flashing. By repeating this process innumerable times, the dog ends up salivating just when it hears or sees the signal, even when there is no meat there to be eaten. In this way, Pavlov produced a conditioned reflex.

I imagined the following experiment. Suppose I wake up the children at the same time each night—say, at 10pm—and have them pee into the pail by the door. Now, I would do this for as many times as necessary until they woke up by themselves to go pee.

I was excited by my idea of the "waking therapy," and decided that later on, when I was completing my advanced studies in child psychology and pedagogy, I would write up this experiment as my research paper.

During four nights, I jotted down and kept track of all the bedwetting incidents. To begin with, I didn't do more than that. But still it was a necessary start. And I had to begin because Miss Groth had just returned from Toulouse with three new little girls: the two sisters Marinette and Pierrette, and Jeanne. They were between eight and nine years old, and apparently Jeanne had a problem with bedwetting. They were given a small room behind the Mickeys' dormitory, where Aurora, Violette (who was slightly disabled,) Friedel and Peggy slept.

At first, only Jeanne wet her bed, but soon after so did Violette and Aurora. Friedel and Peggy complained: "Me too! I want to pee in my bed too!"

That would never do, so I decided it was time to start the waking therapy. I explained individually to each boy and girl concerned that I was going to help them stop wetting their beds so that their beds would no longer become cold, damp and uncomfortable. I told them I was going to wake them up at a certain time every night to take care of them.

We started the following night. At exactly ten o'clock, I went from Aurora to Jeanne, to Violette in the small room, and then to Daniel, Josette, Percy and René in the big room. The little girls slept in shirts and underpants, and the boys in long nightshirts. Jojo had pajamas. I woke them up in the exact same order, speaking quietly, patiently and affectionately to them. Then at 1am I went through the same routine again. But alas! Several of them were already lying in their wet beds. If only I had a few extra pairs of pajamas or underpants. I had to undress each of them and fold the dry part of the sheet over the wet spot so that they could sleep dry, nicely covered up with a blanket of two-ply wool. I congratulated myself that—thanks to the director—I could take care of these children. Lying in their wet beds, some of the children had already caught cold.

At first, waking up the children in the middle of the night was unbearable, especially when my own alarm clock cruelly sounded for me to get up for my task, only to find that most of the children were already soaked through. Some of them got up quickly, others not. René slept with his fists clenched. To wake him up, I had to take him by the hand and walk him around his bed a few times.

When I finished my "tour of duty," dead-tired I dragged myself toward my own bed around two in the morning. Once again, like during my illness, I became the phantom of Canterville dressed in my green training suit. Returning to my bed, I was not able to go back to sleep. That's one reason why later on I often didn't go to bed much before one in the morning. I spent my evenings alone in the salon reading and listening to the news: the German troops were retreating throughout all of Europe! And I would hear these strange bits of personal news: "Grandpa is sick," or "the children are at school." I waited in vain to hear about an Allies' attack.

After a week of the therapy, I was about at the end of my rope, all the more so since I had not fully recovered my strength since my illness. I was able to win over Eugen to my cause, but unfortunately he abandoned the project after three days. So I was left alone once again. I looked up everything relevant to "bed-wetting" for my research paper: the evening meal (no drink!), the weather, the temperature and so on.

Luckily, my efforts were finally rewarded! I had the impression of inventing something useful and positive! I was happy to reconfirm the real connection between Pavlov's conditioned reflex and its application to the children who were able to take care of themselves.

The pride, joy and trust of my child protégés gave me the strength to continue my nightly rounds. How much longer would I be able to keep this up? I didn't know, but it was very important not to interrupt the therapy.

Chapter 21
Edith Goldapper

After the night's work, there was still the daytime to reckon with! Despite the strenuous nights, I was feeling better and better each day. My strength increased proportionally to the decrease in my supply of powdered cocoa! After a rather short convalescence, I figured I'd be ready to take up my own work again. But I didn't know if I was supposed to take over the Middles, whom Heiri had been supervising, or if I was to be in charge of the elementary-school-aged ones among the Mickeys.

Since both possibilities were fine with me, I decided to just wait and see what would come along.

While looking for Walter I made a tour of the entire Château on this, one of my final days of "sick leave." Along the way, I ran into Edith Goldapper and her friend Inge Schragenheim in the small classroom.

Inga was reading and Edith was writing something in a journal. We chatted a bit, and then Edith told me something about her history: her happy youth in Vienna, the precipitous departure in 1938, her stay in Brussels and then in Seyre.

"I was just fourteen years old when I had to leave my parents. Here's a photo of them." She broke into tears. She couldn't bear the thought that they had been deported or killed in a concentration camp. "My poor blind father. I haven't had any news from him in three years," she sobbed.

I was profoundly moved and didn't know what to say. She quickly recovered and put her hand on her notebook. "I've written down everything in this diary, everything I could tell you, and even more. I write nearly every day." She wiped her eyes with her little handkerchief, readjusted her thick eyeglasses, and excused herself. "It has nothing to do with you, Mr. Steiger, but I can't pull myself together any longer."

Edith lives in the United States now. From time to time, she comes to Switzerland with her husband. On the last visit, she brought me her diary and gave me the rights to do with it what I chose. Thus, I photocopied it and inserted parts of it into my book. It tells the story of a young girl on the run, exposed to Nazi hostility, and her arrival at the Château de La Hille with other refugees. But even at the Château, she could never feel entirely safe.

Chapter 22
Edith Goldapper's Diary—Part One[2]

I want to begin my story when I was a small child still living with my parents. At age five I had already begun school in September. Yes, I was tall and strong for my age. During my four years in primary school I did everything I was supposed to do, and I must say: with rather good results. Everyone was very nice to me, my teachers as well as my comrades. We often had a very good time together...

I am ten years old now. They say I am big but also rather dumb. They tease me at home, but not too much. Mama and Papa know what they need to do for my education. Now another life begins with high-school: English, stenography, geometry—all the subjects I am passionate about.

I shouldn't forget the piano and my dear music! I am beginning to take lessons. I'm busy the whole day but at least find time at lunch hour. It is such a pleasure for me! I am so concentrated on my studies that I do not even realize when my time is up...

When I turn thirteen, everyone asks me: what do you want to do later? I don't have to think very long, for I love typing on my typewriter and I'm interested in accounting. I want to continue my studies in a business school. My dear parents certainly agree on this. Unfortunately, "man proposes and God disposes." A great

---

‡ The use of italics for long sections in this book indicates that they are direct quotes from diaries, journals, letters or reports, not Sebastian Steiger's own words.

upheaval suddenly took place: Germany's annexation of Austria. Our lives became much more difficult, but thanks to my poor father, my unforgettable and generous father, we were spared from the horror. When I say "spared," I am not forgetting for a minute that he had to give up his tobacco shop that the State had loaned him under the pretext of reparations. The reparations were for the fact that he had lost both eyes in the war. Now that the State had taken his shop from him we can see what those reparations really amounted to! Alas! we were totally powerless in the face of this affront, totally powerless...

Now I can no longer think about going to business school. But in order not to remain idle, Mama looked around to find me some other training and found me a position in a fashion course. It worked out for me, and I began learning about the fashion world. I enjoyed it and worked hard. At the beginning there were fifteen girls, but after two weeks there were fewer and fewer. Everyone was leaving Austria. I also began thinking seriously of leaving, and I talked to my parents about it. I have never, ever been anywhere alone in the world. The very thought of it made me uneasy.

On the other hand, I thought to myself, at some point I have to live my own life. Every day, I begged my parents, my wonderful parents, to find me the means to leave the country. For four weeks I worked at the fashion school, while I had to begin the process of applying for an official travel visa. Above all, I had to apply to the Bureaus of Culture in England and Belgium. We were in contact with the Baroness Ferstel who helped me a great deal. She had a distant relative in Belgium, a Mrs. Goldschmidt who worked very hard for my passage to Belgium....

On December 18, 1938, we weren't thinking much about my departure when I received a letter from the Bureau of Culture with the order that I should appear on Thursday, December 20, at 12 Ruben Street in Cologne. I was happy, but at the same time my happiness was bittersweet. That I must leave my parents was hard, very hard. But I was young and didn't dwell on that too much. We can say it was the egoism of youth. Parents, homeland, everything was forgotten, and I was thinking only of my future in Belgium, in Brussels, on the sea. All these thoughts were swirling around in my head.—On that very day, Mama took me shopping. Naturally she bought me only the finest of the fine. Everything I wanted she purchased for me. I spent my last day in my parents' house, happy and satisfied. My parents gave me good advice and cheered me up with the thought that soon they would be following me. This was my only consolation. Otherwise, I never would have gone! It never occurred to me that Mama and Papa would not be able to rejoin me, since as an unemployable handicapped person he would not be able to secure a travel visa...

So now we have come to December 19, 1938. At 3pm I had to be at the West Railroad Station in Vienna. For my last midday meal I had my favorite:

Wienerschnitzel with potato salad and a piece of Vienna's famous chocolate cake, the "Sacher torte." It was time to leave the house at 5 Odeon Street, apartment 6—the house I loved so much and would now be leaving forever. This thought broke my heart. And then I had to say goodbye! Oh God! Papa wouldn't let us take a taxi because that might draw the neighbors' suspicions. And so we took the streetcar not far from where we live. My relatives gathered at the railroad station: Uncle Heinrich, Aunt Toni, Cousin Cilly, and Miss Sophie. There were other children and the person who would accompany us to Cologne. We still had a half hour before the final goodbyes. There is always more to say, but now it was time to go. The conductor gave the signal for departure, and I fell into Mama's arms, then Papa's, and back to Mama's. For the first time in my life I saw Papa cry. The tears flowed from beneath his closed eyelids. Mama was inconsolable. Me too! I was crying, but when I looked at Cilly, I had to smile. She was smiling and looked at me with her sparkling eyes that told me to stop crying so as not to make it even harder on my parents. We got on the train that began to pull out. One last goodbye, one last wave! Goodbye, my dearest parents, goodbye Vienna, my beautiful city. I loved you so much, but now it is over for good...

I just turned fourteen years-old, and already I had to throw myself into life, into the world. But then I reflected: the sooner you start, the better. Around ten that evening we arrived at the Austrian-German border in the town of Regensburg. We could go right through without any formalities, since there was no real border anymore. At midnight we arrived in Nuremberg, known for its pretzels and spice cookies. I slept through the rest of the night and woke up only at 8am.

Around three in the afternoon we arrived at the railroad station in Cologne.

The building's architecture is superb, and left a lasting impression on me. Not far from the railroad station, I could see the world-famous Cologne Cathedral. Of course, we went inside, and I will never forget that experience.

Our little group set out in the city and reached Rubens Street around four o'clock. We were led into an immense hall, where perhaps two hundred children on the list for Belgium were already gathered. The six of us sat down, like the others, and we were served a soup of green beans. I will never forget that because a worm more than an inch long was swimming in my bowl. I was immediately disgusted and had a strong urge to vomit. Luckily, it passed. After this "delicious" meal, I wrote a card to my parents as we had agreed. But then I was overcome with homesickness, and felt very much alone and abandoned.

In no time at all, it was 9pm, and we set off again to the railroad station to catch the train to Brussels. At nine-thirty we were off. Toward eleven we came to Malmedy, the border town. There we had a long wait. The border police suddenly burst into our car to inspect our belongings. They didn't bother with me at all, which was a relief, although I had nothing to hide in any case.

We still had a way to go. We arrived at Lüttich around eleven and had to wait another half-hour. I took advantage of the delay to change my pitiful three German marks into Belgian francs. Officially we weren't allowed to bring any money with us, but nevertheless I had taken my three German marks with me across the border.

Without any problem, they gave me fourteen francs seventy-five cents in exchange.

On December 21, 1938, we arrived in Brussels around 1am in freezing temperatures. We had to line up on the railway platform, where our chaperone with the Brussels Jewish Committee called out our names. For our transfer, we were divided into two groups: one group would be placed in family homes, the other in a children's "refuge," or "home," I was put into a taxi with two other girls and driven to the best hotel in Brussels, the Hotel Albert. There Mrs. Goldschmidt welcomed me warmly. I had the impression that she was a kind, wonderful woman. She assured me that she would always look out for me—something she had already promised my parents. Comforted by this meeting, I went to bed and slept until nine in the morning. This time another lovely woman was waiting for me: Mrs. Felddegen. She hugged me, and I immediately felt more at home.

At eleven o'clock a wonderful bus picked us up—at this point there were twenty of us—to take us to the children's refuge in Wesembeck-Ohem roughly fifteen kilometers from Brussels. We arrived just in time for the midday meal. After we got our bags, we went to wash our hands and faces, then were led to the dining hall where thirty children were already assembled. Among them were Walter Strauss, Manfred Kammerer and the Manasse brothers.

From then on I began a new life far different from any I could have imagined. Above all, there was discipline and obedience. On command we had to get up, wash, make our beds, or go for a walk. Curiously, I immediately felt a sense of ease in this children's home. It was quite astonishing. The first night I cried in my bed and felt terribly homesick, but one of the teachers, Miss Mally Schleien, came to console me very sweetly, and my sadness quickly disappeared. Since it was Christmastime when we arrived at the refuge, we all celebrated it together. Each of us received little gifts. The finest present of all would have been a letter from Mama and Papa, but since there was no delivery on Christmas, I had to wait a bit longer for that.

Shortly after Christmas, we began studying French. Since I didn't know a word of French, not even the slightest bit, naturally I participated in the lessons. I didn't learn very much, but just enough to make myself understood. Then I received letters from my parents, not just one but a whole packet of them. They were happy to hear that I had arrived safely. Sometimes the letters would bring on the homesickness again, but with all the children around me, it went away as fast as it had come on. I quickly made friends with the other children, and surprisingly felt extraordinarily well. But this feeling of well-being did not last long. With the best of intentions on my behalf, the committee looked for a better position for me.

[Edith was placed with a family in Antwerp but was very unhappy there. After two weeks the committee brought her back.]

I'm back at the children's refuge! I'm so happy I can't even tell you.

Granted, I am not as free here as I would be in normal life, but I feel so much better. Every two weeks I write a long letter to my parents telling them everything, especially that I am doing fine.

I've been back at Wesembeck for a week. Tomorrow a new transport is supposed to come. All my best friends have already gone. I've become friends with a very nice girl named Käte Kerschen. She's adorable, and we get along so well.

The new transport brought fifteen children, including Leo Lewin, Ruedi Oelbaum, Kurt Klein and Werner Eppstein. We are becoming good friends and are trying to make life as good as possible at the refuge. We've been successful at a lot of things, but this time our luck ran out. It's now February 1939, and we have to leave here next month to make room for the Belgian children. We will be scattered to the four corners of the country.

The momentous day has arrived. On March 31, with heavy hearts we had to say goodbye. I was again sent to a refuge in Zven, not far from Brussels. Mr. Robert Deutsch and Mr. Elias Haskelevitsch accompanied me. The new place seemed very welcoming. It is a Château that bears the name of a Belgian general, the "General Bernheim Home." A very nice eighteen-year-old girl welcomed me. I was told that she is our director Elka Frank. A young man came to get my bags and carried them on his shoulders. He was Mr. Frank. That was my first impression—not so bad! All the girls were nice to me. One day Werner Eppstein came to visit. I was so happy to see him! We reminisced about our time together at Wesembeck.

Every month some girls are sent to live with families or sent abroad. We older ones are roughly the same age, and we hardly ever interact with the younger ones.

Once again I rather quickly became accustomed to life in this children's home, but once again it didn't last long. A very nice woman, Mrs. de Becher, believed that I would be much better off with a family. Since I already knew how I didn't like being with families, my parents wrote to the committee to ask that they pay careful attention to me and act in the role of loco parentis. Mrs. de Becher decided to place me with a family in Malmedy. Whether or not I wanted to, I had to go.

[One more time, Edith had no luck with the family in Malmedy. The family didn't speak to her. Moreover, she had to do housekeeping from five-thirty in the morning until evening. In despair, she cried night and day.]

I'm back at Zven again! How happy I was to see all the familiar faces! I especially enjoyed talking with the Schlesingers. I loved this place so much that I would leave only if I were to be reunited with my parents.

On Fridays we put on plays or engaged in some other fun activity. We also played sports. Almost every Sunday we went on an excursion. Not long ago we organized an outing with the Belgian Scouts. It was marvelous! And now we have been assured the right to get together in Brussels with our parents or friends every other Sunday. I have routinely taken advantage of this by going to visit Käte who lives with her parents in Brussels. Not so long ago the Felddegens invited me to visit for a week. What a joyful life we are leading!

May 10, 1940. The war in Belgium has begun. As horrible as that sounds, it is true. Panic prevails. With every alarm that we hear coming from Ruisbrock or Brussels, we run for cover into the cellars. In our free time, we are digging a trench that may be useful to us at some point. Mrs. Frank is trying to find a means for our escape.

May 14, 1940. We have to pack our bags quickly. Unfortunately we can each take only two small bags the size of a briefcase. We put on as much clothing as we can, and pack only the necessaries. I have to leave my two suitcases behind. Meanwhile, it's four o'clock in the afternoon, and we are all standing at the front door with our meager belongings. With Mrs. Frank and Miss Lea we are thirty-five in all.

Oh, it's a sad sight to see us all walking to the tram, having said goodbye to our beloved General Bernheim Home. At Anderlecht we had to stop at a children's refuge to collect the younger boys. The director there was Mr. Deway Gaspard. Together we headed for Schaerbeck. Since we could not board the train before 11pm, we had to wait five hours in the overcrowded train station. At last, we were able to board—in two "superb" boxcars, one for boys and one for girls. Slowly the train began to move.

We had no idea of where we were going, not even to which

country. Thanks to the provisions we brought with us from Bernheim, we didn't have to worry about being hungry. Besides, at the train stations along the way, there were always generous people who would bring us food. We had been en route for a day and a half when we were finally told we were headed for France.

There were no toilets in our car, so that was a major problem. Getting off the train was difficult, since the train made stops in out-of-the-way places. During the night I barely shut my eyes. Especially the night when we were in Abville near Dieppe where a huge bombardment had just taken place.

We had to make a prolonged stop in Dieppe. We found out that the train just behind us had been damaged. Despite our fright, we remained calm. That made four days and four nights that we have been underway, but we finally arrived at our goal—Toulouse. We didn't get off in Toulouse but had to go a bit further, to Villefranche-Lorragnais. From there we were taken by bus to Seyre by way of Noilloux. We heard that we were going to stay at a Château, but upon arrival we were sorely disappointed. Our "castle" was just a dilapidated old house! The Château was ten kilometers away, but it was designated for other children.

We entered the deserted building. No tables, no chairs, no beds—a real wasteland. We put our things down in a corner and went to ask the nearby farmer for some wood. Soon our boys had put together some tables and benches that we used while eating the light supper the farmers brought for us. In some of the other rooms we put down straw to sleep on for the night. We lived in these conditions for three weeks, until we received some real boards to make real beds. Everything was rudimentary, but we were content. Mrs. Frank was dismissed from her post, and Miss Lea took over her position; Mr. Gaspard became the general director. Mr. Arthur Halot, a friend of Miss Lea, took charge of the boys.

Nothing much changed for three or four months, but then the management decided to return to Belgium. Mr. Frank, who was in military service, was supposed to take over. No sooner said than done: Mr. Gaspard and Miss Lea returned to their homes and Mr. Frank became director.

We hadn't realized to what extent Mr. Gaspard had us live under a reign of terror. The contrast between him and Mr. Frank now made that clear. One didn't shout any more, or at least not as loudly. Everything was much calmer. Above all, the work was much *more pleasantly shared. Moreover, Mr. Frank was looking into the possibility of getting us registered with the "Swiss Aid to Children."' And indeed that's what happened.*

On October 1, 1940 the Swiss Aid Society and the Swiss Help were united. We were extremely glad. We thought that they would really take care of us. For one thing, they gave us sleeping bags.... From day to day things became relatively better. Now Mr. Frank's mother is here to teach us French, and we are making great progress.

It's been five months since I left Belgium, and I haven't gotten any word from my parents. I have a horrible feeling about that. Absolutely no one has responded to the many letters I have sent. But one day I got lucky: I received a thick letter from Aunt Wally, along with one from my dear parents. What a happy day! From then on I received mail regularly, twice a month. The Swiss Aid Society found us some Swiss sponsors who acted as intermediaries for getting our letters to our parents and families. Mrs. Goldschmidt is currently in Switzerland and is looking into the connection with my parents.

Time marches on, and suddenly it's winter. Here at Seyre there was no wood, no heating and no stove. Such a winter I had never experienced in my entire life. In seventeen years it had never been so cold. We were freezing, but nothing held us back. We organized a beautiful celebration for Christmas. Even some folks from the Swiss Aid Society came to visit us, and we put on a play for them. It was really wonderful!

Time passed. In order to secure us better living conditions and at least more comfort than we had at Seyre in the Haute Garonne region, it was decided that we would be moved to a Château in the Ariège. So on a beautiful day in February Mr. and Mrs. Schlesinger gathered a small troop of boys and girls to take them to the uninhabited, empty Château de La Hille to set it up for the rest of the children. Until now, we were always together. In addition to the Schlesingers, there were Ilsa Brünell, Ruth Herz, Walter Kammerer, Kurt Moser, Berthold Elkan, Werner Eppstein and Mr. Elias. They had been interned at the beginning of the war, and had been authorized to rejoin us only recently. As already mentioned, Mr. Schlesinger drove some of us to the Château in order to prepare it for the rest of the children. In March, he made a second trip. In any case, I stayed behind in Seyre where it was getting more and more beautiful. We were perhaps around fifty, including the little ones, and from my point of view, the fewer the better!

The Swiss Children's Aid Society decided to send us a Swiss director. In May Miss Näf suddenly appeared. We were glad to be in good Swiss hands, and for us poor Jews in our situation that seemed to me to be an added security. At the Château, there was a very different sort of work to be done. Miss Näf saw to everything. Our move-in date was set for May 31.

Today we arrived. One could see the difference between Seyre and La Hille right away: here it is much cleaner and more pleasant. Above all, the surrounding countryside is gorgeous. On clear days one can see the mountain peaks of the Pyrénées.

There is always something new at the Château. They installed a water pump, electric lights, and even a piano! What a marvelous place! We often go on excursions, and there are so many interesting things to see and do. Mrs. Frank, Mr. Frank's mother, continues to give us French lessons. I must say that she has taught me a lot.

Unfortunately, Mr. Elias did not stay. On August 1 he had to leave the Château following some sort of dissension with Miss Näf. We were all very sad about that because we liked him so much. But that's life!

It's already September 1941. Tomorrow a Swiss teacher is supposed to come to lighten the load for Mrs. Frank and to help Miss Näf and Mr. Frank.

Mr. Lyrer has just arrived. Because of his strong handshake I will never forget him. Also he talks a lot about sweets and pastries, and seems to me a "sweet" man. He will teach us "older ones" all kinds of subjects: English, French, stenography, and typing. We all love his classes. There's a real difference between Mr. Lyrer's and Mrs. Frank's classes: in her classes there is so much noise, which she cannot control; in his classes we forget about the time and everything runs along smoothly and quietly. We have nicknamed her "Mrs. Bla-Bla," which bothers her quite a bit.

November 12. My birthday. Today, thank God, I am seventeen years old. The girls prepared a wonderful birthday table for me with lots of presents. Ilsa (Schmakkel) especially, and she and I have become very close friends. One has a good feeling when one knows oneself to be surrounded by those who love you.

Now the Christmas preparations begin. The dining-hall has been temporarily set up in the dormitory on the first floor. There we put on plays, and Heinz, Walter and I give concerts. Several visitors come from Toulouse.

Now Christmas is over. It was very beautiful and left us with a warm feeling.

January 1942. The new year begins. Mr. Frank is leaving us tomorrow. He also had some dispute with Miss Näf. One more gone.

February 1942. Today we receive the packet of Christmas letters that were delayed because of the holidays. On this occasion, Ilsa Brünell, Frieda Steinberg, Inge Schragenheim and I have written a long poem that they will read aloud and I will accompany on the piano. It was a huge success. Miss Näf left for vacation in Switzerland, and only Mr. Lyrer remains with us. Everything is going well, and especially our celebration.

March. Today Fritz Wertheimer arrived from Camp Gurs. What he had to tell us! Oh my god! It must have been truly horrible. The poor people! We are truly much luckier than they are.

Spring has arrived with warm weather. Everything outside is so beautiful. The flowers are beginning to bloom. In half an hour I will accompany Inge to Pailhès. From there she will travel to see her mother in Lyon for two weeks. Her mother, Mrs. Schragenheim, has been in Lyon since January after she spent a grueling month crossing the Jura Mountains by foot. This woman is amazing.

Leo came to Pailhès by bicycle to say goodbye to Inge. I will return with him on the bike to La Hille....

Inge writes to me very faithfully. That's how it should be. A friend should always write to her friends. While she celebrated Easter at her mother's, we had fun celebrating here. A whole bunch of people from Toulouse came by. Naturally Heinz, Walter and I gave a concert. In the evening we turned on the radio, and Miss Kasser began to dance. At first, everyone was very stiff. None of the boys wanted to dance with the girls. But after a while, people gradually loosened up, and we had a very enjoyable evening.

Meanwhile, we are almost in the middle of May. Tomorrow May 9 is Miss Näf's birthday. We wrote her a poem, and some of us made her very nice presents. But we all ended up bitterly disappointed. Miss Näf said she didn't want to make a big to-do about her birthday, which certainly spoiled our plans. We were all very upset with her. But luckily Mr. Lyrer's birthday was coming up soon. Now his birthday will be twice as nice. For the third time we wrote a poem. And this time the celebration was a great success.

Now the fruit season has begun. Boy, do we make the most of it! The line of plum trees at the Château invites us to happy picking and eating. The pickers take turns, and we all have a lovely time lounging around outdoors and eating delicious freshly picked fruit.

I think this is the longest period in which I have really enjoyed myself. Today is July 14, and tomorrow is Papa's birthday. Just as I was thinking this, the younger Mrs. Frank called me into her room and showed me a letter she had received from Mrs. Goldschmidt. In the letter she said that my own sweetest, dearest parents had been deported to Poland. At this news I felt sick to my stomach and nearly blacked out.

What they must be going through! That's the kind of thanks Papa got for fighting for Austria and becoming blind as a result. That is the stingy, rotten thanks he got from the cursed Germans. If there were a German standing in front of me, I would cut him to ribbons right on the spot. I am completely devastated. One time my parents received an order to leave, but through some undercover protection, they were able to stay in Vienna. But this time it's for real. Only God in heaven knows if I will ever see my beloved parents again. This is the biggest blow of my life.

August 26, four o'clock in the morning. What's happening? The lights are on in our room. We don't understand what's going on, but we hear voices in the courtyard. Inge, Ilse and I go to the window. What a fright! We see the police!

[End of Part One of Edith's Diary]

Chapter 23
Walter Kammerer; Our Situation Becomes Dire

J ust as before my illness, I often met up with Walter to have long conversations. Generally, I could find him in the "Grand Class"— the large classroom on the first floor above the dining-hall. As usual, he would be sitting at one of the tables made by Mr. Nadal, surrounded by books, with his tin can full of water next to him. He didn't seem to be doing well. He looked haggard and emaciated. His thick horn-rimmed glasses only accentuated his gaunt face.

I said hello, sat down, and asked about his health. He liked to feel sorry for himself and sometimes went on about the evil times when Miss Näf was director, and how she tormented him and accused him of being a lazy phony. He often asked me for some aspirin or some other pain medicine for his headaches, and always concluded with the same remark: "I can barely keep my head above water. If they come for me, I will simply drop dead."

Typically, I sat across from him at the table, and we talked about philosophy and politics. We discussed the situation of the children at the Château, the war, the German troops collapsing on the Russian front, the Allies advancing into Italy. Our region's dense, scrubby forests—the *'Maquis'*—made it favorable for the proliferation of resistance fighters, who themselves were called "the *Maquis*," or the "*Maquisards*." Incidents of sabotage and attacks on German soldiers were rampant. But the Germans did not tolerate this behavior, and retaliated severely. The terror spread by the German SS and the Milice—the horrible

French Gestapo created by Joseph Darnand—appeared in dramatic proportions. The roundups in Toulouse, Foix and Pamiers sowed the seeds of terror among the French. Hundreds of men were arrested on the streets and sent to work in the German factories. Posters showing a mother feeding bread to her child advertised the slogan: "Feed your children, work in a German factory!" But they didn't fool anyone! We knew about the murderous slavery in Germany.

The Gestapo struck everywhere. Hundreds, indeed thousands of people were arrested, tortured or deported. They passed through the Camps of Vernet or Gurs, then through Drancy near Paris, and finally to the concentration camps whose names we did not yet know at the time: Auschwitz, Mauthausen and Bergen-Belsen. Although from all appearances the war was lost for the Germans, the infernal death machine continued to function basically as before. The price paid for the capture of a Jew was still incredibly high. Despite—or rather perhaps because of—the proximity of our National Police headquarters, our Jewish children at La Hille were more threatened than ever. We weren't too worried, however, because we relied on our excellent hiding place.

Despite the Germans' pitiless tracking, the *Maquisards*—the resistance fighters—became more and more daring. They engaged in the riskiest sabotages and, armed with grenades and submachine guns, rashly attacked the German units. In return, the Germans became more nervous and issued a curfew: from a certain hour, one was not allowed to be out on the street. Anyone who broke this law was immediately shot. In our region they shot a young shepherd who was simply watching his flock and knew nothing about a curfew.

Many hostages were taken. One German soldier killed cost the lives of ten or more. In Toulouse, they were torturing captured resistance fighters day and night without interruption.

For the ordinary citizens life became more and more difficult because of the Germans' reprisals, on the one hand, and because of ever-stricter food rationing, on the other. The reprisals often targeted those who had been sent to the German factories but had escaped and returned to rejoin the *Maquis*. As for the rationing, it was virtually impossible to procure basic foods such as butter, milk, meat, sugar or wheat. Ration coupons helped very little. Everyone had to stand in line for hours.

The farmers had it better since they had provisions right on their land. Alas, the majority of them give little to others and instead supplied the black market. We did our marketing in the village of Pamiers. Every Tuesday Miss Groth, our director, took the bus, which stopped for her at the Lèze bridge—or sometimes did not stop! In that case, she made the thirty-kilometer trek into the village on foot. At the market she bought whatever they had to offer: potatoes, tomatoes, cucumbers or carrots. With her ration coupons she tried to get some rice or noodles, and sometimes she even succeeded in turning up some eggs or a bit of meat for enriching the flavor of our meals.

I can't remember a time when we had some real meat—except once. It was the occasion when our three emaciated pigs had to be slaughtered just before they themselves would have starved to death. This event had an unbelievably strong impact on the children and the rest of us too, as we heard the pigs shrieking and defending themselves against the butcher's knife.

That evening every child received one sausage, and the next few days a little piece of meat.

Chapter 24
Rosa, Percy and René

y health had improved, and I had been back on my feet for about a week. After dinner, I was busy with the children in the infirmary, and then, during the night, every night, I would wake the little ones for their "therapy." My work with the bed-wetters was much more tiring than I had imagined. I would not have been able to carry on except on the condition that after I returned to bed, I could sleep until eight o'clock!

In the evenings, we regularly gathered in the salon to listen to the radio.

Every hour the "English"—the name we gave to the BBC from London—brought us the news, introduced by the famous drum-beats of Beethoven's Fifth Symphony. The news was becoming more and more encouraging. The Russians had advanced on all the German fronts and the Allies had gained territory in Italy. After these reports came the "personal news": "Grandfather is in the hospital," "the little girl lost her balloon," "the figs are ripe," and so on. We always wondered about the meaning of these messages.

Rosa Goldmark

I roused my lazy bones rather quickly from bed, and didn't accomplish anything especially noteworthy during the day except for dedicating a little time to drawing the Château.

Eugen Lyrer was supervising the older ones, Heinrich Kägi was teaching the middle ones, and Miss Tobler the little ones. Typically one didn't really have the time to spend with a particular child. That was certainly true for me. What I most regret is that I never took the time to spend with Rosa Goldmark, a child clearly in distress. Her behavior was very strange. Nevertheless, I might have taken the time to be with her. She did everything possible to avoid people and wandered around the Château as if she were living in another world. Was I too young, or was I too preoccupied with my own concerns to help Rosa? I don't know. Perhaps I was really afraid to approach her and even to try to understand her. The idea that she might cling to me like a drowning person clings to a buoy frightened me.

If I had had the least suspicion of how much she was suffering, perhaps I could have helped her. If only I had spent one hour a day with her during my convalescence. Perhaps with the help of Heiri and Anne-Marie she could have been saved. But the best intentions sometimes come too late.

Percy Weinberg

We received a new child only five years old. He was the brother of Robert and Peggy. At first, he seemed to be a little shy. He would walk around with his head lowered like a beaten dog, but he rather quickly became adjusted and more relaxed. He had experienced a lot of sorrow. I will come back later to the woeful fate of the Weinberg family.

Before Percy arrived at the Château, Mrs. Weinberg and her littlest son lived in a wretched apartment in Castelnaudary near Toulouse. Her income was not enough to live on—or to die on. To economize a bit, she ate only at midday, and even then only some fruit.

Every evening Percy would go look for his mother at the train station. One evening he waited for her in vain. She did not come. He stayed at the station long into the night, crying and whimpering. Someone noticed him and some people took him in. Mrs. Weinberg did not come home because she had collapsed in a busy street in Toulouse and was taken to the hospital.

Percy was taken to Château de La Hille to be near his brother and sister. The "disappearance" of his mother and the abrupt change of environment had disoriented him. Consequently, he became one of my "patients." At night I would find him soaking wet in his bed.

René Baumgart

I was pleasantly surprised by some of my longer-term "patients." Aurora, Josette and Jojo managed to remain dry for an entire night. They had gained more self-confidence and that had a stimulating effect on the other children. Violette and René also made progress. Only Jeanne remained a stubborn case. Overall, my waking therapy was a success. I spent less time on it as I had at the beginning, and everything was playing out nicely. The children had managed to wake themselves up more easily and tend to their bathroom needs by themselves.

René, who always seemed to be testing me, still had some problems. For one thing he slept with clenched fists.

I always made my nightly rounds at the same time, but one night I found his bed empty at one-fifteen in the morning. I was immediately shaken. Where is this little one? I searched everywhere, and I discovered him only by chance. I spotted a strange sort of puffy object under his bed, and wondered what it could possibly be. And then I had the hunch that it was a sack under the bed, and somehow René was in the sack. But what sort of sack was it? How could he have gotten in there? I didn't understand it. But then I realized that René must be suffocating! Perhaps he had already suffocated! That thought made me shudder. When I lifted off his covers I solved the mystery. René with his thin mattress had somehow slid through the slots of his bed-frame and landed on the floor. But how could that have happened? I figured it out when I began to try to get him out. The slats formed a kind of lattice-work. One of the cross pieces was missing and caused gaps in the whole bed-frame. When René lay down on one of the gaps, his weight made the gap wider until it became a virtual hole for René with his thin little mattress to fall through. But now René was hanging there like a very fat money bag, and I could not pull him out.

Luckily he was still fast asleep, for otherwise he might become seriously panicked.

I had to free him as quickly as possible. He didn't budge at all, which was good—or was it a sign that he had indeed suffocated? I felt a cold sweat over my whole body. With my legs apart I carefully stood on the bed slots on either side of where René was hanging, grabbed hold of the mattress and lifted it up inch by inch. It kept falling back down again. But finally with all my remaining strength I finally managed to lift the mattress with the boy inside out of the hole. It was a difficult birth! Exhausted, I flopped down on the bed and freed René as quickly as possible from his casing. The sweet little boy was still fast asleep and had noticed nothing.

And he wasn't even wet! I gently woke him up, and told him what had happened—and let him run to the pail.

This was one of those stories that could have ended in catastrophe but luckily had a happy ending.

Chapter 25
My Class of Mickeys

I heard the Mickeys singing in the courtyard:

> *Il était un petit navire,*
> *Il était un petit navire,*
> *Qui n'avait ja-ja-jamais navigué,*
> *Qui n'avait ja-ja-jamais navigué,*
> *Ohé, ohé, ohé!*

> There was a little boat,
> There was a little boat,
> That never ever ever was to sea,
> That never ever ever was to sea!
> Oh-yeah, oh-yeah oh-yeah....

They sang terribly off key, but the sound of their sweet voices was very touching and drew me to them.

During lunch Miss Groth asked me if I would like to take over the older of the Mickeys, those between six and ten years old. Miss Tobler would continue with the pre-schoolers: Daniel, Pepeito, Mireille, Percy and Aurora. I enthusiastically accepted Miss Groth's proposal.

The very next day, October 28, I began my lessons with the elementary- school Mickeys, and they seemed pleased to see me and curious about how the lessons would proceed. At 7am when I went to wake them up in their dormitory on the second floor, they greeted me with big 'hellos,' jumped out of bed, and dressed quickly. Then they happily followed me down to breakfast.

Mealtime was the most important time of the day at the Château. Even more carefully than the kitchen staff, the children obsessively inspected each slice of bread, holding it up to the daylight to see if it was thick enough to hold some jam.

There wasn't any butter to fill in the holes.

After breakfast, we returned to the dormitory. Daniel, Mireille, Percy and Aurora were terribly disappointed not to be able to go to school with the older Mickeys, so I consoled them by promising to take them to the New Mill. Then I had to help those who needed it to make their beds. Their thin mattresses made little hills and valleys, and it was virtually impossible to level out the "hilly landscape" with the sheets. Only the thin woolen blanket laid on top gave the semblance of a smooth bed.

The iron beds were lined up on the left along the long wall, and on the right under the windows. In the middle of the room was enough space for three more beds. Next to the dormitory was a small room with beds for five more children, including Jeanne and Violette.

At 8am on the dot we reassembled in the big classroom. We had four long tables with benches made by Mr. Nadal. The boys and girls took their places, the little ones in front and the older ones behind them. I looked at them in front of me, and I saw how the whole group was excited and curious to find out what was next.

I sat on the edge of one of the tables and observed their happy faces. A deep inner joy welled up inside me. On the one hand, I was still alive, and on the other, all these sweet, happy beings trusted me. I was overwhelmed with a feeling of happiness that I had never experienced before.

I recognized Friedel, way in the back, who had come with her grazed knees to see me on my first evening in the infirmary—so long ago, or so it seemed. Her pretty, black corkscrew curls that had charmingly framed her round face now had grown quite a bit.

Peggy Weinberg, sister of Robert my loyal fly-swatter, sat next to Friedel. She had long black hair, and was eyeing me intently. Her somewhat heavy features complemented her rather pouty expression.

Then I noticed Pierrette, a tall thin girl, and her sister Marinette, who had recently arrived and were still estranged and lost.

In front of the four girls were the two warm-hearted, practical jokers from Toulouse, the brothers André and François Clément. Next to them were quiet René Baumgart and chubby, awkward Jojo.

Pierre Goldstein, a mischievous, good-humored boy was in the second row. Introverted Jeanne absent-mindedly chewed her fingernails, while the mentally handicapped Violette stared into space.

In the very front were my "freshmen," the beginner group who had never been in school before and could neither read or write. Among them was Rosa Marimon, the delicate little six-year-old I have already mentioned, and whose parents work in the garden and the laundry. (Mrs. Marimon was gradually convalescing after her cardiac attacks.) Next to Rosa was Conchita Palau, the other Spaniard—blond, radiant, and happy to be alive. She had a little four-year-old sister named Monique as well as two brothers: Jacques one of the middle ones and Pepito the youngest at the Château. Their mother Mrs. Palau worked in the laundry and did housekeeping. Her husband, our handy man, would be killed two years later. The Palau family had fled Franco in 1939 and came to France by crossing the Pyrénées. At first they stayed in a Swiss home for children in Elnes until they came to La Hille in 1943.

There were two more children at the front table: clever Guy Perry—brother of Raoul and the pretty Mireille—and then comical Josette with the big round eyes. One day Josette came up to me in the courtyard, where I was writing, and tapped me on the shoulder. "Mr. Steiger, I've come to bother you." She gave me a rather mischievous look before running off with her feet comically pointing inward.

Lost in my own thoughts, I scanned my students' shining faces to savor this most important and meaningful moment. These children had become part of my life, and I was going to devote all my energy to them.

"We're not doing anything," said Guy impatiently, breaking my train of thought.

"Of course, we're going to do something," I responded. "We're going to sing songs that everyone already knows." So we tried singing. Then I divided the class into four groups, one level per table. The first class sat at the first table, and so on until the fourth class was at the table in the rear. At that point I would have been all ready to begin the class, but the students didn't have anything, not even a pencil or paper. I myself had only my multicolored drafting pen– my prized possession—and my fountain pen. How could I teach four different classes with no slates, no notebooks and no books? There seemed to be no solution to the problem.

However, I was a bit consoled by the fact that the village school had offered us some blackboards that allowed me to at least begin—but with what? Anne-Marie had drawn on the schoolroom wall a scene from the story of "The Wolf and the Seven Little Goats," but the mural was covered up by the blackboard. So I had the idea of pushing the blackboard out of the way so that all the children could see the picture. "What is the wolf doing in the bed?" I asked. "He wants to sleep," suggested François. None of the children knew the story, so I told them the tale and dramatized it as we went along. They were delighted! The morning passed very quickly, and we went outside for some fresh air.

After recess, we did some arithmetic that turned out to be very amusing. The assignment was to figure out how many feet, hands and noses they had altogether. Friedel and Peggy came to help the little ones. I gave some similar problems to the others, and everyone had a good laugh. Sooner than expected, the dinner bell rang.

Chapter 26
An Outing with the Mickeys

One afternoon we made an excursion to Pailhès. We had to pass the police station on our way to the path leading up to the ruins of the old Château and chapel. The building had only its four walls, but the roof had collapsed. The trees and shrubs growing in the interior had a surprisingly strange effect. We hadn't expected anything like that.

We looked around in the chapel and inspected everything. Suddenly a loud hammering of a bell rang out. It scared me! Was there still some sort of bell-tower attached to these ruins?

I hurried toward the entrance. Indeed, there was a bell way up high, situated in an opening on the façade. The bell was not moving, but something was striking it. Mounting the very narrow, worn stone steps leading to the bell, I saw François on a small landing. He was pulling with all his might on a cord. "Stop," I cried. "The villagers will think there is a fire!" He dropped the cord and looked at me with astonishment. Meanwhile, André had climbed up also, and the other children rushed toward the steps. "Look out, don't fall," I warned them. They ended up sitting on the broken down wall not too high up. Above them, the bell was again silent. From this vantage point, we had a beautiful view of the chapel's nave and the trees growing within it. This was a "natural" chapel in every sense of the word!

The children set to climbing the façade, and again I had to call them to order. "Get down! Do not fall into the bushes!" François and André once more pulled on the bell cord. "This is fun!" François exclaimed with a big grin.

I sent them all down when I heard a man's voice from below. It was a farmer holding Jojo by the arm. "Let her alone, she's not the one who was ringing the bell," I said to the farmer, and he left without another word.

Leaving the chapel, I counted us up: thirteen! One missing! "Where is René Baumgart?" I inquired. No one responded.

"René!" I went back into the chapel. A faint voice issued from the bushes. "I'm here, Mr. Steiger!" Our timid René was indeed there, entangled in the brambles and bushes holding him prisoner.

While I was getting ready to liberate René, the bell began to clang again. "François, stop!" The sound stopped in an instant. "But it's not me," said François, "it's my hands." Again, the bell began to chime, more beautifully this time. I left René to finish disentangling himself, and I raced up the steps toward the bell. "You see," said François devilishly, "I'm not doing anything. It's my hands that are pulling!" He was quite proud of having invented this rejoinder.

I took him by the hair. "Ow! Ow!," he cried, dropping the cord.

"It's not me that's pulling your hair, it's my hands!" I said to him coldly. "Let me go, I won't do it again."

"OK, off you go." We went back down. All the children were waiting for us. They asked, "Did you find René?"

"Yes, of course. Wait here for me."

René was still buried in the brambles and was waiting patiently for me to rescue him, which I was able to do rather quickly. Relieved, he ran toward the others. Famished and exhausted, we managed to get back to the Château in time for dinner. Everyone else was already seated at the table and watched us enter on tiptoes.

Chapter 27

A Day of Joy and Sorrow

I was always moved by seeing the Mickeys asleep in their dormitory in the early morning. The silence, a kind of quasi-divine peacefulness hanging over the sleeping children, touched me like something sacred. My joy at waking them was like a father's, happy and proud to contemplate his children.

Daylight already filtered into the room where the little ones were stretched out in all sorts of positions, as if they had been thrown pell-mell into their beds. I woke them with a jolly "Good morning, children!" "Good morning, Mr. Steiger," responded several sleepy voices. They squirmed and stretched in all directions before jumping out of bed to get in line at the doorway for the first activity of the day: visiting the pail. Then they dressed—which didn't take very long since they didn't have many clothes to put on. Luckily it was still unseasonably warm. The boys put on shirts and pants, the girls dresses and culottes. They didn't have any socks or shoes. Then they filed into the dining-hall for breakfast.

At the Château, mealtime was the most important event of the day. We impatiently waited for it three times a day, as if we were waiting for Christmas. Sadly, we were often disappointed. What could Mrs. Schlesinger do if we had asked for more bread? There wasn't any more—nor was there any more meat, spaghetti, or eggs. She did her best. She had just come in from ringing the dinner bell, and the little ones were sitting up very straight at the table when I entered. I took my usual place and greeted the Palaus, the Nadals, Mr. Marimon (whose wife was again bedridden despite her improved condition), and Eugen

Lyrer who sat across from me. Then came Heinrich Kägi, always seated at the table with the older group, along with Walter Kammerer, Edith Goldapper, Inge Schragenheim and Rosa Goldmark.

I must admit that my first concern when seated at the table was to check out my piece of bread. It was always too small and too thin, prompting in me a feeling of injustice, even offense, directed at a piece of bread. Why were the adults' portions the same as the children's? Didn't we deserve something a bit more substantial? The terrible hunger that haunted me since my illness made me resentful and jealous.

These miserable pieces of bread on our plates annoyed me no end. After the meal I asked Eugen if he knew the reason behind this practice. I suspected that the director Miss Groth, had decreed it so; not only that our pieces of bread had to be identical in size, but that they also had to be the same as the children's. There was never anything extra for the staff. We didn't have the right to an egg from time to time or a sip of wine on special occasions. Everyone was treated the same; that was the principle. Clearly there was nothing intrinsically wrong with that principle, but the result was that we adults became hungrier and hungrier.

And then there was the infamous mail. Eugen went to pick up the mail every morning in Montégut for Miss Groth. There was a strict rule: no mail before breakfast. That was a cause of great discontent among the Spaniards, and in fact annoyed all of us, since mail delivery was one of the most anticipated events of the day. Even more: Eugen Lyrer was not allowed to distribute the mail when he arrived with it, because that "right" was exclusively reserved by Miss Groth to herself. For Eugen the mail was "secret." He would come into my classroom to quickly show me something, only to disappear just as quickly.

But I digress. Let's go back to breakfast, since mail would not yet have been delivered. The director would pronounce her "Bon appétit!" and everyone would begin eating. This measly piece of bread was admittedly better than nothing, and the nondescript chestnut purée, which stained our teeth, was not so bad. Moreover, we did have our "coffee" made of ground acorns.

At the end of the meal, Miss Groth surprised me. Usually she would wait for silence and then say: "You may leave the table." She herself would instantly disappear. But this time she turned to me and said: "I have something for you for your classes. Come see me in my office."

We went up to the first floor, crossed the girls' dormitory as they were making their beds, and finally came to her tiny office. She reached for a stack of what looked like black boxes and handed them to me.

"Here are some slates for your classes." I was shocked! What could I say? It was a gift from the heavens! She also gave me some chalk for the slates.

I thanked her profusely and excitedly ran to my classroom. We were going to have a celebration! "Children, I have a wonderful surprise for you!" Everyone looked at me with big eyes. "Look, look what I have here! Now we can actually write!"

At first the children were stunned, and then let out cries of joy and excitement. I distributed the beautiful, new black slates and a piece of chalk for each child. I wrote on the blackboard: "We are happy. We can write."

For the littles ones in the beginner class I wrote out a string of A's on the blackboard and explained: "With this letter A we can write the word Apple. A is for Apple." Awkwardly but intently, the little ones started to write—for the first time in their lives! The older ones too threw themselves into writing on the slates.

"Don't press too hard," I warmed them, "otherwise you'll break the chalk." The children were absolutely delighted. "Writing is fun!" I added on the blackboard.

But it didn't last. Suddenly Josette broke into tears. Her piece of chalk broke in two. Next, Friedel rested her head on her arms and was sobbing; she had broken her chalk also. That was only the beginning of the catastrophe. François's chalk fell on the ground and broke into five tiny pieces, Guy's into three. What a calamity! By now half the class was in tears. I didn't know what to do. "It's not so bad. I'll sharpen the ends and they will be ready to use again." I wrote on the blackboard: "One big piece of chalk leaves us many little pieces."

The class calmed down, and everyone set to work. I went from table to table to sharpen the ends of their broken pieces with my Swiss army knife. The pieces became so small that there was practically nothing left.

But we weren't at the end of our troubles. We didn't have anything to use to erase the slates, and the children began using their fingers. The most diligent added saliva to clean the slates. "Don't erase everything," I admonished. "Leave something there so you can see how far you have progressed in writing." But they weren't listening to me. Rose ceaselessly erased her line of badly formed A's to write a better one. She rubbed and rubbed her slate until she had stripped off all the black paint!

Realizing what had happened, she was crushed. Astonished, I reached for her slate and confirmed that the yellow color of the carton was showing through the black. These weren't real slates at all, but merely cardboard boxes painted over with black! The little pride and joy I had taken in distributing the slates now turned into bitter disappointment, even anger. How could one make things for the schools of such poor quality?

Suddenly there was a loud cry. Behind me, Peggy stood frozen in a dramatic posture, her eyes fixed on the ground. I knew already what had happened. "Mr. Steiger, come look!"

Everyone gathered around to see. What had once been a nice piece of chalk was now a thousand tiny grains of chalk-dust spread over the ground. Assessing the unhappiness, I finally said to the students: "We've had some bad luck with our lessons. Let's take a recess!"

Chapter 28
Rosa Goldmark

We had gone out of the classroom, and on the staircase I met up with Rosa Goldmark. "How are you, Rosa?" I asked gently. She looked at me for a moment then disappeared without saying anything. Discouraged, I went to sit in the courtyard, going over in my head the story of our classroom slates. I also thought about Rosa, who was haunted by who knows what. I had heard a rumor about a disappointed love affair with Peter Salz. Some said she suffered from his escape into Switzerland.

Why did no one bother about her? Why had I never seen her extend a friendly gesture toward anyone, not even toward her comrades who like she were forced to leave their homes and families to escape the brutal hands of the Nazis? She turned away from everyone and always kept to herself. But I reproached myself for never having done anything for her. I felt that this sick young woman needed immediate care, but I had never succeeded in getting close to her. Whenever I saw her, some inexplicable fear guided my actions. Perhaps it a fear that she would fixate on me and not let me go if I paid too much attention to her. This idea certainly had no basis in reality, but I was too young and inexperienced to deal with a mentally disturbed child.

Rosa seemed to feel completely abandoned. She hadn't received any news from her parents in Vienna in a long time. At sixteen years old, she was small and a bit plump, with wild dark hair. Her round face seemed distorted by her old-fashioned eyeglasses, and her clothing was noticeably unattractive and neglected. She wore a worn-out blue skirt, a washed-out pink blouse, and a shapeless sweater without arms. What must this poor, pale creature have endured that so much unhappiness is written in her vacant stare and repellent appearance! Just like Edith Goldapper, she was just eleven years old when she had to leave her home in Vienna and flee to Belgium by way of Cologne.

Miss Groth interrupted my reflections. She had just gotten back from Montégut five kilometers away with the mail that she refused to give out to anyone before breakfast "for pedagogical reasons." There were only some French children who received mail anyway, those who had come to the Château to replace the Jewish children that had fled. The Jewish children Gustav, Henri, Mane, Pierre and the "older ones" never received any mail. Friedel, whose parents were hidden in Nice, was the exception.

Miss Groth approached me and said in a rather disdainful tone: "I thought you were teaching today."

"I was, but now it's recess." She left in a hurry, clutching the leather pouch containing the mail tightly under her arm. I wondered if I had any news from my parents. Oh, this director! She could at least have told me! Always so secretive!

Mail was our second major preoccupation, next to meals. By holding on to the letters that had been underway for weeks, she frustrated us when she could so easily have made us happy. Her secretiveness seemed to be an integral part of her personality. She was the Château's sphinx, carrying out her duties in silence.

Children would come and go, but we were never informed in advance and were left to deal with *les faits accomplis*.

Chapter 29
Paulette Abramovitsch

We all knew that the director went to Pamiers every Tuesday to do the marketing. The bus stopped near the Lèze bridge and took her on her way. But when she got up at four o'clock in the morning and walked as far as Pailhès to take the Toulouse bus, we knew something was up. We could be pretty sure that some of the children would be gone that morning. I'm thinking of Paulette Abramovitsch who one day simply disappeared without saying goodbye.

When I arrived at the Château, I was immediately impressed by Paulette. She wore a short, shiny red dress, and her job was to set the table in the dining-hall.

Since I was a stranger, she looked at me with a mixture of astonishment and anxiety, and timidly said hello. Eventually we got to know one another better. Around eleven years old, she was small, pretty and lively, with long black hair. Her eyes were flecked with brown and seemed to change color. When she looked at you, it was with an odd, unsettling stare. Indeed, this was particularly uncomfortable because when she was talking with you she would come up very close, as if she were terribly near-sighted.

One day during one of my inspections in the bedroom next to the Mickeys' dormitory, she waved at me to stop by to see some photographs of her parents. "I've had no news from them. Perhaps the Germans have already killed them!" she said with a mixture of resignation and sadness. I was startled by her ability to speak so frankly. Her face nearly touched mine. "They are surely dead. Otherwise they would have written to me." She looked at me intently. I noticed that she had some tiny particles of dust in her eye.

"Paulette," I said, "you have something in your left eye. Doesn't that bother you?"

She stepped back from me, and with her index finger and thumb grasped her eye and pulled it out of its socket. I was shocked! She showed it to me, and then reached for a tin cup under her bed, dropped the glass eye into the water, and rubbed it with her fingers, and reinserted it into her eye-socket. She came up very close to me again and asked, "Is that better?"

That was Paulette. One day she left with the director at four o'clock in the morning.

Chapter 30
Egon and the Mysterious Visitor.

The occupation of France became more and more brutal. At the Château it was as if we were living on an island. All around us horrible tragedies were being played out. The Germans were on a death hunt for *Maquisards*—the resistance fighters—and Jews. They would arrest people on the streets or in their homes and send them to work in the German factories.

In Toulouse everyone was terrified of the roundups. The Germans would barricade the streets to trap passers-by as if they were fish being caught in a net. At the general headquarters of the Gestapo, located on the street now called the Street of Martyrs, the SS would torture people day and night. The French trembled with fear, and so did we.

After an interruption of several days, I listened again to the "English" on the BBC. The Allies were steadily advancing on Rome. I thought I had misunderstood when they announced that Italy had declared war on Germany. Unbelievable! We knew that the worse the Germans were doing on all fronts, the more dangerous they would become in France.

Our director Miss Groth, true to form, never visibly reacted to this increasingly dire situation. She never asked our advice and never suggested we talk about the dangerous situation of the older group. There were never any staff meetings called to discuss what provisions we should make or how we should handle the difficulties. Each of us was on his or her own. The director made all the decisions by herself.

One fine day a stranger came to the Château. Since there were never any visitors, we were highly curious about his visit. He came to talk to the director. What did he want? He left shortly after, without saying one word to us. He was evidently on an important mission.

The mystery was resolved a few days later. The man had come to take Egon to Spain. Inge Berlin, his sister, had successfully crossed the border early in 1943 and had arranged for this "smuggler" to take Egon. But Inge had done so in vain.

Miss Goth did not let Egon go. She considered crossing the border, where several of our children had been sacrificed, too dangerous. This decision proved fatal for Egon, as we would see later on. But perhaps if we had been in her shoes, we would have made the same decision.

Chapter 31
The Trip to Toulouse

The children in my class remained in a funk. I did all I could to console them, and I still tried to sharpen their pieces of chalk, but finally I gave it up. They were reduced to tiny stubs, and the blackened cardboards had become unusable.

Another miracle came our way! To our great astonishment, Miss Groth came into our classroom with some twenty slates—real ones! These slates still had traces of the beautiful writing of Swiss schoolchildren. It was fantastic! I was in seventh heaven! Delighted, the children clapped their hands and tapped their feet. I distributed the slates so that they could begin writing. They applied themselves diligently with their stubs of chalk, as long as they lasted. But one by one they raised their heads: no more chalk! Now what? We had beautiful slates but no chalk! Miss Tobler, who had already been in charge of my Mickeys while I had been sick, agreed to take them while I went off in search of some chalk. So I got up at four the next morning to arrive in Toulouse around nine-thirty. I went from shop to shop, and met up with Germans on every street corner. They were downright terrifying with their machine guns under their arms and the skeleton insignia on their caps. More than once, I patted my passport in my pocket out of fear of being arrested. Marshal Pétain's picture was plastered on every wall and building. The piercing look of this once valiant officer who unfortunately allowed himself to be manipulated by the Germans followed me everywhere. Next to his picture was a poster showing a mother feeding some bread to her child. The caption read: "Feed your children, work in Germany!"

In truth, there was very little to eat. The people of Toulouse were ravenous. I saw long lines in front of the food shops. Luckily I was not looking for some beans or potatoes! For purchasing chalk there weren't any lines. I asked in all the shops likely to have some—the tobacco stores, the bookstore, the newspaper stands, the paper stores—everywhere. If I had asked at the butcher shop, I would have heard the same reply: "Chalk for chalkboards? Are you crazy?" I might as well have been asking for the moon! My search was futile, hopeless. One could find neither notebooks, nor crayons, nor paper. All the shops were empty.

Somehow I had to find some chalk! At any price! I ended up stumbling upon a large department store called The Capitol. With renewed hope, I entered The Capitol. But as soon as I viewed the interior, I was again downhearted. It was as if Ali Baba's forty thieves had made off with everything! The store was virtually empty.

The German army had bought up everything not nailed down to ship it off to Germany. All that was left were a few very expensive items that no one would need or want: some huge ugly vases and an over-elaborate tea set. I went from one floor to the next. The search for chalk now seemed ridiculous and absurd. I was famished and longed to be back with my children at the Château. I felt lost and abandoned in this plundered "Capitol," in this distressing town. I went back down to the ground floor and by chance wandered into the book and stationery department, which was not completely empty. After all, the Germans didn't have much interest in French books! I went up to a saleswoman who was standing around looking bored. But I couldn't bring myself to ask for the chalk; I couldn't bear another disappointment.

"Do you have any notebooks?" I asked politely.

"No, Sir," she responded.

"Writing paper?"

"No, Sir, I'm sorry."

"Pencils?"

"No, sir."

"You don't have anything?"

"We do have books and other things that no one would want, like blackboard chalk."

"You have writing chalk?" I cried out. "Unbelievable!" I was afraid I had misunderstood. "You said you have chalk?" I repeated more softly.

"Yes. Is that what you want?"

"Indeed! Right! Exactly!"

Astonished, the saleswoman brought me a box of chalk. It was real blackboard chalk, thin and strong, still wrapped in paper. I remembered this kind of chalk from my own school days. I had been searching for hours, and I finally had my supply of chalk! I took the whole box, which came to sixty pieces—five dozen. I couldn't wait to get back to my students to see the excitement on their faces. Now we could really begin our lessons in earnest.

I left The Capitol in a good mood. The dark presence of the Germans didn't get to me now. Even Marshal Pétain's face seemed less threatening. Thanks to a ration coupon Miss Groth had given me, I was able to get a meager bite to eat in a tiny restaurant. Then it was time to think of going home.

One more time, alas, I did not get to the station ahead of time and all the tickets for the seats were already taken. Wedged in the crowd, I waited for the bus that, like some pre-historic monster, would swallow up this mass of humanity and squeeze it more and more inside its guts. Luckily I didn't have any luggage this time, and a little later found a seat.

Exhausted, I got off in Pailhès. Because I was famished, the hour's walk to the Château just about did me in. The sun was setting as I got to the gate. An unusual, somewhat ominous silence greeted me in the deserted courtyard. Everyone was in the dining hall. I could distinguish the muffled sounds of voices and plates, the familiar sound that warmed my heart. A wave of happiness passed through me as I anticipated reuniting with my pupils. Only at the Château de La Hille did I feel at home in France. What's more, I had their chalk.

The dinner of tomatoes and potatoes reinvigorated me, and I gave a full account of my adventures in Toulouse, proudly displaying to all my precious acquisition.

As every evening, I went up to the dispensary on the second floor to do my duty as the infirmary doctor. The little children filed in with their booboos. Friedel Kriegstein always came last, but she did come every evening. Every day she acquired some new injury, even if it was just a little redness on her arm.

Friedel was not the only one to come every day. Monique, a girl from Nice, as well as many others also came like clockwork, especially the girls. They all needed to feel they belonged here as members of our "family," so a bit of ointment gently applied to a finger could sometimes do the trick. Of course, they didn't have any trouble getting themselves into scrapes, and serious injuries were also not uncommon. They would frequently injure their feet on the jagged stones and the prickly bushes and dried weeds covering the fields. They were all barefoot, after all! The path to the New Mill is a good example. Where we climbed the hill toward Blanca Borda, the narrow footpath was overgrown with broom, that yellow-flowered shrub found on sunny dry hillsides, but also littered with dried, thorny twigs and branches that we called "*picots*," or sticklers. These "sticklers" would lodge in the sole of the foot and were terribly hard to remove, even with tweezers.

In the evenings, I would have my work cut out for me to extract these nasty sticklers from the children's feet—a laborious and painful process.

But it wasn't just foot injuries that were a problem. We had very impure water—that sometimes flowed red from the pump near our woodwork shop—and very poor nutrition, food lacking in essential vitamins and such, so that our immune systems were severely compromised. Even the slightest wounds became infected, and we were subjected to periodic epidemics of boils.

I don't know exactly how many children I would care for each evening—at least fifteen or twenty. The little ones always came first, followed by the middle ones and then the older group. I loved working as a doctor, for it gave me the opportunity to get to know the children individually, both the girls and the boys.

Afterwards I would generally meet up with Eugen Lyrer in the salon around ten in the evening. The news report told us nothing especially new: The Allies were advancing in Italy, and the Russians were advancing on all their fronts. That particular evening we were alone in the salon. After the puzzling "personal news" on the radio, I enthusiastically told Eugen all about my luck in finally tracking down the chalk after my initially distressing and depressing search in Toulouse. I told him about the endless lines in front of the food shops, how the stores were empty, and how the huge "Capitol" had been bought out by the Germans. "I saw so many German soldiers armed to the teeth, with the skull-and-bones insignia on their caps. Each time I encountered them, I was paralyzed with fear and patted my Swiss passport in my pocket and..."

"You are not telling me you don't have an identity card, are you?" he sharply interrupted. Confused, I shook my head no. I didn't know anything about identity cards. Eugen quickly got up from his seat and exclaimed:

"Are you kidding me? You don't have an identity card? That is incredibly dangerous! During routine inspections, whoever does not have an identity card can be arrested, tortured by the Gestapo, and in the worst case scenario, shot!"

"What about my passport?" I asked, deeply shaken.

"Carrying a passport is also dangerous," he responded more calmly. "They suspect someone with just a passport as being a spy or a Jew. So many phony passports are floating around these days. You have to get yourself an identity card as soon as possible! An identity card is absolutely necessary!"

I was devastated. As if I hadn't already been through enough! I went to bed utterly exhausted.

Chapter 32
The Trip to Foix

My students were in seventh heaven with their new chalk sticks. They could write all they wanted! My trip to Toulouse was not in vain after all. What I needed now were some beginner readers, and since I had to get an identity card as soon as possible, I decided to go to Foix. You might remember that we were already in Foix with Anne-Marie Piguet and my middle ones to explore the ruin perched on the hill overlooking the surrounding countryside.

Anticipating a long journey, I left at the crack of dawn the next morning.

There was no connecting bus. "Our" bus that on Tuesdays picked up Miss Groth—or not!—today traveled only in the opposite direction. I don't recall how I actually managed to get to Foix that morning—undoubtedly mostly on foot and on a local bus—but I arrived there around noon. Since it was the custom that parents bought their children's school supplies at a bookshop, I immediately began looking for one. I figured correctly that I would surely find the readers I needed. I bought five small copies of *Papa and Mama* illustrated in color, four copies of *Anna*, and seven of *Robert in the City*. I was happy to have purchased all these for a relatively small amount of money. I looked forward to getting home to my children to see the joy on their faces when they saw these news books.

Now I had to get my photo taken for the identity card, so I began looking for a photographer. There were many small shops, but no photography store in sight.

More than once, I ran into a group of German solders with their machine guns, as well as the French gendarmes in their khaki uniforms. I detested them! They were serving the barbarians. I froze with fear every time I saw them, for I not only did not have an identity card, but on top of that, I stupidly left my passport at the Château.

"Let's hope they don't give me any trouble," I kept repeating to myself as I paced up and down the streets, absorbed in my own thoughts. Again I saw a group of German soldiers ahead, and crossed over to the other side of the street.

"Where does the third Reich get all these Soldiers?" I wondered. "They are everywhere, in Norway, Russia, Greece, Africa..." I came to a large square, where I noticed a photo shop. I went in, and a young man with a straggly beard greeted me. I told him what I wanted, and he led me into a small room, a sort of dark room.

"In these days, we've got to have papers, that's for sure," he said while setting up his equipment.

Then he said to me: "You sit over there on the hassock." When I was seated, he continued. "My neighbor, Mr. Durand, was shot because he didn't have his identity card with him." After a pause, he asked: "Do you want an identity card for a green card? If so, I have to take your profile as well. Turn and look at the picture over there." He pointed to a photo on the wall.

"But that's Laval, the worst criminal in the French government!" I asserted with astonishment.

"But of course," he replied. "You work for the Germans?" "That depends."

"In that case, I'll go to another photographer," I declared.

"But you're German! You are wearing glasses without frames!"

"A German would have papers," I retorted.

"True enough."

"I'm Swiss and I work in the region."

"Swiss! Well then, are you perhaps against the Germans?"

"That's for sure!"

"Me too, I'm against them."

"I hope so!"

The photographer took down Laval's picture and replaced it with one of General de Gaulle. He said to me sheepishly: "You never know. There are so many traitors. You certainly prefer de Gaulle! Look at him. That's better, right?"

A light flashed in the studio, and then another. "OK, it's done," the photographer said, adding nervously: "But don't tell anyone that it's de Gaulle."

"Certainly," I reassured him. "Please develop my photos and mail them to me." I paid him and gave him my address at the Château.

It was still fairly early in the day. I was hungry, as usual, so I went to buy some grapes. I had scarcely sat down on a bench when a group of German soldiers came around the corner. I learned later on that the Gestapo had set up a headquarters in Foix. This time there were two SS in black uniforms heading my way. I feared the worst. But nothing happened, and they went on their way. Whew! Once again I felt I had a narrow escape.

I was safe for now, but for how long? I had to get home as quickly as possible. I was filled with dread. Why did I leave my passport at the Château? How easy it was to lose one's life by a simple act of negligence!

Without being stopped, I arrived at the station and headed to Varilhes, where I could catch the bus for Pamiers that passed by La Hille on its way to Mas-d'Azil.

Safe and sound, I arrived just before dinnertime, and was greeted by quite a hullabaloo. Guy Perry was shouting at the top of his lungs: "Anne-Marie is back!"

Chapter 33
Anne-Marie's Return

Later that evening, the Swiss and Spanish staff gathered in the salon. Anne- Marie invited us for some real coffee she had brought back from Switzerland. That was an invitation no one would refuse!

You are already familiar with our salon, our meeting place. It still had some of the furniture from the last heir, Mrs. Péreau, who had died some twenty-three years ago. Since her death, the Château remained uninhabited in this isolated location. It had come back to life only with the arrival of the Jewish children.

Soon everyone was gathered, with the exception of Eugen Lyrer, who typically remained aloof. We made ourselves as comfortable as possible on the rickety wooden chairs, the old red armchairs, and the sagging couch. Mr. Marimon excused the absence of his wife who had some housework to do, especially since she had just recovered from her latest cardiac problems. Luckily Dr. Pic's predictions did not come true. The Palaus and the Nadals were seated by the window, Miss Tobler and Anne-Marie were on the couch, and Heiri and I had taken a seat near the radio. As usual we were discussing the current situation. We were constantly preoccupied with the same question: When would the Allies arrive? We had made some bets: "I bet you two slices of chocolate crème cake—from Switzerland—that the Allies will not come anymore this year," I said. Heiri raised the stakes: "Three cakes and three pastries of your choice that they will still come this year."

Shortly before, the Germans had jettisoned from an airplane some large paper leaves in brown and red. Ironically they had written:

"It's autumn. The leaves are falling but the English have not come." This was of course a sarcastic allusion to the liberation that had not taken place.

We hadn't noticed that Mrs. Schlesinger and Miss Groth had come in carrying the special cups rimmed in gold. Mrs. Schlesinger was accompanied by her helper Cilly Stückler. One of the nineteen children from Vienna, Cilly was a pretty girl with dark eyes and beautiful dark wavy hair. She poured the precious coffee and distributed the cups. In order to make the occasion even more special, everyone received a cube of sugar. Mrs. Palau smiled while watching me stir my coffee with my little finger, since there were no spoons. "Look at what Mr. Steiger is doing," she exclaimed.

"Would you like me to do the same for you?" I proposed. Everyone laughed good-naturedly. It was rare to have real coffee other than for special occasions like this evening. Wanting to get back to the facts, I asked: "Anne-Marie, would you tell us about your trip to Switzerland with Addi?"

Anne-Marie took a deep breath, and everyone quieted down to listen as she began her tale:

Before telling you about our trip to Switzerland, I would like to quickly explain why I have been away for such a long time. When I left here, I was already running a fever and had terrible headaches. I had to stay in bed for fifteen days with a terrible flu. But our trip was a success. The first part, the four-hour walk at night to Saint-Jean-de-Verges, was difficult, but after that everything went like clockwork. We got the train from Saint-Jean-de-Verges to Toulouse, after passing through Pamiers. We finally left Toulouse in the evening. That didn't bother us at all. In fact, we felt more secure.

Because the train was so crowded it would have been impossible to conduct a careful inspection. The train was so packed that people were sitting in the corridors. We had to stand, jammed in like sardines. The whole time until we arrived in Lyon, the only light we saw was like lightening from the train stations we zipped through at full speed. We were happy to see the dawn, although that presented a new danger. We were approaching Lyon, the stronghold of Klaus Barbie, the SS hangman. The train entered the station filled with noise and confusion. Groups of German soldiers were already on the platforms just waiting for their prey.

Or at least, so it seemed to us. Luckily, we could stay on the train that would soon be heading toward Mulhouse- Strasbourg.

"Addi and I got off at Lons-le-Saunier, a little town in the French Jura, in order to catch a bus for Champagnole. This was tricky for us, since there were already some German soldiers at the station in Lons-le-Saunier. Several of them wore black uniforms, and we knew that the black SS was something to fear. Indeed, we were petrified, and felt particularly conspicuous with our large backpacks. But we were lucky again. Apparently the Germans were there to check just the passengers on the train, and we were able to leave the station without any difficulty to catch our bus.

"The bus drove us into the Jura Mountains. I had an excruciating headache, and the interminable curves on the mountain road drove me crazy. My friend Victoria greeted us warmly in Champagnole. I was completely exhausted and running a fever, so I went straight to bed.

"What else can I tell you? I had to lie in bed two days to get over the fever. The waiting and inaction made Addi extremely nervous. He feared falling into the hands of the Germans, and imagined himself already arrested by the Swiss and sent back to the border. In short, he was terrified.

"Finally we set out again with Victoria as our guide. She knew every tree, every rock, every fork in the paths we hiked for hours crossing the forest. As we approached the border our path became increasingly steep. We didn't talk at all; from time to time we stopped dead in our tracks at the slightest noise. We surveyed our surroundings like a hare that freezes on its hind legs to check for danger. We knew our life was in the balance.

"In short, I can tell you that everything went very well. We saw not one German. We arrived at "Chapel of the Woods" and after a long, strenuous climb of Mount Risoux we crossed the border. We said goodbye to Victoria, thanked her for her tremendous help, and couldn't help expressing our concern for her safety on her way home. She laughed and said: "You don't have to worry about me. I'm very much at home in these forests."

"I too was able to find my way in my father's forests without much trouble, but coming across a Swiss patrol still posed a great danger. The moment we were alone, our fear took over. When Victoria was with us, her confidence and assurance had been a huge support. But now, alone and so close to our goal, we were overcome with anxiety.

We threw ourselves to the ground at the slightest sound. Addi dreaded being arrested and delivered over to the Germans at the last moment by the Swiss border control. Night had begun to fall when we arrived at my parents' house—exhausted, but safe and sound. My parents' joy at seeing us was indescribable. We were saved!

When Anne-Marie finished her story, there was a long silence. We had been intently focused on listening to her account. Each of us tried to imagine this drama of crossing the border into freedom. We sipped our coffee that had become cold, and gradually we relaxed a bit and began talking again. But then we quickly became involved in a heated discussion. We couldn't understand why Switzerland— supposedly a land of asylum!—could so pitilessly refuse the Jewish refugees at the border, including some of our own children from La Hille, and send them back to a near certain death. What a horrendous shame!

Had the Swiss government sold out to the anti-Semites? Is it possible that the Swiss didn't know about the death camps in Germany? No, that was not possible.

Since 1943 we all knew what was going on in Dachau. There was enough information to support those claims, not to mention the testimony of innumerable refugees: the articles in the *Neue Züricher Zeitung*, or the dailies such as *Die Nation* and *Der Beobachter*, plus the radio reports by Mr. von Salis or Mr. Oeri to the Basler Nachrichten. I was thinking also of the suggestions of Leonhard Ragaz in the *Christlicher Friedensdienst*. Already in 1933 Rausching's book *Conversations with Hitler* made perfectly clear the intentions of the German Führer. Moreover, the accounts of the horrors of Kristallnacht in Berlin on November 9, 1938, brutally revealed the Nazis' project against the Jews. Wolfgang Langhof's book *Moorsoldaten*, which received a great deal of notoriety in 1934 in Switzerland when it was published, concluded by informing us about the Nazis' activities in the concentration camps. Indeed, we were well informed!

We remained together for quite a while, for we didn't lack for topics of conversation. Unexpectedly Heinrich Kägi posed a troubling question: "How many children from La Hille have been subjected to the consequences of being turned back at the Swiss border?"

At that point, we turned to Mrs. Schlesinger who had been at the Château for a long time. She reflected for a moment, and then said emphatically: "Many, too many! The attempted escapes by our older ones ended tragically for many of them.

Walter Strauss, Inge Helft, Fritz Werdenberg, Manfred Vos—little Heinrich Vos's brother—and Dela Hochberger were arrested and deported by the Germans. But not all those who were refused at the border died. Some tried two or three times to escape into Switzerland. For example, Inge Joseph tried a second time and again had bad luck. Before the Swiss Border officers sent her back to France—after she had just traveled over a thousand kilometers to get to the border—they showed their compassion by offering her some soup. Inge threw it in their faces!"

"And so she was deported?" asked Miss Tobler.

"No, her third attempt proved successful. She sent us a letter from Zürich.

Among other things, she said that those who manage to get as far as thirty kilometers over the border into Switzerland can consider themselves safe. (That was quite a daring letter!)"

"Curious, these policies of Switzerland," commented Heiri while shaking his head.

Once again silence descended on our group, as we were caught up in our own thoughts. Then Miss Tobler spoke up and asked: "Mrs. Schlesinger, perhaps there are other children from La Hille, besides Inge, who successfully fled into Switzerland?"

"But of course!" responded our cook. "There are a dozen who have been lucky and are being safeguarded in Switzerland as we speak. Hans Garfinkel was the first to leave. Alone. Right after his arrival in Switzerland he sent us a letter full of enthusiasm. That was in December 1942, almost a year ago. Around that time, in December 1942, the Germans occupied France, spreading terror and fear throughout the whole country. BBC London spoke of deportations. For us here at the Château that triggered a terrible confusion, turning quickly into panic. Everyone wanted to leave as soon as possible. It was a veritable exodus. After Hans left alone, small groups formed to leave the Château during Christmastime, and they fled toward Spain and Switzerland. There were twenty in all, boys and girls, and nine were arrested en route or at the border to be sent to the death camps in Germany and Poland.

"The older ones who stayed behind—Walter Kammerer, Ruedi Oelbaum, Inge Schragenhein, Edith Goldapper, Edith Jankielwitz, as well as Onze and all the others—could tell you in greater detail about these frightful times, filled with such despair. And to think that was just a year ago."

We couldn't budge from our seats, as we tried to form some idea of the magnitude of this catastrophe. This wasn't the first to hit the children at La Hille. Nine young people full of hope and the joy of living were caught in the throes of this dreaded fate and sent to their deaths. Their exodus covering thousands of kilometers, far from the security of their homes, to the far reaches of a foreign country could not save these children. The madness of the German Führer had motivated thousands of individuals, without a hint of bad conscience, to engage in a death hunt for their fellow human beings.

At eleven o'clock we were still gathered in the salon. Only the Spaniards had said goodnight. We were deeply engaged in discussing the precarious situation of the Jews. The manhunt took on ever more dangerous proportions. They looked for Jews in every nook and cranny. Luckily, we had our secret hiding place! The hunt for resistance fighters, members of the FFI (French Forces of the Interior), and for other potential workers for the German factories continued unabated.

More and more people were seeking refuge in the *Maquis*. The "forests" of this region are totally unlike what we think of as forests in other parts of the continent. They are more like impenetrable thickets, consisting of thorny bushes and brambles among scraggly trees of varying heights. People could hide out in there, but winter was approaching and many of them had no weapons.

We turned to the question: why did the older ones try to flee a year ago instead of hiding in the *Zwiebelkeller*? Mrs. Schlesinger explained to us that this hiding place didn't yet exist at the time and that the children no longer felt secure at the Château since the police started showing up to interrogate everyone.

The gong of the BBC London shook us out of our reflections. The news was good once more. The German aggressors were suffering setbacks on all fronts. After the fall of Naples, the Allies advanced slowly but surely toward Rome. In Russia, the Germans were in dire straits; the Dniepre line was broken.

"If things continue this way," commented Heiri, the war will soon be over.

The invasion will surely take place no later than February."

"But in winter a landing is virtually impossible. The waters are too rough," I remarked. "You lost our last bet. You want to make another?"

We ended up making another bet: patisserie of your choice! Then we all went to bed.

Chapter 34
The New Readers and an Incident

The next day, all my students—with the exception of the youngest—had received their new readers. What joy! My littlest ones, in contrast, sat there empty-handed and looked at me disappointedly. They had received nothing to be happy about.

"As soon as you can read, you will get your little books," I told them consolingly. "Look here! I've already purchased them." I showed them the reader *Papa et Maman*, but they didn't seem convinced.

"When will we know how to read?" asked Guy morosely. "In a week, but you will have to work really hard!" I said. "In a week? I don't believe that!" said Josette, the sharpest.

"And why not? You will already know how to read today. Look: what is this letter?"

"It's a P," answered Conchita, very proud of her knowledge. "Very good. And this one?"

"An A!"

"And together, Rose?" "PA!"

"Everyone!" "PA!"

"You see? You already can read! So, what do you say, Josette?" She didn't respond. I fished into my shirt pocket. "I have a surprise for you," I said emphatically. I had cut out the letters written on a box, and I pulled them out and showed them to the children. They read: "PA"

"Very good. Now repeat that two times." "PA—PA!"

"Perfect. You can read 'Papa.' For now, you can write on your slates as long as you want to, and afterwards you can tell me about your own papa. You older ones—Friedel, Peggy, Jeanne and Pierrette—you can read your little book. And you, René, Jojo, Marinette, Violette, François and André, open your books to the first page. We are going to read a funny story about Anna."

The rest of the morning went by happily. The children were eager to read and write, and worked very hard. After that, we sang one of our favorite songs *Il était un petit navire*. The noon bell surprised us; the morning had gone by so quickly. We were hungry and looked forward to our lunch. But for me, this mealtime was spoiled by an unfortunate incident.

Anne-Marie, Eugen Lyrer and the Spaniards were already at the table when I arrived. As usual, I took my seat next to the director, Miss Groth, and glanced out of the corner of my eye at the mail she had placed on the table. In the little stack of letters, I noticed a Swiss postcard with the letters EXPRESS written on it. I immediately recognized my father's handwriting, and jumped to the conclusion that something had happened at home. Maybe an accident or a death? Mechanically, I chewed and swallowed my potatoes. I was upset. I knew very well that express postcards do not arrive any quicker than ordinary letters; they both take three weeks. Whatever the bad news it had already happened quite a while ago. Why didn't Miss Groth give me the card? Should I simply take it? I just had to know what happened at home! Perhaps one of my brothers was ill, or my sister.

I couldn't stop looking at this postcard with my father's handwriting. The meal took forever. I was imagining the worst. Finally, everyone was finished, but the director... forgot about the mail! She merely said: "You are free to go." I thought I was going to have a heart attack! This was the last straw! I wanted to shout: "What about the mail?" but I was short of breath. Miss Groth was already at the door when Mr. Palau reminded her that she had brought the mail for us. I rushed straight up to her, and was beside myself with anger. I had to restrain myself from yelling. "My express postcard," I said through clenched teeth. "Why didn't you give it to me this morning?" Quite taken aback, she looked at me and gave me the card. Then I shouted: "From today on, I will no longer eat at the staff table!" And indeed, from that day on, I sat at the table with the middle-schoolers.

Meanwhile, all my aggravation was pointless. Nothing terrible had happened at home. My father simply wanted to find out whether an express card would arrive more quickly than a normal letter. On the one hand, I was certainly relieved, but on the other, I couldn't understand why there was such a fuss about the mail, which annoyed all of us on the staff.

I was sitting in the courtyard reading and rereading my postcard and trying to calm down. Heinrich Kägi came up to me. "Don't get so upset," he offered. "It's not worth it. It doesn't matter to me whether the director distributes the mail or not." I was astonished. For me, this could never be a matter of indifference.

Heiri seemed to me as solid as a rock. Nothing got under his skin. Since my illness, he was in charge of the middle ones. He would get them to fetch water and carry wood for the kitchen, and also taught them in the little classroom next to my big one. The middle ones had absolutely refused to go back to the village school.

Heiri was also involved with the older ones who usually were under the supervision of Eugen Lyrer. How this all worked out I really didn't know. I was responsible for the Mickeys, and that was enough for me.

Chapter 35
Boils, Wooden Clogs and Rats

During morning recess, I was sitting in the courtyard surrounded by my little ones when I saw Heiri come in by the large entrance in the tower. He was walking slowly and strangely stooped. I went over to see what was going on. Since I was worried, he said he had a boil on his leg that was more and more painful and made it difficult for him to walk. I tried consoling him by saying that as long as he doesn't have jaundice he should consider himself lucky.

A year later, when I came down with boils and could barely take a step without pain, I conceded to him that this illness—allegedly caused by a vitamin deficiency—was really something to complain about!

Heiri had to stay in bed for several days. His boil became larger and larger and turned into a very worrisome tumor that went from red to blue and then purple before erupting into something looking like a cauliflower. That eruption allowed Miss Groth to drain the pus. After that Heiri had one boil after another, always on the most delicate and sensitive spots.

It was quite a while before he was able to sit in the dining hall at the table with the older ones facing the kitchen. On his right were Edith Goldapper, Inge Schragenheim, Martha Storosum, and Rosa Goldmark; Rosa was in a relatively calm state at the moment. On his left were Ruedi Oelbaum, Walter Kammerer, Onze, Egon Berlin and Gérard—when the latter wasn't off working for a farmer.

After my blow-up with the director, I sat with the Middles. On my right were Daniel Reingold and Hervé, who were new, as well as Bernard. On my left was Pierre Bergmann whose mother was killed on the boat called the "floating sarcophagus" carrying her to Israel, but which hit a mine en route. Also there were Jacques Palau, Conchita's borther, and Isi Bravermann. Across from me were Pierre and Jacques Costeseque, Mane and Gustav Manasse, and Jacques Pedrini, also new. The older girls sat at the table in the rear near the kitchen: Eva Fernanbuk, Trude Dessauer, Irène and Guita Kokotek, Cilly Stückler, Edith Jankielevitz and Irma Seelenfreund, the loyal helpers for Mrs. Schlesinger, who also sat at that table.

Sitting with the Middles, I felt liberated. Miss Groth could hand out the mail whenever she wished and it no longer bothered me. Moreover, the Middles were proud to have me sitting with them.

Late that evening, after my duties in the infirmary, I had the habit of going back to my classroom to clean the slates and sharpen the chalk, a time-consuming, boring task. The upside to this task was meeting up with Walter Kammerer who was always sitting on a stool in the classroom, absorbed in his reading, with his perennial mug of water at his side. Going from table to table to sharpen the chalk sticks with my Swiss army knife, I had the chance to observe him rather closely.

When he sat slouched over like this he seemed so fragile. His prominent, high white forehead and pale, haggard face contrasted sharply with his long black hair tied back at the nape of his neck. He seemed to be very ill. I could indeed imagine that he would fall over and die, stiff as a board, were the police to show up to arrest and deport him. Indeed, it was possible at any moment—a fact not to be forgotten—that the police could come to hunt us down like wild animals. The Château was not that far from the National Police Headquarters in Pailhès. We lived in constant apprehension, jumping at the slightest unexpected noise outside. Access to the *Zwiebelkeller* was always ready, and the older ones could disappear at any moment.

In mid-November, the temperature suddenly dropped. The sun barely shone through the cloud-cover. From time to time, it rained.

My daily joy was school. We were all doing well. My beginner class got to listen to a funny story for each new letter they learned. My third- and fourth-graders were making great progress in arithmetic and reading. When the afternoon was sunny, we would go for a walk to explore the magnificent countryside, happily losing ourselves in the hills and landscape as yet unknown to us but marvelously preserved. We didn't encounter a living soul! We would hunt for the fruit trees, especially the apples, because the farmers rarely picked them and they were often nice and ripe and would assuage our hunger.

Despite the cold, we would run barefoot in the fields and meadows—and come home with cold feet! Even in the typically sunny Midi region in France, winter had to come someday. I was concerned about how long we could manage to go barefoot. The weather was turning colder and greyer, with more frequent rain. One day I had to leave the children under a tree for shelter while I ran home to shut my dormer window.

The rain brought with it an unexpected chill. Our need for shoes became acute. But where would we find them? Who would be able to give us shoes for so many children? I was faced with a serious problem. I hesitated a long time, but finally went to Miss Groth to discuss the issue. Contrary to my expectations, she was not at all alarmed.

"We have anticipated this problem. All the children, even the older ones, will have wooden clogs," she said with uncharacteristic good humor. She was right: we all received wooden clogs, and each of us got to choose a pair that fit. Those who didn't have socks could go look for some in the laundry room.

The children were delighted! The Château was filled with the sound of wooden clogs clunking on the bare floors, stairs and hallways. But the happy excitement did not last! Most of the children soon stopped wearing their clogs because they hurt so much. Joy gave way to bitter disappointment. Our first walk in the country was quite a drama. We started out very slowly, not getting very far, but the children whined and complained that their shoes were rubbing the tops of their feet and numerous other places. What a situation! I had to help so many that I finally lost my patience.

I ended up gathering them around me to explain what we had to do: "Listen, everything has to be learned. Even walking in wooden clogs! We are going to practice every day, and you'll see that in a couple of weeks you will have it down pat. For now, you may take them off and go barefoot." The clogs brought a record number of children to the infirmary that evening.

Their feet were in a pitiful state, and I needed many rolls of gauze to wrap their sores and blisters.

During this period of "practicing" with our clogs, I would meet up with Heiri in the dining hall from time to time. Usually we would talk at the table, especially about the unpleasant topic of boils. When Miss Groth unexpectedly came in, Heiri stopped talking. But she had come to make us a surprising proposal: "Would you two like to move into the woodshop?" she asked. "The room next to Nadals on the first floor is free. In former times pears used to be stored in there."

Her proposal suited me just fine, for my "tomb" was really getting on my nerves. At night, I had to close my tiny window, but then it would get terribly stuffy. Moreover, the mice were bothering me again, for they had chewed a new entrance hole into my room.

Heiri was just as enthusiastic as I, and with the help of Ruedi Oelbaum, Onze and Egon Berlin we made the move that very day. While Heiri and I were sorting through our belongings, the young men carried our two iron beds, our two thin mattresses, and our four miserable woolen blankets over to the workshop and then up to the first floor by way of the steep wooden steps. They came up with a lovely old chair and a little table. Our new room was perfect! We were delighted. We even had a real window that faced out onto the ancient, majestic chestnut trees.

Unfortunately, we couldn't ignore the big haystack about three meters high that somewhat blocked our view. We called it "the mattress," and it belonged to the neighboring farm of Mr. Dedieu. In former times, he owned the workshop as well as the water pump, and used the old building as a stable and barn.

That evening, after the move, we went to bed exceptionally early. Heiri had the bed to the right of the big open window, and I had the one diagonally across, near the door. Finally we no longer had to live in "solitary confinement" in our tiny attic cells. What a pleasure to have a good friend so close, to be able to share our thoughts, and to have a sounding board for our feelings.

We talked long into the night. Scarcely had I fallen asleep when I was startled by a terrible noise that like a thunderbolt came at me from above and then quickly passed alongside my bed. It gave me the shivers! In a few seconds, there was silence, then as if by a secret signal the noise came back. It was like the scampering and scurrying of a thousand tiny feet, back and forth from the door to the window. They were living creatures—no doubt, rats! Yes, hundreds of crazy rats. Again, a moment of silence, and then the noise returned. I heard the rapid stamping of feet and tails rustling along the floorboards. I lay paralyzed in my bed! Then, like a nightmare, it was over.

"Did you hear that?" I whispered to Heiri.

"Yes, the rats. They're in the loft," he said sleepily.

"They're not in our room?"

"No, certainly not."

"But I heard them pass right by my bed. I was terrified that they would jump up on me!" Heiri didn't respond. He had already gone back to sleep.

The next day we decided to pay back those ghastly rats. Mr. Palau found an old rattrap that we set up in the loft that very night. The night was quiet, but since we were on the alert, we didn't sleep well. The next morning we did find a big fat rat in the trap. Heiri buried that one, and I promised to bury the next. But luckily there were no more. The following day the trap disappeared—and remained nowhere to be found. That night, our sweet dreams resumed.

Chapter 36
"Fight to the Final Victory!"

For various reasons we didn't listen to the news on the radio very often. On the one hand, we were totally immersed in our tasks, without a day off or a Sunday rest. No one, with the occasional exception of Miss Tobler, had the time to take care of my children. They were after all "my" children, and every day, from morning to night, I was responsible for them. Evenings I spent taking care of them in the infirmary, and nights I would wake up my bed-wetters. I didn't have much time to spend listening to the radio, and neither did Heiri. I should also add that listening to this old dying radio was not so pleasant: it would hiss and crackle, whistle and groan like an old steam engine.

We Swiss and the Spaniards would take turns listening and reporting to the rest of us, so that we were not completely uninformed, despite the lack of reliable newspapers. The newspapers available only printed lies anyway. Rommel was finally beaten in Africa, the Allies had landed in Sicily and Calabria, Naples had fallen long ago. Since the fall of Stalingrad in February, the Germans fought desperately for each square foot of land, and tried to reinforce their bloody counter-offensives. But the mighty Russians advanced inexorably, like a gigantic steamroller crushing any obstacles in their paths. The German Corporal Hirnschal, well-known thanks to the BBC London, wrote the absolute truth to his wife from Russia, saying: "The Eastern front accompanied me all the way back to Zwieseldorf [his home in Germany]."

Every night, for hours on end, we would hear disturbing booms and blasts in the distance, or not so far in the distance. From the courtyard, I would often look up into the night sky and imagine innumerable British and American planes flying toward German targets. The bombings were becoming truly terrible. We heard about the systematic destruction of Berlin, and thought of that as retaliation for the bombing of Coventry.

"Never will the bombs land on German soil!" declared the Führer in one of his many speeches filled with his delusions of grandeur. The Germans' struggle had become hopeless long before, but still they fought on "to the final victory." The more desperate their situations became in Russia or Italy, the more brutally did they treat the French population. There were more curfews and round-ups, arrests and deportations. The Germans continued to act as if they were an invincible power. The Jews did not know where to hide, and the danger that threatened them was greater than ever. The increasing threat targeted the Château as well. We had to be on constant guard, for the criminals in uniform we most feared could violently swoop down on us at any moment. As the resistance fighters and the FFI made the lives of the Germans increasingly difficult, the Germans lost their heads. They arrested people and deported them like never before, twenty-four hours a day, every day.

Why did the capture and annihilation of the Jews take priority over the destruction of the FFI? It made no rational sense. The Germans had nothing to fear from the Jews, but everything to lose from the FFI. The explanation lay in the racial theory adopted by the Nazis. In their eyes, the Jews were an inferior race. Thus, it was necessary to exterminate them before others. What utter nonsense!

Unfortunately, they practiced this madness systematically. Fear reigned in our Château filled with children. Despite the good news about the Allied advances on all fronts, the BBC London spoke of the Germans having a secret weapon that would give them a final victory.

Chapter 37
Marinette and Pierrette

Toward the end of November the sun was no longer shining and the mornings were downright cold and crisp. We had to put on whatever sweaters and outer clothing we had on hand—that is, if we had any. In short, the children did not have enough warm clothes, especially Marinette and Pierrette, the two sisters from Toulouse. They didn't resemble each other at all. Marinette, nine years old with short blond hair, was small and strong, with a face expressing her aggressive nature. "If it bothers you, I'll fix it," was her motto. Pierrette, more than a year older, was totally opposite: tall and thin, gentle and endearing.

Our first really cold morning I noticed the two of them, white as a sheet, standing there freezing. All the others had on sweaters, but they had none. I motioned for them to come over to me. They were holding hands, wearing their little summer dresses with short sleeves, shivering with the cold.

"Why don't you have on your sweaters?" I asked them.

"We don't have any," answered Pierrette, embarrassed. "Not even a little shirt," snipped Marinette.

I was seriously concerned. "You'll catch your death of cold! You're almost naked in those thin little dresses."

Marinette raised her skirt to show her panties and said defiantly: "But we do have our culottes."

"Of course," I agreed, "but a dress and culottes are not enough in this season. I'll find you something else to put on!" Turning to the rest of the children I told them "to keep busy, write or draw on your slates. I'm going to look for some clothes for Marinette and Pierrette."

I took them by the hand and we went to see the director in her office. She was busy pasting ration-coupons on large cardboards. I showed her the half-frozen girls and asked if she had any extra clothing for them. "We have some things in our reserves," she said upon reflection. "Or perhaps you will find what you need in the laundry." The laundry was washed in the cellar or outdoors, and in the so-called laundry room it was sorted and mended. In the laundry room we found Mrs. Palau and Mrs. Marimon. Mrs. Marimon had just returned to work and still looked rather run-down.

We quickly found two sweaters that fit, as well as two sets of shirts and woolen pants. Marinette and Pierrette put them on right there on the spot. Satisfied, we returned to our class that was about to begin. We sang one of our favorite songs—about the wind:

Mister Wind, said the cherry,
Do you want me to get bruised?
Mister wind, Mister Wind,
Go away! Go away!

You-ou-ou!
You-ou-ou!
Frivoli-vola, frivoli-volette!
You-ou-ou! You-ou-ou!
Frivoli-vola, frivoli-volette!

Mister Wind, said the swallow,
Do you want to break my wing?
Go away! Go away!

Chapter 38
Jojo's Accident.

An unpleasant incident usually brings on another. Just as we finished singing our first song, Jojo raised her hand for permission to go to the toilet. Of course, I said yes.

We had sung a second and third song when Jojo reappeared in tears. She stayed at the doorway, but it wasn't necessary for her to tell what had happened. We all knew right away from the horrible stink.

"I fell into the hole," she cried.

"Go on out, Jojo, go out and close the door," I called.

One more time I left the children by themselves to deal with this disaster, which was "polluting" the atmosphere.

The toilets were behind the house, between the Château and the wall, in two small outhouses made of cement-blocks. Each little house had a hole in the ground that tilted around the edges toward the center. All the children dreaded this scary hole, and unfortunately, to say the least, Jojo had accidently stepped into it.

The poor little girl, with her soiled leg, stank to high heaven! What could I do?

I didn't know where to start. Moreover, a dark, stinking trail led from outdoors through the corridor to our classroom. I had to pluck up my courage to control my nausea and despair. I asked my class to be patient while I led Jojo to the water pump.

Chapter 39
The Stove

It was getting colder and colder. The thermometer I had brought from Switzerland showed eight degrees centigrade. Even with our sweaters and pullovers we were freezing. "Why don't we light the stove?" demanded Peggy in her direct manner. Indeed, there was a stove at the back of the classroom, but I had never paid any attention to it. Why not use it? I sent the children down to the courtyard where they could get warm by running around and getting some exercise. Meanwhile, I went to the director's office. She had just returned from Montégut with the mail. "What do you want?" she asked in an irritated tone of voice, thinking I would ask her for my mail. But I explained our predicament.

"We are all cold," I said, "and winter has not even begun. It's just December. There's a stove in the classroom, couldn't we light it?"

"The problem is wood. We don't have enough, and what we do have we use for cooking."

"I see. But we are really cold. The children's fingers are so swollen with the cold they can't even write. Surely they will get sick."

"All right," she said. "I'll ask Egon to heat the classroom. By the way, that is the only room in the Château that one can heat."

The next morning, I entered the classroom before breakfast, lost in thought, but immediately had to step back. The place was completely full of smoke! I thought there was a fire, but I could glimpse the stove at the back of the room, spitting out fire and flames like a volcano. Blinded by the smoke, I stumbled toward the window and opened it as quickly as possible. Then I turned back to the stove. It certainly looked dangerous! I saw that Egon had not put the lid over the fire, so the flames were reaching almost to the ceiling. Looking for a way to shut the fiery opening, I saw that there was no lid in the vicinity. Luckily Egon arrived on the scene. "Look at that! You didn't shut the opening!" Egon just shrugged his shoulders indicating his helplessness.

"I don't understand!" Egon said. "One cannot close the stove! Since there is no opening at the bottom, I have to feed the wood from the top."

"What kind of a miserable stove is this anyway, if it doesn't have a lid!" I exclaimed.

Since the flames were already lowering we approached the fire monster to get a better look at it from all sides. Indeed, there was no means of closing the stove. Completely unusable! We thought we'd extinguish the fire, but it was going out on its own, retreating in the black cylinder as if exhausted by its spectacular display.

We went down to the dining-hall for our breakfast without exchanging a word.

After school, I went in search of a large flat stone near the old, crumbling towers. I went around the Château twice: first, from inside the wall and then from outside the wall. I had some luck, for near the western tower I found a lovely stone slab that looked perfect. I carried it to the classroom, and indeed it fit the opening of our mini volcano perfectly. I was impatient to have to wait until the next day to try it out, but in fact it worked just fine! I helped Egon light the fire, and the smoke was drawn up the chimney just as it was supposed to do.

I started class at eight o'clock. The room was still rather smoky, but I could feel the heat. The thermometer registered 13°C [55°F] and we were all feeling much better and looking forward to the room's becoming even warmer. As usual, we sang Mr. Wind and some other songs before our lessons, which put us in a good mood. The noise of the chimney draft provided the bass. After the songs, we did arithmetic. Each group, according to their age, had to solve some arithmetic problems suitable for their level. We were fully engaged in our work when a terrible explosion shook the whole classroom. Frightened to death, some of the children jumped up from their seats, but soon sat back down at their tables. Others ducked in anticipation of a second explosion, but nothing happened. Silence—except for the crackling of the fire and the flames that triumphantly escaped from the stove and were heading toward the ceiling along with plenty of smoke.

We were in a bad spot. The stone cover was shattered by the heat, and the room was quickly filling up with acrid smoke.

"Mr. Steiger, open the windows! Ouvrez les fenêtres," cried François desperately, rubbing his eyes. Resigned, I opened one of the windows. My dream of having a cozy warm classroom was foiled a second time. But I wasn't going to give up! I was convinced there must be a way to close the stove.

That afternoon, making the rounds of the Château, I was lucky again—this time finding an old spade without its handle. I was pretty happy, for this could be just what we need. I took it to Mr. Nadal to flatten it out, and he brought it back to me that evening as flat as a pancake!

During the night as I was tending my bed-wetters, I was imagining the pleasure of entering a warm, cozy classroom. It had been really cold the whole day, and of course the dormitories were freezing also. It would be a miracle if more of the children don't wet their beds. I had made a special effort to find an extra blanket for Jeanne because she is the most prone to "accidents," but miraculously indeed her bed was dry. When she returned from her visit to the pail, she gave me a rather annoyed look as if she had read my mind. She asked, "Mr. Steiger, will we have a warm room tomorrow?"

"Certainly!" I replied while covering her up. "Yes, tomorrow will be fine." Satisfied, she closed her eyes and went back to sleep.

And it was really cozy in the classroom the next morning. A little bit warm and a bit smoky, but I didn't so much mind the smoke. The important thing was to have a fire in the stove, and I was happy to have a warmer classroom at last!

We began our lessons in high spirits, but something wasn't quite right. The children couldn't seem to concentrate. And the truth was that I couldn't even see them all that well. The smoke was really getting to us. My eyes were burning and tearing. "Mr. Steiger, look at the stove," called Peggy. I could barely make her out in the smoke. I stumbled toward the stove when a loud cry left me paralyzed. "Mr. Steiger, Mr. Steiger!"

Right beside me was André with huge tears running down his cheeks. "Mr. Steiger, open the window!" he desperately implored.

With a heavy heart, I opened the window and the door. The children ran into the corridor to gulp some clean air. Thick, biting smoke continued to pour out from the stove. I had put all my hopes in the flattened metal spade, but it just couldn't contain all the smoke that continued to escape all around my marvelous lid. I was deeply disappointed. Could it be that Egon used wood that hadn't dried?

Outside the doorway my little children were trying to suck in the fresh air while they continued to cough and rub their eyes. My dream of a heated classroom had vanished. The temperature again fell to eight degrees.

That afternoon Egon came to see me in the classroom. I was busy correcting the arithmetic lessons on the children's slates. He looked questioningly at the stove and then at me. At lunch I had told him about the hateful smoke that nearly asphyxiated us. He went over to the stove and examined the piece of iron that served as the lid. "And the smoke can get out here?" he inquired doubtfully.

"And how!" I responded, "just like a real steam engine! You should have seen it this morning!"

"I'm really sorry, but there's only green wood," he said despairingly.

"It's not your fault," I reassured him. "Why don't you help me correct the arithmetic assignments. Here, take a piece of chalk and underline the errors."

We got the work done in no time at all.

Chapter 40

How Egon Survived
Kristallnacht

Worn out, I sat at my little desk by the window. It was no longer so cold. As it happens sometimes in the Midi area of France, the sun had come out a bit during the morning and warmed up the air. Egon was still busy cleaning one of the blackboards. When he was ready to leave, I asked him to stay a while. He sat directly across from me in François' seat. For a long time I had wanted to speak with him. I knew absolutely nothing about him. It is strange to address someone in the familiar way without knowing him at all. I thought this was the perfect time to remedy that situation. I broached the conversation by asking him about his background.

"Tell me, which part of Germany are you from, and how did you manage to end up in this godforsaken corner of France?"

As if he had anticipated my question, he began to tell me his whole story. He told me about his parents in Coblence who had a clothing store, and his older sister Inge who had come to the Château de La Hille with him but then had escaped to Spain. (He never knew that Inge had sent a *passeur*, a smuggler to get him too, and I didn't have the heart to tell him.) When I think back on this conversation, what stands out is his last day at the Jewish school. Here's Egon's story:

"I was still a little boy, around ten years old. One morning, as I was walking on my usual way to school, I saw three or four men armed

with rifles storming toward a watch and jewelry shop, using the butts of their guns to smash the windows. They threw the clocks, watches, jewelry—everything they could get their hands on—onto the street and climbed through the broken window into the shop. I was glued to the spot. A second group of armed men were hurriedly moving behind me. They threw all the stacked fruits and vegetables from a food shop onto the ground. The fruits, potatoes, tomatoes— they threw them all on the sidewalk. I stood there paralyzed, terrified—literally petrified. I wanted to run when I heard the sounds of shattering glass above my head. I jumped with fright just as a chair came crashing down next to me. Then another chair, a table...I leapt to the side. I thought I had gone crazy. All around me was chaos—noise, confusion, destruction. These men, armed with cudgels, clubs and shotguns, were running loose like wild animals. I ran zigzagging between the debris and falling objects, and somehow managed to evade the men who were threatening to beat me to death by ducking into a relatively quiet alleyway that led to the synagogue. But the synagogue was on fire, inundated by flames pouring out from all its windows. There was fire everywhere! Again I ran for my life, and arrived at my school completely out of breath. My teacher was still there, as white as a sheet. "Go home," he cried. "Take the little streets." I made a quick u-turn and ran as fast as I could through the alleys towards home. I was out of my senses; I couldn't see or hear anything more. I arrived at home ready to collapse. Mama, Papa and Inge were waiting for me outside the house. Mama and Inge were weeping, and Papa was holding a small, brown leather suitcase. I can still see them clear as day. "God be praised, you are here!" he called out when he saw me coming. "Hurry up, we have to leave immediately. They could arrive any minute."

"We took the tiny streets and alleys that were still deserted. We didn't have to go very far, for a Christian colleague of my father's took us in. He must have been one of Papa's clients. This man was taking a risk by helping us. If he were found out, he could be beaten up or even deported.

"We returned home later that afternoon. The nightmare was over. Unlike all the other Jewish shops in our street, our shop was the only one that had been spared. Nearly all of our friends had endured frightful experiences. Some of them had even been beaten to death, while others were arrested and deported. The Jews

that were left were made to clean up the broken glass while the SS watched, beating and harassing them. It was horrible.

"Several days later my parents put Inge and me on a train for Brussels. Since that day, I have not seen or heard from them."

I was floored. Egon recounted this traumatizing final day at school with such vivacity and expressive gestures, as if it had happened only yesterday. I had never heard about such things except under the vague category of the long-ago persecution of the Jews under the Russian czars.

After a long moment of silence I asked: "All this really happened exactly as you have reported? But it's not possible. What were the police doing?"

Egon shook his head and looked at me with astonishment. "You mean you've never read or heard about Kristallnacht? It was a massive pogrom. All these men who shattered and destroyed everything were hired by the government, by Hitler and his henchmen. In all the cities and towns in Germany Jews were hunted down, their synagogues, houses and shops set on fire. It was reported in all the newspapers. It happened about five years ago, for I was only ten years old at the time."

At that time, I was still a student in the Pedagogy School in Grisons, an isolated village in the mountains. No information about these terrible occurrences had reached this location.

Later, Walter Kammerer told me more about what had happened on Kristallnacht, and I understood that Egon had lived through the most devastating pogrom of the Third Reich. On this subject I read:

On November 7, 1938, Herschel Grynspan, a Jewish refugee, shot the secretary of the German Embassy in Paris because his father, along with ten thousand other Jews, had been deported to Poland. Kristallnacht, the worst of the German pogroms, so named because of the slivers and shards of glass sparkling on the streets of the large German cities, was the consequence.

7,500 shops and 171 homes were destroyed and pillaged, 276 synagogues were set on fire, of which 76 were entirely destroyed, and 30,000 Jews were arrested and deported. The estimated number of deaths was not confirmed.

When I was editing Egon's story—and it was truly a swan song since six months later he suffered a cruel death—I realized all of a sudden what it meant that this lad had lived through such a nightmare on his way to school that fateful morning. But the riots of Kristallnacht occurred the night of November 9, 1938. We speak of Kristallnacht, but Egon was overwhelmed by the riots on the morning of November 10. Something seemed odd about these dates, so I consulted William Shirer's book *The Rise and Fall of the Third Reich*, and found this report:

On the night of November 9 at 1:20am an urgent message was sent to all the State Police and Security offices, along with the Party and SS leaders to settle the arrangements for the demonstrations.

Further on down, Shirer notes:

According to a top-secret report from Major Walter Buch, on the evening of November 9, Goebbels had already given the order to organize and execute these "spontaneous demonstrations" during the night.

The order was clear: it was a matter of destroying Jewish shops and setting fire to the synagogues. That these persecutions lasted through the morning of November 10 is not at all surprising.

Chapter 41
An Outing in Wooden Clogs

Mrs. Palau, Mrs. Marimon and Mrs. Nadal solved the problem of the wooden shoes by fashioning socks from any bits of material and yarns they could find. The Mickeys, who were used to going barefoot around the Château, now could slip on their new socks before putting on their wooden clogs, and as a result no longer complained about blisters.

From then on, we were able to resume our customary walks in the countryside. Most of the time we would walk along the county road toward Pailhès, or in the opposite direction toward Montégut. One day we took a tiny path that cut across the fields and led us to an isolated farm we had never seen before. We didn't hear any dogs barking. The farm was totally quiet and seemed abandoned. Full of enthusiasm, we decided to go and have a closer look. As usual, Guy and René led the pack, followed by André and François, the two inseparable brothers. The rest of us followed in single file, with Rosa at the tail end as always. Every few steps she would stop and take the time to examine something, whether it be a huge beetle, a flower, a pretty pebble or whatever. In the middle of my tribe, I was chatting happily away with Friedel and Peggy, when all of a sudden we heard some shrieks coming from the head of our line. René was wildly waving his arms like a crazy person: "I'm sinking! I'm sinking! Mr. Steiger, come help me!"

I wanted to run to help him—René and Guy were already standing by the stables—but I too was stuck in the mud and the slime. It had been raining heavily the day before. The two boys were bellowing even louder, so I took off my wooden clogs and socks, and left them there in the mud as I hastened toward the boys. By the time I got to them, they were already sunk in the mud up to their knees—and still sinking. What a frightening scene! I felt myself slipping too, so I had to act quickly. I grabbed René and with all my strength yanked him out of the black slime and dragged him over to the field grass—minus his wooden shoes. Then I liberated Guy from his trap, but he too had lost his clogs to the morass.

I had scarcely caught my breath when André and François began to scream. The whole time they had been making fun of my rescue efforts and gloating over the others' bad luck without even noticing that they too were beginning to sink!

I saved them, but not their wooden clogs, which just at that moment disappeared into the oozing mud. The girls—Friedel, Peggy, Pierrette, Marinette and the others—were quite amused by this whole incident, and couldn't keep from laughing. In the end all of us were laughing. Invigorated by our latest adventure, we returned home to the Château, clomping along in our clogs. However, four boys clomped no more.

And by the way, from that farm all the way home, we didn't meet up with a living soul.

Chapter 42

The Assault—Children from Château de La Hille are Arrested and Sent to a Camp

uring our mostly carefree walks, we were completely oblivious to the war and tragic events taking place all around the Château. Cut off from nearly everything, we lived as if on a little island. On our hikes, through the peaceful countryside and the quiet, undisturbed fields, we never encountered anyone. We were always alone with just our comrades, as if we were enjoying a beautiful Nature Park isolated from the rest of the world. But this idyllic peace was a sham. Not far from us, the resistance fighters were hidden in the forests and brush. They were mostly young men who had fled from the Germans and sought refuge in the *Maquis* to escape the torture by the SS or the forced labor in the German factories. In hiding, they faced a miserable life of anxiety and hunger, not even counting the approaching winter conditions. Besides all that, they were outlaws at the mercy of anyone who might denounce them to the Germans in exchange for a sizable reward. The nights at the Château were peaceful and uncannily quiet—except for the distant roar of the bombers heading toward Germany.

As I have already noted, after my duties in the infirmary, I would often meet up with Walter Kammerer in the classroom, where he sat surrounded by books, with his tin carafe of water next to him. Seated at the table facing Walter, I was sharpening my students' sticks of chalk and colored crayons, the whole time talking with him about current events or stories from the past. I knew so little about the Château and the children. The following conversation especially has stuck in my memory.

"The nights are so quiet and peaceful," I began. "If one didn't know it, one would never believe we are in the midst of a terrible war."

"True enough," he responded. "Yet all the same, we know it. We Jews know it better than anyone since we had to flee, leaving our parents and our countries behind. It's been four years that we have been on the run. Every minute we feel endangered and threatened. It is like a pain that does not let up. It wasn't like that last year before the German occupation of France. We felt protected from everything here at this isolated Château. We never imagined that one fine day the police would come to search us out. Nevertheless, against all expectations, at a moment no one thought would happen, they did come.

"It was in August of last year. At four o'clock in the morning a dozen or more policemen had surrounded the Château. A vague anxiety had awakened me. When I was up, I saw them in the early morning light advancing toward us with their guns in their hands, as if we were criminals. They entered the Château, and stormed the dormitories and rooms, surprising the little ones as well as the middle and older ones in their beds. I can recall the scenes of terror and despair in the dormitories as if it were only yesterday. The girls were crying, some of them screaming. The boys also lost their heads. The police gave them hardly any time to get dressed and to gather their necessary belongings. After calling the roll in the courtyard—at the time there were forty-five of us—they led us out in single file toward the Lèze where a bus was waiting. They didn't take the little ones. And the worst of it all for us was that we were so suddenly attacked out of the blue, like a deadly storm breaking over us. We believed we were lost!"

Walter's story shook me to the core. I wanted to know: "Why did you think you were lost? After all it wasn't the Germans who arrested you. Surely the French aren't as dangerous as the Gestapo."

"I wouldn't say that," he retorted. "We know that the French police search and arrest all foreigners and all Jews to put them into the French camps. That could be Gurs, Saint-Cyprien or Rivesaltes. We were taken to Camp Vernet, fairly close to the Château. From there, the Jews are taken to Drancy, near Paris, where the Germans take over and regroup them for transport to the concentration camps. That is equivalent to a death sentence. "

"But do you actually know something about these concentration camps?"

"Yes, of course. They are most likely death camps. A bunch of us—Egon and others—lived through *Kristallnacht* on November 9, 1938. We saw how the houses and synagogues were burned, how Jews were beaten and arrested. There were many thousands of arrests. The German newspapers presented the Jews as inferior people, as the perpetrators who could not be trusted. They claimed it was Germany's duty to get rid of this scourge. But how can one get rid of the Jews?

Deport them. And then what? We at the Château counted deportation as a death sentence. With this assault by the French gendarmes, our destiny seemed clear. As I said, we were at Camp Vernet...."

During the time I had left before waking my bed-wetters, Walter recounted what had happened on that terrible August 26, and how the children of Château de La Hille were liberated by an unexpected miracle. Here is how Edith Goldapper described it in her journal.

[Edith's Journal, Part Two]

"August 26, 1942, 4am. The light in our dormitory was suddenly on. We didn't know what was happening, but we heard voices in the courtyard. Inge, Ilse and I ran to the window to see—what a shock—policemen! We dressed as quickly as possible, and at that very moment Miss Näf came into our room with the gendarmes. We jumped into our beds fully clothed and pulled the blankets over us to cover up any suspicion that we were trying to get away. Then Miss Näf said that all the older ones needed to get dressed immediately and pack up our belongings. We quickly headed to the attic to get our suitcases—accompanied by the police. We felt panicked! A bus was waiting for us. We hurriedly tried to eat some biscuits, but we could barely choke them down.

When we dropped our bags in the courtyard, a policeman immediately went over to rifle through them to make sure we hadn't hidden any scissors, knives or other objects that could serve as weapons. Then they led us to the bus. I will never forget that moment for goodbyes. It was terrible. Miss Näf completely broke down. On the bus they told us we were going to Camp Vernet.

We arrived around 11am. Then we were called one by one to the commander's office to fill out a thousand lists, after which we were led out, undressed, and searched to make sure we didn't have any false papers or other documents on us.

After all these procedures we ended up "safe and sound" in barracks. There were beds lined up against the walls, one over the other like primitive bunk-beds. Inge and I were on top, Frieda and Ilse below. Next to the beds were a little table and two benches. The person in charge of our barrack gave us each two thin blankets and a work-apron. Unexpectedly, they served us some hearty, thick soup. After this good meal, we had a bit of time to arrange our things. Meanwhile, there were constantly more arrivals. Horrible scenes. The lights were left on all night in the barracks. I barely got through my first night. Camp life is hard. Roll call is early in the morning. Then we have a cup of strong coffee and 325 grams of bread. While we are busy in the mornings peeling potatoes, the time goes by fairly quickly. Of course, Werner is our cook. In general, La Hille is well known in this camp. Because of our red "kittles," or Swiss smocks, we stand out from the rest—but also because of our good spirits. We always wear a smile on our faces to bolster morale in the others.

For lunch we again have a good soup with two potato halves, plus lots of fruit—plums, peaches, and pears. Then we return to the kitchen to peel onions for supper.

Because we work in the kitchen we are allowed hot water to bathe every day. Of course, in the afternoons, there is roll call again. Around 6pm we have soup and fruit. Then it's the "Vernet Parade": the two hundred detainees from our camp go for a walk. We talk with each other, and we think a lot about the Château. Often we sing, to renew our courage...

Today is the second day. We are very happy because Miss Näf has arrived. We don't leave her alone for minute. She gives us a feeling of security.

We've been here now for half a week. We no longer think about getting out.

September 1. The commanding officer comes into our barrack. He yells: "In half an hour you are to be ready to leave. Pack your bags!" We suddenly felt sick all over, with headaches, sore throats, stomachaches, leg pains. We felt weak. In short, we were panicked. What we secretly dreaded the most—deportation to the East—was really about to happen.

It was frightful. But at that moment Miss Näf entered our barrack. She said that we should stop packing our bags and help others. We weren't going to be deported after all! Naturally we didn't believe it, and took it to be some sort of mental lapse Miss Näf was experiencing. But she insisted, and we ended up believing her. Indeed, the commanding officer showed up half-an-hour later, and his voice sounded like a death knell: "Kohn, Katzenstein..." It gave us the shivers. We helped those whose names were called to carry their bags. Toward noon, almost the entire "block" was empty, with the exception of us and a few others. In my entire seventeen years, I had never seen such a sight. Although their fate was far more dubious, those poor, unlucky people were still happy for us that we were going to be free. My god! That's hard. I believe there is no more human justice left on earth. We gave all our food provisions to the deported ones, so we didn't have anything to eat that day. But we had no desire to eat anyway. We had lumps in our throats....

The same day: Mr. Dubois [the director of the Swiss Red Cross, Children's Aid Society in Toulouse] and Miss Kasser [a colleague of the Taur Street branch] come to see us in our barrack. They bring us the good news that we are allowed to return to Château de La Hille the very next day! Our joy is overwhelming. Mr. Lyrer comes to see us in the camp that evening. [He had been in Switzerland during this difficult time and returned to La Hille as soon as he found out what had happened.] He brings us some jam. After his departure, we have a little goodbye party and give a jar of jam to those in charge of our barrack. Kurt plays the harmonica. [Kurt Moser, brother of Edith Moser, was arrested a little later on, with Charles Blumenfield, Werner Eppstein, and Fritz Wertheimer at the Spanish border. They were deported.]

We have a really good time. The next morning at 10 o'clock we say our goodbyes to everyone at the camp. Those in charge of our barrack are inconsolable. Although they are glad for us that we will be safe, they are sad that without us their lives will once more be dreary.

As sad as we were arriving at the camp, we are as happy and excited to leave. We all depart together by train for Saint-Jean-de-Verges, where Louison and Roger will meet us with a horse-drawn wagon to take our bags. Mr. Boubilar, the green grocer, will come to take us back to La Hille by car...

We were liberated thanks to the Swiss Children's Aid Society. I *don't think in our whole lives we can ever repay them for what they did for us—and continue to do. One is hard pressed to find such good people in our world today.*

On our way we meet up with Mr. Lyrer and the children who had come to greet us. But I was not able to adjust to life at La Hille again. I had changed. I felt different, and it took me a long time before I was able to feel at home there again.

We "older ones" are now incredibly bonded. I think we would walk through fire for the sake of the others. We are really, really good friends (and in spite of all that happened to us, our morale is very high).

Autumn slowly arrives. October, November. Soon it is my birthday. But while we are listening to Radio Toulouse, we hear that on November 11, 1942 the Germans invaded France. We know right away what that means. I don't know how it happened, but suddenly we were all in a panic. We wanted to flee. We hurriedly packed our bags and were ready to go. My birthday was the next day, November 12. Amidst all this turmoil Inge and the others were really sweet to think of giving me a present for my eighteenth birthday. Miss Näf tells us not to get so upset, to unpack our bags, that it is silly, that nothing will happen to us. But one always hears about the deportation of the Jews....

Winter arrives. Nevertheless it is still not cold. Irma Seelenfreund, Cilly Stückler, Inge and I are on kitchen duty. It's really fun, partly because Werner Eppstein is there to help us. We can't stop joking around together, and happily the work gets done anyway....

It is December 21, 1942. Exactly four years ago I left home. But today there is something else going on. There is talk of the imminent deportation of the Jews, and some of us at La Hille have decided to leave this very night. My dear friend Inge Schragenheim and Leo Lewin left today. They want to go to Switzerland. Our goodbyes were heartbreaking. Just think of it: two young people venturing forth alone into the ever more threatening world. How unsettling! The next day Luxian Wolfgang and Norbert Stückler set out for the Spanish border. And so it goes, day by day, someone else goes off. But I have to add that the police are not letting us off the hook. They show up all the time asking for information about someone or other.

This year Christmas time is not as joyous as it was last year.

Walter, Heinz and I give a concert. (I play Hayden's "Symphony of the Bells" four-hands with Walter, though I usually play with Heinz.) The director tries to make everything as beautiful as possible, but half our thoughts are with those who at that very moment might be crossing the border.

In January we learn that some of our friends have made it safely into Switzerland: Hans Garfunkel, Régina Rosenblatt, Else Rosenblatt, Jacques Roth, Peter Salz, Margot Kern, Ruth Klonover, Ilse Wulf, Leo Lewin, Lotte Nussbaum and Almut Königshofer. The "Hillers" who arrived safely in Spain were Luzian Wolfgang, Norbert Stückler, Mr. and Mrs. Frank, and Inge Berlin, Egon's sister.

What a relief! Those caught at the borders were sent back to us safe and sound, except for the three taken by the Germans: Dela Hochberger, Inge Helft, and Manfred Vos, Henri's brother. These three were first taken to Drancy, then elsewhere. We do not know where. We live in an atmosphere heavy with anxiety and oppression.

Chapter 43
The Miraculous Liberation of the 45 Children from Château de La Hille

Rösli Näf, our director at that time, was a very energetic person. Like Miss Groth, she had spent several years with Albert Schweitzer in Lambaréné in Gabon, Africa. Miss Näf was driven totally beside herself by the startling action of the French police to dispatch forty-five children from La Hille to Camp Vernet.

Desperately, she ran to the post office in Montégut to telephone Mr. Dubois in Toulouse to inform him what had happened. He promised to do everything he could to save the children, and requested a list of names of those sent to the camp. Miss Näf ran back to the Château to get the names of those children and then again ran to Montégut to send him the list of names by phone. Without hesitating a second, Mr. Dubois took the train to Vichy that very morning, arriving late in the evening.

The next day Mr. Dubois showed up at the Swiss Embassy in Vichy.

Unfortunately, the ambassador—Mr. W. Stucky—was not in. His secretary welcomed him and advised him on how to proceed. The secretary introduced Mr. Dubois to a very influential person, the General Secretary of the Ministry of the Interior, who had the power to liberate those who had been arrested. Presenting himself as the "Director of the Swiss Red Cross, Children's Aid Society," Mr. Dubois had a long conversation with this Interior Minister. Mr. Dubois spoke of the three thousand French children, war-victims, who are being taken care of by Swiss families. He spoke of other children as well, those who are the victims of the war in France, that the Swiss Red Cross is sheltering in refuges called "Swiss Colonies of the Red Cross, Children's Aid Society."

"What are you suggesting I do about all this?" the influential man inquired. "That's just the point," replied Mr. Dubois. "A great misfortune has occurred, and that is why I have traveled from Toulouse here to Vichy. You see, in Toulouse we are supervising the Swiss Colony La Hille that is attached to the Swiss Red Cross. The colony shelters about one hundred children. Yesterday, around four in the morning, the French police arrived to arrest forty-five children and sent them to Camp Vernet near Pamiers for later deportation." He brought out the list of names of the forty-five, and continued: "This was an irresponsible over-reach by the French police that the Swiss Red Cross cannot tolerate. This infringement and disrespect of the conventions established between France and Switzerland calls into question the stay of French children in Switzerland. I have taken the precaution of sending my wife to Bern to tell the government about our reaction to this turn of events."

The Secretary of the Ministry of the Interior was floored by this news. He apologized by saying that this action by the French National Police must have resulted from a misunderstanding and that he would immediately see to it that this whole situation would be cleared up and all necessary measures taken to liberate the children.

He immediately wrote the requisite order to the officials at Camp Vernet, affixing the list of the children's names to the impressive ministerial letterhead. His signature and official stamp sealed the deal. Mr. Dubois held in his hands the most important letter of his life. It was a moment of grace! This conversation had allowed him to save the lives of forty-five children.

While Mr. Dubois was in Vichy, Mrs. Dubois visited the Swiss government headquarters in Bern. She went as quickly as possible to the Federal Council to tell them about the danger of death threatening the children of the Swiss Colony of the Swiss Red Cross at La Hille near the Pyrénées. She spoke of the arrest of forty-five children, their transport to Camp Vernet, and their eventual deportation to a death camp in Germany. She said her husband was in Vichy to obtain the liberation of these forty-five children who were under his supervision as a director of the Swiss Red Cross. She insisted they authorize all

Jewish children of the Swiss Children's Aid Society who are still threatened to be allowed entry into Switzerland without delay. Having learned from her husband that he had managed to secure their liberation from Camp Vernet, she demanded that the government issue entrance visas to these Jewish children who remain in mortal danger.

But no one would listen to her.

On my request, Mr. Alfred A. Häsier, author of the book *The Boat is Full*, sent me some explanations and clarifications on the subject of the strange behavior of the Swiss politicians:

According to the decision by the Assembly, the borders have been hermetically closed as of August 13, 1942, even though a report at the end of July from a section of the federal police affirmed that it was irresponsible to turn back refugees since we are now certain about the way in which Jews are deported and the horrible living conditions in the East. After humanitarian associations, politicians, the press, and artists sounded the alarm, the borders were provisionally reopened. In Zürich-Oerlikon in 1942, Federal Counselor Edouard von Steiger coined the expression "the boat is full," comparing Switzerland to an over-burdened small rescue canoe. This expression was to have grave consequences. Walter Lüthi defined Swiss politics concerning the refugees as "without charity, hypocritical and ungrateful."

At the September session of the National Council, a parliamentarian spoke of "Sacro egoismo"—sacred nationalistic egoism—while the liberal Albert Oeri asked: "Should we be cruel, cruel by precaution?" While the federal and state ("cantal") administrations practiced a politics of turning back refugees, the clergy, people of the press, writers, artists and prominent scientists tried to perpetuate the Swiss humanitarian tradition. The Swiss people themselves have shown their good will. No one knows how long the war will last and who will win. More than five million Swiss francs were collected to help the persecuted. This amount represents more than fifteen million Swiss francs in our day. Many simple people have illegally welcomed refugees and have hidden them so that they would not be expelled.

Scarcely had the humanitarian spirit subsided when the borders were once again closed. The applied principle stated: "Refugees on account of race, such as the Jews, are not political refugees." Only political refugees could enter Switzerland. The Jews were systematically escorted back to the frontier. The vigorous anti-Semitism at play since the early centuries of the Confederation (Switzerland was 'free of Jews' since 1349), plus the fear of overpopulation have inspired in large part the politics of the refugee question. This is evident in police documents.

Alfred A. Häsler, Doctor of Theology

Unfortunately, no one at the Federal Council had the heart to advocate for the forty-five children. Had Germany contaminated Bern with the virus of anti- Semitism? One has to believe that was the case.

Chapter 44
The Fate of the Group of Five

I t's too bad that Edith didn't develop in her journal the story of the hastened departures of so many of the children from La Hille. I'm going to try to fill in those gaps here.

Hans Garfunkel left alone. It was a wise choice. He managed to cover the thousand kilometers to the Swiss border without any problems. He also succeeded in secretly crossing the border and sent an enthusiastic letter back to the Château.

All the others that Edith mentions in her journal fled in small groups. The biggest group, with five members, was taken prisoner in the Saint-Cergues forest, near the Swiss border. It was a tragic catastrophe for them and for the Château.

Before I again turn to Edith's journal, I will recount the events of this catastrophe that for more than a year traumatized the older ones who had stayed behind at the Château.

On December 21, 1942, Inge Helft, Inge Joseph, Walter Strauss, Manfred Vos and Adele Hochberger left the Château. They couldn't take the bus to Pailhès because it stopped directly in front of the police station. Instead they hiked the mountain path that led to Saint-Jean-de-Verges, between Foix and Pamiers. (Anne- Marie would take this same route later on with Addi and Edith Goldapper.) In the deepest silence, they set out at midnight with their backpacks in order to arrive early in Saint-Jean-de-Verges where they planned to take the 5am train. Before fate caught up with him, but after his return to the Château, Walter recounted in detail all the misadventures of his group of five.

The trip from Toulouse to Lyon, and then on to Annemasse was relatively smooth. The train was packed, with the corridors full of people, making any sort of careful inspection impossible. The train stations in Toulouse, Lyon and Annemasse were very dangerous, however. The very presence of the Germans was petrifying. Nevertheless, the group made it safely to Annemasse, near the Swiss border, but that's where the troubles began. How can one inconspicuously, undetected, without being stopped or questioned cross the heavily guarded border, teeming with Germans and French on the one side, and Swiss on the other?

(Twice I myself was apprehended without the required papers—for I was traveling illegally—and sent back into Switzerland, one time near Geneva and the other near Basel. I must confess that I had never before done anything so exciting. With this attempted illegal border crossing, my heart was beating so powerfully that from time to time I thought I would pass out.)

At the train station in Annemasse, the five felt scared to death. They were so close to the "promised land," to safety. Now they didn't just feel afraid but knew for sure that what they were doing was a matter of life and death.

They had planned to cross the border near the tiny village of Saint-Cergues.

They had all chosen this route near Saint-Cergues because close by there was a Swiss Colony that would give them a good excuse if they happened to be caught.

They could always say that they were on their way to this colony. We don't know if they did actually show up at the colony. Nor was it clear that they would be able to find places there since there were five of them. It would have been too risky for the colony—and formally forbidden—to simply take them in. It is more likely that for unknown reasons they didn't try to join the colony. One cannot explain otherwise why they ended up taking a different route—one that led straight to their death. At the colony, they would have been told exactly which route to take. But lacking this information, they were lost.

Nevertheless, they did miraculously succeed in getting to the Saint-Cergues forest. They believed they were safe in this peaceful forest and breathed a bit more freely. But then unpredictably they were again overcome with dread. They became aware that a patrol could appear at any moment. Continuing on their path they risked being thrown directly into the arms of the Germans or the French.

What to do? Where was the border? They were confused, and

jumped at the slightest noise. Every step further into the forest, every movement in an uncertain direction seemed to them like a step into the abyss. In their state of heightened alert, they saw death snarling at them everywhere, and imagined the guns pointed at them. Inge Helft, a little blonde seventeen-year-old girl, sobbed despairingly. They were crouched down together in the brush at the edge of the forest. They had already set down their packs next to them. Only Walter Strauss was standing. He was the tallest and strongest of them all, just a year older than Inge Helft. He was standing watch, and looked around in all directions. No one dared to make a sound. It was dead quiet. They heard not even a bird, only Inge's stiffled sobs. Did she feel the presence of death? Manfred Vos was hunkered down next to Inge, withdrawn into himself. Did he divine the horrible fate that was inexorably befalling him?

Walter was getting impatient. "We can't just stay here indefinitely," he said in a low voice.

"But with the five of us I can't go on, not a step further. It would be crazy," asserted Inge Joseph. Her voice resonated so loudly under the trees that everyone jumped. She was a tall, thin girl, a bit younger than Walter. There was a moment of silence—and then a noise. Frightened, they all held their ears. It was nothing, maybe a rabbit.

"I can't bear to stay here any longer," Walter said again, in a choked up voice. "I'll leave my backpack here. I'm going off to look for a path to the border. When I find it, I'll come back. If I'm not here in an hour or two, that means they've caught me. In that case, you're on your own!"

Having stated his decision, Walter took off. He followed a little path that unexpectedly led him straight to a customs house. At that point he no longer had any choice. The customs agent had seen him and signaled him to come closer. He put a finger to his lips and said in a low voice: "Be quiet! The Germans are in the house. You're lucky you stumbled upon me! Follow me!"

The customs officer led him back to Annemasse and handed him over to the French police. In a "trial" that happened instantaneously, Walter was sentenced to fourteen days in prison for attempting to cross the border illegally, and was taken to the jail in Annemasse.

Meanwhile, back in the forest, Inge Helft, Inge Joseph, Adele Hochberger and Monfred Vos waited and waited for their friend—who never returned. After a good three hours, almost evening, they set out, unfortunately on the same path Walter had taken only hours before. They were right on track to their own slaughter. Like Walter, they suddenly found themselves at the customs house. But this time, there wasn't a single Frenchman in sight. The Germans in their well-tailored uniforms nabbed them before they could even think of fleeing.

The worst nightmare that had haunted them night and day for several years was coming true. They were handed over to the Gestapo in Annemasse for interrogation. If they didn't talk, they were threatened with death. In the end they gave the name of the Château and the other children there. It was horrible. Suddenly, Inge Joseph cried out: "I have to go to the toilet!" Someone went with her, but she locked herself in and climbed through a window into the courtyard that led to the street. She ran through the town screaming like a madwoman. She was arrested by the gendarmes and led to the police station. Inge told them about what had just happened, about being arrested by the Gestapo and her own attempted escape at the last minute. She gave them a false name and showed them her false identity papers. (Nearly all the older ones at the Château had false identity papers.) Finally, she told them a totally fictitious story about her past and her current business in Annemasse until she was suddenly interrupted with the question: "Do you know Walter Strauss?"

Inge was so taken aback that she lost her breath. She hadn't given him a thought! Hesitating for a moment, she said yes, she knew him, and then had to tell the truth. The police were already on her trail, for they had listened to Walter's story just a few hours before. Inge, like Walter, was sentenced to fourteen days in prison for attempting to cross the border illegally. She was taken to the prison in Annemasse, luckily having avoided the Germans and certain death. Once in her cell, she broke down sobbing. She saw how Manfred had been beaten, and these images stuck in her mind.

Once, she was allowed to see Walter. Her visit was a stupendous surprise for him! He hadn't let himself even dream of such a thing: a reunion in prison! After fourteen days they were both freed at the same time, with a strict warning: "Never again try to cross the border illegally. That would cost you dearly. We French would put you in prison, the Swiss—who are refusing to take in any Jews—would send you back, and the Germans would deport you, amounting to a death sentence."

Walter let this all sink is. He was tired of these hopelessly failed attempts to escape to Switzerland. He decided to return to his friends and comrades in La Hille, believing he would be most secure with them. He couldn't know that the Gestapo in Annemasse had alerted the National Police in Pailhès to be on the lookout for him. So he made the long, strenuous trip back toward Château de La Hille, which for him was going to turn into a death trap.

Inge Joseph made a different decision. She tried to cross the border a second time, and succeeded! On the other side, however, she was apprehended by soldiers from the Swiss army. (The customs officials were not able to handle the influx of refugees, so the Federal Council had sent in military reinforcements to beef up their staff.) Before sending Inge back into France, which now posed a real danger to her, they offered her some soup. Out of anger and despair, she threw the soup in the officer's face. What a scandal! She was sent back to the border without delay.

We don't know if the soldier who accompanied her took pity on her and let her go her own way, or if she succeeded in crossing on her last try. Whatever happened, several months after Christmas we received a card from Zürich—with best wishes from Inge Joseph!

The fact that thousands of women, men and children driven by fear to try to escape were cruelly refused entry into Switzerland and were sent back into the arms of their torturers was a tragedy of incomparable dimension and remains one of the blackest chapters in Swiss history.

How to explain the inhuman behavior of the Swiss border guards? I cite Alfred A. Häsler's book *The Boat Was Full*, page 90:

> *Following the decision by the Federal Council on August 4, 1942, Dr. Heinrich Rothmund closed the borders on August 13, 1942.*

That's supposed to explain everything!

But it doesn't stop there. This decision was followed up by a further clarification that had even graver consequences for the Jews. I cite the same book and same page:

> *A confidential message from Dr. Rothmund sent to the directors of the state (cantal) police contained this fatal phrase: "Refugees on account of race, such as the Jews, are not political refugees."*

The Jews were not considered political refugees, so they had no chance of entering Switzerland.

The horror goes on. To be able to more quickly identify Jews at the border in order to refuse them, Mr. Rothmund proposed stamping their passports with the letter 'J'. To convince the Germans to take up his proposal, he took the trouble to travel all the way to Berlin.

The criminal decision of the Federal Council to hermetically close the borders and the discriminatory orders addressed to the police force remained secret for a long time. At the Château, however, we were no longer in any doubt. When these decisions became more widely known, they provoked a storm of indignation among the people and the press, and prompted a relaxation of these orders.

Walter returned to the Château, but he was deeply marked by his terrible experiences at the Swiss border and in the Annemasse prison. The tragedy of the group of five was our main topic of conversation for many days. The presumed deportation of Inge Helft, Adele Hochberger and Manfred Vos weighed deeply on all of us. The atmosphere was grim.

The days became progressively longer, and the sun reappeared. Time passed quickly in the everyday routines that created for us the illusion of forgetfulness. The older ones became more carefree. Nothing alarming happened. For two months no police showed up. No one thought of planning further escapes, especially to Switzerland. Our lookout system, normally so vigilant, became lackadaisical. Even Walter Strauss let himself be lulled into a complacent sense of security and returned to life among the large family of children at Château de La Hille. He worked diligently and made himself useful in the house and garden.

Walter was in the courtyard, busy cutting wood for the kitchen, when they came. The raiders in this sudden attack came roaring through the entrance gate in a police van. In a second the gendarmes were everywhere. For Walter Strauss the trap had sprung…

[Edith's Journal, Part Three]

[Just as Edith had given few details about the arrest of the La Hille group at the Swiss border, she wrote very little about this assault by the police. Here is what she did write:]

February 23, 1943. We were completely crushed by the unexpected arrival of the gendarmes. This time there was a warrant officer and a brigadier general as well as many others. We saw right away that things were not going our way. In fact, we were all called for roll. The brigadier read out the names: Manfred Kammerer, Heinz Brünell. Mr. Schlesinger, Berthold Elkan, and Walter Strauss. They were told to pack their bags. An enormous van was waiting there to take them to Camp Vernet. We were deeply dismayed, for we knew that if they left, they would never return. We broke down in tears. Mrs. Schlesinger was sobbing uncontrollably...

From Camp Vernet they were sent to Gurs where they met up with Emil Dortort, Norbert Weiner and Mr. Elias. Soon, they sent Mr. Schlesinger, Walter, Berthold, Emil and Norbert to Drancy, near Paris, the transit camp that was the most dreaded and well-known. Heinz and Manfred returned to the Château. Everyone was very nervous.

We again set up our system of sentinels, and every time they spotted police coming our way, they called out "Short circuit!" At that point all the older ones would disappear, as if swallowed up by the earth. Luckily, this lookout system worked very well.

[End of Edith's Journal, Part Three]

In the next chapter, I would like to recount in more detail the gendarmes' visit. On that occasion several children from La Hille and Mr. Schlesinger were taken away from us, never to be seen again.

Chapter 45
The Roll Call

What follows was told to me by Eugen Lyrer.

Walter Strauss barely had time to set down his hatchet before he was arrested. The brigadier went to ring the bell in the courtyard. Everyone had to show up for the roll, the little ones as well as the older ones. That provoked incredible confusion. Everyone was running here and there, gesticulating and crying. Finally, a good number of children were gathered in the courtyard, but not many of the older ones, who had had time to hide.

The brigadier stood up on the cover of the cistern in front of the kitchen.

Without paying the least attention to the confusion around him, he began reading the names. "Walter Strauss!" Walter acknowledged his presence though he had already been taken prisoner.

The brigadier continued: "Inge Joseph!" Inge's card had just arrived from Zürich.

The brigadier repeated: "Inge Joseph!" Silence. Everyone expected an outburst. But nothing happened.

The brigadier read out the other names on his list. After each name, he paused and looked over at us. "Peter Salz!"—"Hans Garfunkel!"—"Ruth Klonover!"—"Ilse Wulf!"

Silence. None of them was present.

The brigadier started to have enough of this, and yelled: "Where are they?"

"They've all left," said Eugen Lyrer. "We don't know where they are and have no way of getting in touch with them."

"They're hiding," grumbled the officer. "We will search the house!"

The brigadier was angry and called his men. He put two of them in charge of keeping watch on the courtyard, while the others disappeared into the Château.

"I wasn't afraid," Eugen said to me in recounting this story. "They weren't going to find the *Zwiebelkeller*!"

After a rather long time, the gendarmes showed up again in the courtyard: they had found no one. The *Zwiebelkeller* could not be found! Every one of us breathed a sigh of relief. The brigadier climbed back up on his "podium" and again started reading names in a shrill voice. This time he had some success. "Manfred Kammerer!"—"Berthold Elkan!"—"Heinz Brünell!" The three of them stepped forward. They hadn't had time to hide. Manfred and Berthold had been surprised while they were carrying water, and Heinz was right there in the courtyard. The brigadier was satisfied. Manfred, Berthold and Heinz knew they were condemned.

But the reading was not over. "Mr. Schlesinger!" and again "Mr. Schlesinger!" No response. It was deadly quiet in the courtyard. Everyone loved Mr. Schlesinger, and we all knew he was hiding somewhere on his own, not with the older ones. Only Mrs. Schlesinger knew exactly where. We waited.

Suddenly someone cried: "No!" Eugen told me he could not believe his eyes. Mrs. Schlesinger appeared with her husband.

What on earth had happened? I've already told you about this earlier. The police shamelessly abused Mrs. Schlesinger's naïveté and convinced her that they were only interested in checking Mr. Schlesinger's ration coupons. Above all, they lied to her that Mr. Schlesinger would be right back.

Mr. Schlesinger was arrested with the others, and Mrs. Schlesinger began howling with despair when she realized her mistake. Her cries penetrated to the marrow of our bones.

The brigadier got down from his perch and gave the signal to depart. His victims were already stashed in the police van. It was horrendous to see. All the older ones were crying with Mrs. Schlesinger, and the middle ones—typically so brazen and fierce—watched teary-eyed as the van disappeared through the gate.

Chapter 46
Miss Näf Departs

At Château de La Hille other changes took place as well. Once more I will cite:
[Edith Goldapper's Journal, Part Four]:

Mrs. Frank senior is gone now too. I think it is better that the Franks are no longer here. Otherwise we would surely have had more arguments and disputes.

We regularly receive mail from Inge Schragenheim with good news. But she has been in some real trouble too! She had been in Switzerland for four days when she was sent back to the border. Now she has found a young man, and they live together in Nice. She seems very happy but I would much prefer that she were here.

Spring is gradually approaching. Miss Näf thinks that all the boys over eighteen years of age have to go and work on a farm. Fifty percent of them are happy with that decision, but the other fifty percent are not. As it happened, the Vichy government's "Mission to Restore the Farmers" was gaining momentum, with the result that sooner than expected there were plenty of openings for our boys on the farms. The first to go were Werner Epstein, Edgar Chaim, and Charles Blumenfeld, followed by Kurt Moser and Fritz Wertheimer.

The Château was becoming rather empty. Meanwhile we got a letter from Inge saying that she and her boyfriend were arrested.

I turned pale from fright. Mr. Lyrer immediately took a train for Nice, and he succeeded in arranging that Inge come back here. I don't know how we can ever make it up to him.

Oh, I am so happy! Today, April 17, 1943, Inge returned with Mr. Lyrer. For her it is not so easy to be back here at the Château. She had gotten used to another life, but for the moment this is her best solution.

Today Charles and Edgar came for a visit. Besides, it's Easter, and we are having a very good time. You see, we are still very much bonded with one another, and I believe that this bond will not ever be broken....

It's the month of May, and there are rumors that Miss Näf will leave us for good.

It makes me really sad to think that I will never see her again. Even though she often has her moods, overall she has been good for the colony.

Meanwhile, Ilse Brünell has also left us. She is going to work for Mrs. Authier in Foix. Another one gone.

It's really true. Miss Näf is leaving. Another director, a woman, is arriving today.

May 7, 1943. Miss Piguet, Miss Näf, and Walter Kammerer leave for Saint-Girons. Walter is also leaving us. Too bad, for we will never be able to listen to such wonderful piano playing. (I am no competition for him!) At seven o'clock that evening Miss Piguet comes back with Walter! She says they couldn't find him anywhere to stay! But it's true that Miss Näf will not be coming back, so we have to send her things to her tomorrow.

[End of Edith's Journal, Part Four]

In light of her outstanding, exemplary intercession on behalf of the forty-five children so unexpectedly rounded up and sent to Camp Vernet, Miss Näf received orders from Bern to leave Château de La Hille and return to Switzerland. The Swiss Red Cross was uncompromising. They had to bow to the wishes of the Germans, just like the Vichy Government did. Vichy slavishly adhered to the orders and wishes of occupying Germany in every instance and in every institution, including the police. After all, the Vichy regime was put in place by the

Germans; Marshal Pétain and Pierre Laval were fully subservient to Germany.

Miss Näf never did like Walter Kammerer. That she always regarded our thin, pale pianist in his unique position in the Château as a slacker and a phony was not terribly surprising; she never believed that he was really sick. As it was later verified, he did indeed have a serious case of tuberculosis. Whether consciously or not, she tormented him as only she could. Walter often regaled me with his sorry tales of Miss Näf.

Miss Näf was a thin, goal-directed person with small, steel-grey eyes that demanded the strictest obedience.

Before leaving the Château and the children, she made a strange decision. One assumes in the first instance that she wanted to protect Walter from the police in Pailhès. It is also possible that she intended to spare her follower, Miss Tännler, any trouble with such a willful musician. She may well have had other reasons also. In any case, Miss Näf decided without further ado to place our pianist in a psychiatric clinic.

According to Edith's journal, Miss Näf and Walter left the Château early on May 7, 1943, along with Anne-Marie Piguet. They took the bus from Pailhès to Mas d'Azil, and then another bus to Saint-Girons. There they registered at the psychiatric hospital. After a brief conversation with Miss Näf, the chief doctor and director of the clinic met Walter in the waiting room and led him into his office. The doctor was amazed to find that Walter was not at all a mentally ill person but a fully normal young man. The doctor seems not to have understood Miss Näf's putative intention of hiding Walter in the clinic. Perhaps she had not clearly enough expressed her intentions or she had simply hoped that Walter would be admitted without any further ado.... But after examining Walter, the doctor asserted that there was nothing wrong with the patient in question and that he could not possibly admit him into his psychiatric clinic. Moreover, psychiatric internment for such a sensitive musician could have grave consequences.

"It is totally out of the question that I keep you here!" he asserted exasperatedly. He considered the whole affair as an imposition and bid the anxiously awaiting Miss Näf to come back into his office. He must not have treated her in a very friendly manner, for she returned to the waiting room utterly shaken and humiliated.

"I am never going back to the Château," she said curtly, and immediately left without even saying goodbye. Anne-Marie accompanied Walter back to the Château.

Miss Näf and Miss Groth were civil servants. Both of them had spent several years in the Albert Schweitzer Hospital in Lambaréné in Gabon, Africa. They were experienced in dealing with the sick and had generally been held in high esteem.

Both of these women had boundless energy that they expended in their work. Self- sacrifice became second nature to them. One could not imagine more ideal Red Cross workers! They had the capacity to be effective in all sorts of extreme situations—for example, as rescuers of the wounded in Solferino. The only problem was that they had no pedagogical training and no professional experience with children.

As directors of the Red Cross Colony of La Hille, they were in an extremely difficult position. After all, this colony was full of children who were war victims and, more specifically, Jewish children hunted down by the police. Given the situation, their work was in many ways over their heads, and they were bound to make errors despite their very best intentions.

One can't help but conclude that their training in the harsh conditions of the Albert Schweitzer Hospital in the jungle had deeply and permanently influenced them. The authoritarian model of the famous doctors, who made the most strenuous demands on themselves and expected total dedication and effort on the part of their co-workers, must have had a profound effect on both our directors. Perhaps these features of their previous work led to their hard, apparently unfeeling, authoritarian comportment as well as the self-sacrificing nature of their efforts.

The Red Cross Children's Aid Society had sent Miss Näf and Miss Groth to the difficult situation of the Château de La Hille and appointed them directors of the colony. These women themselves had not applied for this position, but as civil servants they were prepared and willing to take on this mission. It is not hard to see that this mission was highly stressful. The Director's tasks at the Château were barely achievable. For example, they had to travel thirty kilometers each way to do the marketing and get supplies, to deal with hundreds of rationing tickets, to oversee the staff and the children, and to carry out numerous other duties. The two "sisters" from Lambaréné did their best under often hopeless conditions. They cannot be blamed for mistakes in pedagogical and similar matters. Sooner hold the Red Cross itself accountable! Retrospectively we can say that both directors found themselves "between a rock and a hard place." They were strictly forbidden from engaging in illegal activities, but the parameters for accomplishing anything at all at La Hille were terribly narrow.

Chapter 47

Inge Schragenheim, Edith's Friend

E dith has often mentioned Inge Schragenheim in her journal, but now it's time for me to make the reader better acquainted with her in the following chapter.

Shortly after *Kristallnacht* in 1938, fourteen-year-old Inge left her parents' house in Cologne. Like most of the older girls, she came to Château de La Hille after a prolonged stay in the General Bernheim Home in Brussels and then another in Seyre near Toulouse.

A general panic swept through France in December 1942 as the Germans occupied France. Inge was also caught in its thrall. She packed her bags and left the Château with Leo Lewin (as did a group before them) in hopes of safely crossing the Swiss border. Near the Red Cross Colony at St. Cergues, they had better luck in making the illegal crossing than the fated group of five. They had passed by two border control stations undetected and were on their way to Geneva when they were stopped by a patrol of Swiss border guards and were brought to the transit camp Claparède in Geneva.

After a long investigation and even longer interrogation, it was decided that Leo could stay in Switzerland since he was not yet eighteen years old. (The restrictions were constantly changing. For a long time no child was allowed in, and then later at least children up to sixteen were admitted.) In contrast, Inge who was a year older than Leo, was sent back to France after her four days in Switzerland.

Another refugee, also a Jew, was also sent back with her to France.

His name was Peter, and they became intimate friends. They traveled together to the Côte d'Azur and hoped to be able to cross the Italian border near the town of Ventimiglia, but they were stopped in Nice. During a round-up Peter was caught by the Germans and—apparently during an attempted escape—was shot.

Inge inadvertently ran into the arms of the French police and was imprisoned for carrying false papers. Fortunately she was allowed to write to friends. She sent Eugen Lyrer a letter explaining her situation, and he immediately left for Nice to visit her. In the course of fourteen days, Eugen traveled back and forth to Nice three times. Finally he was able to secure her freedom by paying three hundred francs, and brought her back to the Château.

[Edith's Journal Part Five]

✳

Today already marks two years since Miss Näf came to Seyre. Yes, the time goes flying by. But in these two years so much has happened. I think the years 1942 and 1943 are the worst I have ever lived through. I strongly hope that my future will be rosier!...

Rikon, December 31, 1943. As I promised myself, I will continue my journal. This time I am not sitting at the Château but in Switzerland! Indeed, I have to backtrack quite a bit.

I was writing about May 1943, when Miss Näf left us for good. Miss Tännler took over her position as director, and Anne-Marie did the marketing. For the rest of us life went on pretty much as before. But out in the real world, things were looking grim. There were more and more deportations of Jews and French. Charles, Werner, Edgar and even Addi Nussbaum want to go to Spain. Also Kurt Moser.

The next few weeks are full of secrets. People are whispering in every corner, for the boys planning their escape come to visit us often and are constantly discussing the details. They decide the day and the place where they will meet for their flight into Spain. Even Addi our scholar wants to go. But at the last minute Addi and Edgar change their minds and stay here. [They don't know yet how lucky they were for backing out!]

On June 24 we receive shocking news. Our beloved Fritz Wertheimer and Kurt Moser were arrested on their trip to cross into Spain. Who knows what will happen to them. [Later on I will hear what does happen to them: they both were deported and killed by the Germans.] *We are convinced that Charles and Werner have successfully arrived in Spain.*

On July 22 we find out the terrible news that Charles Blumenfeld and Werner Epstein have also been arrested while crossing the border. Then we receive a final card from Werner that he throws out the window from the train where they are packed in. Our four good friends are there where many of our faithful have been sent. But I still hold out the hope that one day we will meet again, for they are young and can put up with a lot. [I have already talked about this tragic, ill-begotten escape to Spain in a previous chapter.]

Time doesn't stand still, and the days pass quickly. Before you know it, it's already autumn. September: We again hear about more deportations of Jews. We are again panic-stricken by the thought of being taken by the Germans. That's why our wonderful Zwiebelkeller *is made accessible again. In fact, one day "our dear friends" from the police headquarters do indeed pay us a visit and ask whether Manfred Kammerer, Heinz Storosum, Heinz Brünell and Addi Nussbaum are still at our colony. We are immediately suspicious, and our comrades go hide in the* Zwiebelkeller. *I am working in the office, when I hear the gendarmes in the house. They are here again to pick up the four boys. Miss Tännler explains that she has no idea where they could be, and it is certainly understandable that they have run off since everyone is fearful of the police. Then the aide-de-camp shows up too. Naturally, Mr. Lyrer also has no idea of where the four might be. I continue working at a feverish pace in my accounts book so that I don't burst out laughing. It is really a sad situation, but right now it seems almost comical.*

For the next several days, the Château is under strict surveillance day and night.

It would be impossible to escape. A dark, heavy mood hangs over the Château. Every day we are afraid that we too, the ones still here, will be arrested. Oh, it is a horrible way to live, in constant fear of being deported.

Meanwhile, we hear that Ruedi Oelbaum, who is working at Mr. Roubichon's, has been arrested and is now apparently in Camp Vernet. Immediately Mrs. Authier, the administrator in charge of the police in Foix, has been informed that Ruedi is not yet seventeen years old and therefore must be set free. A few days later he miraculously returns to the Château. He was let go just shortly before a deportation. Thank God that everything has turned out well this time. Meanwhile, our comrades in the Zwiebelkeller are holding up well.

Miss Tännler and Miss Anne-Marie have so much to do. The whole day they are running here and there to find suitable places for the children. Mr. Lyrer is also very busy.

In the meantime, a new teacher from Switzerland has arrived: Mr. Sebastian Steiger. He is still very young.... Since many French and Spanish little children are still with us, we are in need of more teaching staff.

Today little Betsy Schütz has also left us. She will try to get into Switzerland.

Mr. Lyrer is going to accompany her to the border.

Today is a very nerve-racking day. Miss Tännler has picked Inge and me to stand watch at ten o'clock tonight, because the four boys in the Zwiebelkeller—for whom some suitable places have been found—want to leave the Château. We are very nervous about this, but all things considered it is our duty to help our friends.

Mr. Lyrer is often away. Heinz Storosum has a lot of work. He is the Château's great violinist. We hear that Heinz Brünell, Ilse's brother, is doing well on a farm in Pau, and Heinz Storosum has found a place in a Jewish children's home. Manfred Kammerer goes back and forth from Toulouse and Foix. That's a very risky business for him!

Our dear mathematician Addi Nussbaum is in Switzerland, thanks to Anne-Marie's great help. [I have already told you the story of Anne-Marie's trip to Switzerland with Addi.] She says that she will bring all the older ones to Switzerland this way.

From all the turmoil she has had to deal with, Miss Tännler has become ill. She has jaundice, and therefore has gone to the Schmutz family in Tambouret to recover.

I've been playing the piano a lot recently and taking lessons from our great pianist Walter. In exchange for the lessons, he is dictating to me his philosophical work, which I am taking down in stenography and then later type out on the typewriter. It's very busy in the office, and I am allowed to do the bookkeeping. I really enjoy this work and learn a lot by doing it.

Yet another teacher has come to the Château: Mr. Heinrich Kägi. There are still so many French children here with us that we really need more personnel, especially since Miss Tännler has put in an application to return to Switzerland. Her recovery is proceeding slowly, but soon she will go back to Switzerland. Now we need to find another director. We all wish that Mr. Lyrer would be our director, but I think a woman from the Swiss Aid Society has already been appointed. We are not overjoyed by that, but there is nothing we can do about it.

The rest of us here at the Château no longer want to stay. Gerti is going to work for a family in Pamiers, Edith Moser is going to Varilhes, and Onze often works at Mrs. Melanie's. The Château is becoming more and more empty. Are Inge and I supposed to remain here with just the Mickeys and the Middles? That will not do!

Mr. Lyrer asks Inge and me if we would like to go to Switzerland. What a question! I would fly there in a minute! Inge and I are no longer allowed to work in the office. The new director, Miss Groth, has taken over all the office work. Now we don't have anything fun to do at the Château. But according to Miss Groth, if we want to leave the Château to go to Switzerland, we first have to find positions here in the area. So for this purpose I may use the typewriter for the last time: to put in an application for Inge with a Mr. Pick, and for me in Bordes-sur-Arize with a pastor. If all this works out, we can under the circumstances start in our new positions in fourteen days. But of course, we don't really want to go work with these families but, instead, to flee to Switzerland!

Fourteen days pass with no responses. We are really discouraged. Irma Seelenfreund is supposed to come along with us, and so she is also waiting impatiently to hear. To be quite honest, I have to say I would prefer that she not come along. But if it comes to saving her life, then I must indeed be understanding and agreeable.

Miss Anne-Marie has already arranged with the guides who will accompany us into Switzerland. We are supposed to depart La Hille on October 27, 1943.

Still no word. Mr. Lyrer is staying with Mr. Dubois on vacation in the Haute-Savoie. He said goodbye to us and told us he was absolutely sure we would already be in Switzerland when he returned. I am ninety-nine percent sure that the responses to our applications will not arrive in time and we will not be allowed to leave.

Tomorrow, October 27, we are really supposed to depart if we are going to be in Champagnole on Friday as planned. We are on pins and needles! No response. We continually pester Miss Anne-Marie and Miss Groth. Miss Groth remains adamant. She insists that we may not leave without first obtaining working positions because the Château will get into trouble with the police. Inge and I are terribly sad! We are so close to having a great chance, but now we have to miss out on it!

Oh, it's frightful. Inge and I feel deeply disappointed. We are so eager to get on with our lives. We try to console ourselves by saying: If we cannot go, then at least Edith Moser ought to take advantage of this opportunity. Anne-Marie Piguet immediately takes the bike to Varilhes to tell Edith about the situation. On her return, Anne-Marie tells us that Manfred Kammerer is also going along to accompany Edith to the border.

To a certain extent, I am happy. At least this rendezvous is not completely wasted.

Now we are constantly worried that the two of them will be nabbed by the police. We received mail from them from Toulouse, and then from Lyon—after that, nothing. No word. Walter Kammerer is deeply worried. He is constantly telling us that Edith and Manfred have most certainly been taken by the Germans. Miss Anne-Marie is also terribly nervous....

Finally a letter arrives from Champagnole. Edith and Manfred write that they have safely gotten into Switzerland! What a tremendous joy! At lunch, Miss Anne-Marie jumps up from her place to hurry to tell Walter the good news.

Naturally Inge and I are very happy about this report. But we can't get it out of our minds that we too could have been there....

Mr. Lyrer returns from his vacation to find us still at the Château—just as I had predicted!

Now there are many discussions with Miss Groth and Miss Anne-Marie to the effect that we should also be able to try our luck. Because of the approaching snow season, we would have to act quickly in any case. Our bags have been packed for several months so that we are ready at any opportune moment to quickly disappear.

Our applications for positions have not been answered. We have already lost every thread of hope and have reconciled ourselves to the thought that we must remain at the Château.

It always turns out this way: If you constantly think about something and obsessively hope for it to happen, it will be guaranteed not to happen. Something lucky happens only by chance, out of the blue. Today the work permits arrived for Irma and me, but not yet for Inge. So we can't think about leaving eventually because it seems too unlikely.

Today, Tuesday, November 9, Irma left for Varilhes to work at a hairdressers' salon.

At eight o'clock in the evening, as I was coming out of the infirmary where Mr. Steiger had given me something for a cold, Miss Anne-Marie spotted me and told me to go fetch Inge and bring her immediately to Anne-Marie's room. I have a funny feeling that I can't explain.

Shortly thereafter, Inge and I are in Miss Anne-Marie's room upstairs. She says that we should gather all our things and count on a hasty departure. I suppose that she means tomorrow evening, but then she explains to us that the departure will be this very night! It's as if we are hit by a lightning bolt! This is something we never expected. Irma is now in Varilhes and can't come along....

Anne-Marie very carefully explains the route to us and writes down all the important reference points. We still can't comprehend it. Right now it's ten o'clock and at three o'clock in the morning we need to be on our way toward Saint-Jean-de- Verges. We need to be as quiet as possible so that no one notices us. Our roommates know we are leaving because they see us get our things together.

Mr. Lyrer is so sweet and generous; he has offered to lend me his backpack.

Without that, I don't know where I would have put all my things. Whatever I don't take along, I am putting into a suitcase for storage in Miss Groth's office. Mr. Lyrer will keep my books and most important letters. Everything left behind will be in good order.

The time approaches: eleven o'clock, twelve o'clock... Inge and I dress warmly, for outdoors it is bitter cold.

Two o'clock in the morning. We sit in the salon and listen to some music. We try to distract ourselves. Until twelve thirty Anne-Marie, who was writing to her parents and friends, stayed with us in the salon. Mr. Steiger was there too, preparing some kind of theatrical piece. Mr. Lyrer joined us since he wants to accompany us for a bit.

2:30am. We are in the kitchen drinking coffee and eating

biscuits. *My throat feels like it is tied in a knot, so I can barely get anything down. We go upstairs one more time, to put on our coats and fasten our backpacks. My backpack is not light, but I will manage.*

Farewell, you beautiful Château! So many wonderful hours— you were my second home. Now I am leaving you. My heart tightens when I think that I will no more run through your familiar rooms, no more reign in the laundry room shouting at the girls to get them to work more diligently at their mending so that on Saturday I can distribute the washing...

All of that is over now, but the Château will remain and I must see it again sometime. Come what may, I must somehow return!...

Outside it is light as day. The moon is bright in the sky. Inge is on the left, Mr. Lyrer in the middle, and I am on the right. No one speaks. Our thoughts are already far off. We don't even feel the cold; on the contrary, it seems to be getting warmer. One last time we pass the post office in Montégut. Here is the bus stop where I have often taken the bus to Foix.

Now the path gets steeper. We arrive at Loubains. Mr. Lyrer is still with us. It is eighteen kilometers to Saint-Jean-de-Verges. We are about half way. Mr. Lyrer leaves us at Loubains, and we walk on, alone. Once more we turn around and see a faint silhouette— then nothing more—as Mr. Lyrer heads back to the Château. We set out on our way into a new world.

Gradually we get tired, and our backpacks are a tremendous pain. But one thought urges us on: keep going! When we pass farmhouses, we walk very quietly and if possible in the grass. We always have to be on our guard! We have our false identity cards with us, but mine is totally unusable since it was issued in 1942. It would be unusable for a real French person as well. [The new identity cards in use are valid for one year.] Inge's card is also problematic since the stamp is completely faded out. We just have to hope that we get through all right. From here on we use the names 'Danielle Pascab' and 'Eve Germain'—obviously French. I was born in Alsace! I have to imprint all of these new personal details deeply into my brain!

Finally we arrive at Saint-Jean in barely under three hours. We sit down on a stone near the train station. It is November 10, 1943, at six o'clock in the morning.

At 6:30am we board the train for Toulouse. It's really cold, and we are freezing. We arrive in Toulouse around 10am. We have to be very careful not to meet up with any inspection agents. So far, so good. We leave our bags at the station and take a walk in town. We find a pleasant café and sit down. We immediately write a card to the Château. A hot cup of coffee nicely warms us up.

Our train to Lyon doesn't depart until 8pm, so we have all afternoon to go see a film. For me this is really funny because I haven't gone to the movies or even been in a big city for so many years. The film "Gold on the Streets" is totally stupid, but at least it provides some distraction.

We go back to the train station to look for our train. A nice young man in the Air Force notices us, picks up our bags and stows them in his compartment. He saves two places next to him, and we three settle in quite comfortably. I decide to try to fall asleep as soon as possible. That way, if an inspector comes by, I will already be in a deep sleep. But our airman doesn't let us alone. He wants to know where we are going, what we are doing. Inge quickly takes charge of the conversation. I am not at all interested. He offers us some bread and ham and tells us about his activities in the black market. But after all, it is very pleasant to share his compartment. If a passport control officer suddenly shows up at two in the morning and sees the airman, the airman can right away declare that everything in his compartment is fine. That certainly lifts a weight off our hearts!

At 6am we arrive in Lyon. It is rather cold, so we go into the train-station restaurant and have some coffee. Later on, Inge will show me the city, since she has already been here. But unfortunately, because of an attempted assassination, Lyon is strictly barricaded. I regret not being able to take advantage of being in Lyon.

Our train for Lons-le-Saunier departs at 11pm. We arrive around midnight.

Then Inge and I consider what we should do: either stay in the station waiting room or look for a hotel. Without having resolved the issue, we go back outside. At the station exit, someone gives us a permission slip to circulate in the town until 1am. What to do? Here we are after midnight, in the middle of the street, in a strange town, with our gigantic backpacks. We can't very well hunt up a hotel, and in our situation it would not be wise to even try.

Luckily we meet a young lad from the "Youth Camp," and

we ask him if he could arrange a place to stay for us. He says no, but nevertheless he begins looking for a hotel. It's a nightmare! Nothing can be found in this little hole of a place. We are completely discouraged. It's already 1am, and the police could arrest us at any moment. And with our poor identification!

In deep despair, we find a house door partly open and go in. Our young man leads us to a corner tucked way in the back. Later on we figure out that it is a police station! Luckily we didn't notice that earlier on.

Meanwhile we make ourselves as comfortable as possible on our backpacks.

Because we had been walking around, we feel quite warm, but soon it gets colder and we realize that our limbs will get stiffer and stiffer. We had scarcely nodded off when a blast of cold air awakened us. It was terrible, but I had the impression that I simply couldn't do anything about it. Every hour I heard the nearby church bells chime.

And today is my birthday. It is the saddest one I have ever experienced. Inge softly whispers happy birthday to me, but that's all I have. I am nineteen years old now. Where will I spend this year? In Switzerland—or Poland? [in a concentration camp]

If it were only morning already!... But we get through this night, and on the dot of seven we go to the station restaurant to get something warm to drink. Gradually we thaw out, and the time passes.

At 9am we take the bus to Champagnole, our final destination. But I still have the feeling that we will have to go through some kind of check-point. But it is a miracle: we do not go by a single one!

We arrive in Champagnole around noon, and now we look for the address we have been given. We find it rather quickly, along with our dear, unknown friends. Two nice young women around twenty-three and twenty-five years old welcome Inge and me with the utmost kindness and immediately make us feel at home. I am so tired. I think I have never been so tired in my whole life as I was on that day. After lunch they send me to bed. Later on we will need to discuss so many important questions.

Around seven we have our Abendbrot, "evening bread" or supper. Then the two sisters explain to us that at this time of year it is just about impossible to get into Switzerland. The snow is already too deep. If we perhaps want to wait a week, they would be happy to put us up. Perhaps the snow will melt enough to allow us to get through. When I heard all this I was very disappointed. I had been so convinced that tomorrow, Saturday, I would be safely over the border. But now, everything has fallen through. And whom shall we thank for this situation? None other than our Director Miss Groth who wouldn't let us leave earlier! Oh well, perhaps we will be lucky and the snow will indeed melt. Last year at this time it was still warm—why couldn't that be true this year also?

Despite our initial disappointment, we feel very much at home, really like family. The two young women are so nice. Naturally, we help in the household and try to make ourselves as useful as possible.

November 19, 1943. I have never waited so impatiently for something as for the snow to melt a bit. But nothing like that happened. It's really not all that cold, and I go around the house in socks. Today the sun was shining nice and warm—but in the morning it was snowing again! It drives me to despair. I am very discouraged. We receive mail from the Château, that is, from Mr. Lyrer, and that makes me feel very homesick for La Hille. Switzerland seems out of the picture for this year. I just have to drum it out of my head. Before April or May 1944 we cannot do anything. Anne-Marie sent a telegram telling us we should go to Montluel, but our new sisters suggest that we try to find positions in Champagnole until spring. That would make the time go by. Victoria's boss—Victoria is one of the sisters—would like to take one of us. Inge jumped at the chance, and so from now on goes by the name Danielle Pascal!

We spend many beautiful days at our sponsors' house. Their mother comes to visit from Chapelle des Bois, as well as several friends. One evening they made a delicious fondue! Every Sunday we go to the movies!

Inge is nicely settled in with her family. Mr. and Mrs. Girardet are very kind. Besides them, there are three other young girls, as well as two boys nineteen and twenty years old. Inge feels very happy there, and is counted as one of the family.

Now people are actively looking for a family for me. A family turns up that is looking for a young woman to help with their children. I go to meet them in their gorgeous villa! The father asks if I can cook, since they are in need of a cook, but unfortunately cooking is not my thing. He's sorry, I'm sorry too. But deep down I *feel content and return "home." What to do now? I can't really stay with my new sisters until spring. I fret about this, and still hope that I can somehow be in Switzerland before the end of the year 1943!*

[End of Edith's Journal Part Five]

Chapter 48
An Old Jug

L et us leave Edith on the Swiss border in the ice, the snow and the cold, hoping for some good luck...

At the Château, we have absolutely no snow, but it is very cold here too—biting cold! The thermometer in the big classroom regularly shows between zero [32°F] and three degrees centigrade. Once in a while Egon tries lighting the stove, but there's nothing to be done. The thing simply smokes too much.

Not only in the classroom but in the entire Château the temperature is the same as outside. When the icy winds from the Pyrénées sweep over the landscape, we soon have the fabled "Drafty Castle." During our lessons, this scenario constantly repeats itself: in the front hallway the door bangs shut, the door to the classroom springs open, and the window flies up with an explosive noise. The draft chills us to our very bones. André and François run to shut the window, Jojo closes the classroom door, but then someone walks through the hallway and leaves the door open—which promptly bangs shut...

We freeze the entire day.

It is almost as bad during meals. The benches are icy and the table is too cold to touch. In the mornings, the staff gets a "bowl" of warm "coffee" substitute. (I've already mentioned this earlier in the book.) But at least holding our coffee bowls we have a way to warm our hands—what a pleasure! Once a day, then, we have a tiny bit of warmth.

Of course the beds are also ice-cold. The shabby, worn-out mattresses and the two pitifully thin wool blankets give no protection against the penetrating cold. For Heiri and me the result is predictable:

our bladders rebel, causing us to find our way at all times of the night down the steps into the frozen outdoors, no matter the wind or weather. Once back in bed, which feels like no one had ever been lying on it, our bodies shiver and our teeth chatter. One tosses and turns, trying to get back to sleep, but then all too soon wakes up, to begin the circus anew.

That was our pattern for a good many days, until Heiri had an idea on how to radically shorten our route to pee in the great outdoors. He climbed out onto the window ledge and peed into the darkness. From our window ledge high on the first floor [the second floor on American reckoning], came the sound of a steady stream hitting the gravel below. In the stillness of the night, this unfortunately made an awfully loud sound. Worst of all it woke up our neighbors the Nadals.

The very short walk to the window had its distinctive advantages: we were back in bed in no time flat. However, this practice was rather dangerous. I nearly had to pay for it with my life, or at least serious injuries. Without thinking of the risks involved, I got out of bed, half asleep, and for the second or third time in the night climbed out onto the window ledge—but suddenly lost my balance! Luckily, with my left hand I was able to grab the window frame. For a moment I was looking death in the face, hanging from the second story window over the dark abyss, cold sweat covering my brow...

As I said, our noisy splashing during the night had awakened the Nadals. The next morning, without any comment, Mrs. Nadal appeared with an old, cracked jug that handily saved us from having to climb out onto the window ledge in the middle of the night.

Chapter 49

Saint Nicholas

In her journal Edith wrote that on the evening of her flight from the Château, I was still up at 12:30am in the salon rehearsing a play. I can't recall anything about that. Perhaps I was preparing something for a Saint Nicholas pageant. In any case it must have been some sort of long humorous or satirical poem.

At the Château, we were consciously and unconsciously building a family. In this context it was always important to organize a little celebration or festive activity that everyone could enjoy. December 6, Saint Nicholas day, is a perfect occasion for a joyous evening when all cares can be set aside. Acting out skits, charades, word games and other kinds of play puts the children into high spirits.

The highpoint is always singing the *Schnitzelbank* song, with various funny verses about the teachers and staff inserted between the chorus. Here are two examples:

> *Mamsell TOBLER veut nous quitter*
> *Les enfants l'ont trop fâchée,*
> *Malgé son amour pour les petits*
> *Qu'elle met soigneusement dans leurs lits*

> Miss TOBLER wants to leave us bad,
> 'Cause the children drive her mad,
> Though she tucks them into bed,
> Lovingly it must be said.

Le visa ne veut arriver,
Le dossier s'est égaré
Le Préfet de l'Ariège
Ne veut comprendre que ça presse.

Miss Tobler's visa will not come,
Her file lost to kingdom come,
No one in Ariège does heed,
Her visa she does desperately need.

Everyone had such a good time at our jolly Saint Nicholas party. Even the Mickeys were allowed to stay up later than usual. But Miss Tobler, who on my birthday (as I lay deathly ill with jaundice) had the children come up to my doorway to sing happy birthday to me in such a touching if off-key way, was visibly upset. It is true that we had often made fun of the fact that her visa never arrived. But she took that very badly. She really wanted to leave; she had had enough of the children and life at the Château. She wanted to go home. And on top of that came the *Schnitzelbank* verses making fun of her situation. It was too much! One dark night, she disappeared without even saying goodbye, taking with her two girls, Toni Rosenblatt and Inge Bernhard. Neither Miss Tobler nor the two girls had visas. In the letter Miss Groth found in her room, Miss Tobler wrote: "I can't stand it here in the Château any longer. I'm going to Switzerland and taking Toni and Inge with me."

They arrived in Switzerland but not without difficulty: even a Swiss citizen without a visa does not have the right to enter her own country!

Some weeks later Miss Tobler sent a letter saying: "The Germans are not all as bad as you think." We wondered for a long time if a German had helped her cross the border into Switzerland. (A later chapter in my book will reveal what really did happen on the Swiss border.)

I haven't yet had the opportunity to mention that at the beginning of December Miss Annelies Keller arrived without any fanfare from the Château Avenières, a Red Cross colony situated on Mount Salève near Annemasse close to the Swiss border. Annelies is Heiri's fiancée, and she will replace Miss Tobler in caring for the pre-school Mickeys.

Chapter 50
My Idea for an "Eiderdown" Comforter

After eight weeks, I successfully ended my "waking therapy," based on the Pavlovian theory of conditioned reflexes. My little "subjects" wet their beds only occasionally. Like good little children, they all used the pail by the door. Even Jeanne now stayed dry for several days in a row. I myself, however, seemed to be at the end of my rope: I hadn't given myself enough time to recuperate after the jaundice.

The children were very happy to be over their problematic condition, especially since it was getting colder and colder. As a precaution to avoid any unexpected relapses, I still woke them up promptly at 10pm. I was proud of my success and determined to write a groundbreaking Masters research paper for the University of Zürich's Health and Pedagogy Department. With this end in mind, I had already gathered all the necessary support for my thesis. I had all the essentials written down, including the weather conditions and the menus for the evening meals for every day.

It seemed to us to get colder and colder every day, although the temperature officially never fell below freezing. Since the Château had no heating, the inside could well have been colder than outside. I would wear my coat in the classroom, but I still froze. The girls wore socks. There were no long stocking, leggings or long pants. Only a few of them had woolen undergarments. The bare legs of the boys, who had only short pants, turned blue. We were all freezing, and our fingers became so stiff with the cold that often the children could not write. School was no longer much fun, but all the children were doing their best. The first graders—Rose, Conchita, Guy and Josette—had all learned their letters and could read reasonably well. Conchita proudly walked around with her book under her arm. For François reading was no real joy but it was no longer any torment either. The fourth graders could add, subtract, multiply and divide in writing. They all did their best and did not let the smoke from the stove or the coldness in the room spoil their desire to learn.

I don't know if my reader can imagine life in the dead of winter in an unheated Château that is slowly but surely falling into ruins. Some of the rooms did indeed have fireplaces whose size would be proportional to the size of the room.

However, there was no wood to burn. The wood we did have was used in the kitchen for cooking. Only in the kitchen under certain circumstances—if one was lucky and Mrs. Schlesinger had just made some "coffee" in one of the two wash- kettles—could one warm up a bit.

In short, the Château was a giant icebox. From morning to night the cold penetrated our very bones. Often we could barely stand it. We dreamed of a nice warm room. We would have gladly given our entire monthly stipend—pocket money amounting to 800 old francs [$30]—to be able to sit in a cozy warm room for even thirty minutes.

Remarkably, none of the children got seriously sick. Mornings, the Mickeys would be shivering under their skimpy wool blankets, but they didn't get sick. One reason was that we very rarely had visitors, so no dangerous viruses were carried into our environment. In any case, our children were astonishingly hardy and resistant. Moreover, they seemed to have enough to eat.

The nights in the ice-cold beds were the worst. Heiri and I decided that we couldn't go on like this. "We definitely have to be able to cover ourselves adequately," Heiri declared. "One thin wool blanket is clearly worse than nothing!"

Over several days I was working on an idea, and had a prime opportunity to bring it to fruition. First I went to Miss Groth to ask for two extra woolen blankets, which she gave me. Then I went into the laundry room to find Mrs. Palau, Mrs. Marimon, and Mrs. Nadal, and asked them please to sew together the two woolen blankets on two sides. They did that for me right away. Now I had two "sacks" and all I needed was something to fill them with. I had in mind some hay, since I was sure I could easily get some at the neighboring farm. Farmer De Dieu did indeed have hay, but he wouldn't give me any. I could have some straw, he grumbled. He was definitely not friendly. So I had to make do with the straw, but I figured it would keep me just as warm. Having filled my sacks with the straw, I went back into the laundry room to ask Mrs. Palau to sew together the ends of the sacks now full of straw. It wasn't so easy! I had to help her keep the straw stuffing inside the sack while she was sewing. But in the end, I had two nice big "eiderdown" comforters for our beds! They weren't exactly soft, but they were good and heavy. That boded well for some warmth!

Late that evening I surprised Heiri: "Look what I have! These 'eiderdowns' are fantastic. My own invention! They will be perfect on our beds!" Heiri was astonished, but he didn't get what I had in mind. "From now on, we will be nice and warm in our beds," I said triumphantly. "We're done with freezing our butts off. We even have an extra wool blanket that we can lay directly on the mattress to protect us from the cold beneath us."

Heiri gradually became interested in my plan.

Up till now, before getting into bed, our routine was first to get undressed and then to put back on all available clothing. A thick puffy vest, our long underwear, pajamas, hand-knit woolen socks, two sweaters and a scarf around the neck, which I wore every day in any case. But now, with our new "eiderdowns," we looked forward to our first real warm night this whole winter. We were so convinced that we would be warm that we went to bed freezing, half-naked, dressed only in our pajamas. We climbed in under our thick, stiff, straw "eiderdowns" expecting to be cozy. Unfortunately, to our great surprise and consternation, our straw comforters were supremely uncomfortable. First of all they did not conform to the shape of our bodies, so we had this enormous weighty thing lying on top of us, stiff and hard as a board, and letting in the pitiless cold air on both sides.

That was our first disappointment. The second—although we were not quick to admit it—our super straw pillows were not at all warm.

So as not to freeze, we had to get out from under our traitorous comforters as quickly as possible. But that wasn't so easy! We sat up, only to find that my genius invention made a straight bridge from our shoulders to our feet.

In and out of the cold, and back in again, we rapidly dressed ourselves in all our clothing, hopped around for a while in our room to get a little heated up, and crawled back under the weight of the straw— hoping against hope that we would be cozy.

Given how annoyed we were, at first we just wanted to get rid of this heavy thing. But we didn't have any time for another solution. Christmas was knocking at the door, and we had a lot to prepare for the celebration. So we left the straw sacks on our beds. Despite everything, they gave us an incomprehensible illusion of warmth. I don't know how it happened but at some point we started to call them "our children." And so every evening we engaged in the same dialogue: "How's your kid doing?"

"Fine! He's gained a little weight and is heavier! And how's yours?"

"Also good, but he's still irritating. He's constantly pricking me!"

Chapter 51

Rosa Goldmark's Abandonment

For quite a long time I had not seen Rosa around in the Château. Curiously, she had never come to see me in the infirmary. All the others, beginning with the Mickeys right on through the Middles to the older ones, showed up between 6:30 and 9pm. Only a very few—perhaps Rosa was the only one—never came at all.

The infirmary situation had basically not changed since I took over. Many children, especially the little ones, wanted to be taken care of on a daily basis. So they would come day in and day out, over weeks and months. They never lacked for some kind of "booboo."

"Look! This really hurts!"

"But there's nothing there," I would reply.

"But yes there is! You can see—it's red!"

"Does that feel better now?"

"Yes, that's better. Thank you very much, Mr. Steiger!"

On the hand, leg, face, arm—a little booboo was always to be found. Besides these mostly little patients, many girls and boys came with various serious injuries or wounds that needed attention. The bitter cold was the cause of horrible frostbite on fingers and toes. For Percy, I had to wrap each of his toes individually. In addition I had to deal with wounds and boils on every possible and impossible place: under the arms, on the buttocks, behind the knee, in the groin area.

But sadly, Rosa Goldmark never came. Seeing her in the infirmary would have allowed me to connect with her and possibly win over her trust.

One evening after my infirmary duties, I met up with Walter in the classroom, as usual, and asked him how Rosa was doing. "She's not doing well," he offered, "but also not worse than before. Most of the time she sits somewhere in a corner and stares into space—or she flits about like some kind of startled bird. Sometimes Mrs. Palau succeeds in getting her to work in the laundry. By the way," he continued after a long pause, "I have written up a report on her for the doctor."

He handed me a copy of the report and at the same time a letter from Rosa to her father, which I was allowed to copy.

What follows is Walter's report on Rosa Goldmark. Walter knew Rosa very well.

[Walter's report on Rosa Goldmark]

❋

Rosa is Jewish. She was brought up strict Orthodox. She suffers from the fact that she has never paid sufficient attention to the Jewish instructions and cannot rightly participate in the Jewish feasts. She would like to live in an environment where that would be possible. She would like to speak with a rabbi about a problem that constantly obsesses her. Once when she was in a hospital she was sprinkled with holy water, and on another occasion recited the "Our Father" in German. That was several years ago. She incessantly reproaches herself, especially for the latter event. "We are strictly forbidden to recite that!" she claimed. I tried to explain to her that this prayer fundamentally contains the same content as the Jewish prayers, and that for God, whatever language one uses to address him—whether Hebrew, German, French—is unimportant. She admitted that that was so and that it is stupid for her to worry so much about it, but nevertheless in the next breath she returned to her lament that "we are forbidden to do that, we may not pray in that manner."

She was in love with a young man who had left the colony a year ago and who had never paid any attention to her. Rosa's attachment to him was intensified by his absence and turned into adoration. The story seems to have begun toward the end of 1940. At that time, three years ago, Rosa had taken the train to Toulouse to see an eye-doctor—and by chance Peter Salz had been on the same train. Rosa interpreted this coincidence as some sort of divine providence or predestination: "Why was it that he had to take precisely the same train as I did to go to the eye-doctor's?" I told her that there wasn't anything special or supernatural about this, since Peter had the same reason she had to travel to Toulouse—namely, that he also needed eye-glasses.... To this day she will have none of it, and will not admit that Peter wore eyeglasses. I point out to her that Peter always wore his glasses for reading and writing. I expressed my astonishment that a person who claims to love someone remembers him so badly. Her answer: "Oh, I did like him very much, in fact so much that I dared not look at him."

She was bored. "What must I do so that I'm not bored?" she asked me. "You are lucky, you are never bored." But the truth is she avoided any work.

She loved looking at the sky, and at night she loved contemplating the moon. She never stopped asking certain questions: How is it that one can think, that one can dream, that one has a memory, that one can have children? Often she suddenly demanded of someone to explain something to her. She asked: How is it possible that someone lives, how long is a human life, and how is it possible that one wakes up every morning? (She believes that she dies during the night and is perplexed to find herself alive in the morning.) Sometimes she asks, suddenly astonished and frightened: "Where are all the others?" (the girls and boys who have left the colony). "Tell me, where are they? You know it, right? It is not possible that they simply went away!"

Often one tried to explain everything to her that she wanted to know, but unfortunately either she didn't listen—she was so deeply sunk in her own thoughts—or she would promptly forget what she had been told and recall it only months later. At the end of a conversation she sometimes suddenly would say, as if she had just awakened: "What did you say? I wasn't paying attention."

About a year before, she believed she was pregnant. This crazy idea came to her after reading a novel by Cronin: "The Hatmaker and his Castle." For weeks on end we tried to free her from her overwhelming panic. In the end we just stopped talking about it, but for a long time after she was visibly tormented by her worries. About two weeks ago, during a conversation, she referred to this period and made fun of herself for being so stupid.

She suffered from her isolation and was ready to do anything to get through to the others. "How can I be as smart and likable as Peter"—and Peter was indeed both—"so that others will talk to *me?" She wanted to study and become more intelligent. "I so much want to be liked! What do you do so that others will like you? Tell me, please, please, I really want to know, and you can tell me, right?"*

Practically on her knees, she wouldn't stop begging her comrades: "What do I have to do to be as well liked as you are?" Totally in despair, she repeated: "You know it, most definitely you know it, please tell me."

She had stolen, mostly photos from absent roommates but also things from the laundry. From time to time she would confess what she had done and return what she had taken. Moreover, she would offer all of her own things in recompense. She wanted to be punished, beaten, confined.

This wish to be punished that she often expressed without any apparent reason resulted from her having often been punished, sometimes physically, earlier on.

Someone wanted to convince her that she had done something "on purpose" and that "being punished" for it was "exactly what she deserved."

Her roommates were constantly mocking her and making fun of her, scolding her and bullying her at the slightest opportunity. That is one reason for her attempt to flee. Another reason is that she wanted to find some former roommates who had left the colony but who had liked her. Although she didn't have any addresses for them, she somehow hoped to get Peter's address from one of these girls. (Since 1943 Peter was living in Switzerland. We all knew his address, but Rosa did not believe it was the correct one.)

[End of Walter's report on Rosa]

✳

Rosa gave Walter the following letter from November 9, 1943, with the desperate hope that he could somehow get it to her parents. Rosa had such confidence in Walter! She did not want to believe that her parents had been arrested in Vienna and were probably dead....

Walter held on to the letter for safe-keeping. Recently he showed it to me and allowed me to copy it. This document is a "swan song" from one of the children at Château de La Hille most deeply troubled emotionally and spiritually. Five years earlier as a young girl she was ripped out of the security of her family home and sent alone and defenseless on a long journey into a world filled with evil, where death was lurking at every corner.

Here is Rosa's letter, originally written in German:

Château de La Hille, November 9, 1943

My dear Father,

Everyone has recently gone away. Peter Salz, who is so dear to me, has gone to Switzerland. What shall I do without him? I love him so much, you can't even imagine. I want most of all to sleep with him. With him I would never make any scenes. When do you think he will return? I love him more each day, and dream only of him. I would like all of them to come back: Walter Kammerer, Betty Schütz, Pauli Schlesinger, Peter Salz, Manfred Vos—I like all of them very much. Sadly they have all gone away. [Rosa mentions all of them, although Walter and Pauli are really still at the Château.] *What will I do without them? I also get along well with Norbert, and with Luzian...* [Norbert Stückler and Luzian Wolfgang successfully escaped to Spain at the beginning of 1943.] *I am very sorry that on Yom Kippur I didn't fast, though I should have fasted all day. When do you think I will get married? I am really still just a kid. I'm way too young for all that. But without Peter what should I do now? I miss them all.*

Helga Klein, Else Rosenblatt, Régina Rosenblatt, Ruth Klonover. I am so sorry not to have fasted on Yom Kippur. One time I did a very bad job mending a stocking. Ruth Schütz blamed Fanny, but Fanny hadn't done anything wrong. I'm sorry for that, and I will apologize to Fanny. I have sinned so much that nowadays I am sorry for everything. Ruth Schütz, Betty Schütz, Ilse Wulf, Inge Helft and Manfred Vos—how are you all doing? I very much long to see them again. Once I received a parcel of food and I am sorry to say that I ate most of it myself. [Some of the older ones did in fact have sponsors in Switzerland, but to my knowledge during my stay at the Château no one ever received a food parcel.]

Tell me, dear Father, is it true that once when I was in third grade I recited a Christian prayer? Tell me, what shall I do without all the boys that I love? How I would like to see Leo Lewin and Fritz

Werdenberg, the rabbi from Ausbach. One time I swiped a photo from Inge Berlin and burned it because I looked too ugly in that picture. If I see Inge again, I will ask her forgiveness. What shall I do without my sweet Peter Salz? In front of him I didn't dare open my mouth. When we would play "capture the leader," I couldn't bring myself to run after him. What shall I do without him, I love him so much! I don't even trust myself to talk to him—he is so intelligent, and I'm so utterly stupid. I would very much like to see Leo Lewin and Jakob Roth again. I wouldn't feel ashamed in front of them.

I miss Peter Salz so much! I dream of him day and night.... I long to be with you, dear Papa, dear Mutti, and with you, Peter Salz whom I love to this day. I pray morning and evening, but I often forget to pray. But I always repeat the same prayer. I wish that Peter Salz and Miss Tännler return to the Château. I want Miss Tännler to punish me once more.

All my warmest wishes,

Your Rosa Goldmark

[end of Rosa's letter]

On the one hand, this letter disturbed me very much. On the other hand, it didn't seem to me so "abnormal" or strange. Many young girls could have written something quite similar, I said to myself, especially young Jewish girls who no longer have anyone to confide in and have already had so many dreadful experiences.

In any case, one thing stood out for me: something must be done to help Rosa. Her repetitive fugue states, when she would disappear for days on end, were a clear alarm signal for us. How can we prevent her from engaging in these obsessions?

Our director was not approachable. She seemed to be absorbed in very different issues. Unperturbed, she went along her own path, which to me was difficult to comprehend. She never asked for our opinions and typically presented us with faits accomplis that often exasperated us. I was reluctant to meet with her to discuss Rosa's case, for Miss Groth and I did not get along well. Moreover, the thought of closely following Rosa, of "spying" on her, of intruding into her private world was very troubling to me. And so I came to the conclusion that it was best to let Rosa go her own way.

Here I must note that the director, Miss Groth, was definitely paying attention to Rosa. She did something very intelligent, that I heard about only later when the situation had already played out. She sent Heinrich Klägi, in strictest secrecy, to accompany Rosa to a doctor in Toulouse. Perhaps on the basis of this doctor's diagnosis Miss Groth decided to take a step that had disastrous consequences.

For my part, I did nothing—an unpardonable error! I rationalized my decision in this way: "Rosa has problems just as others do, and she will eventually sort them out. I'll keep an eye on her, and when the opportunity presents itself, then I will try to have a conversation with her as a friend."

But according to the nature of the case, Rosa isolated herself more and more, so that for weeks on end I never laid eyes on her and consequently she slipped from my mind also. Meanwhile she was on a path leading to disaster.

Chapter 52
Burned Children Do Not Fear the Fire

The cold weather hung on; the days were gloomy and overcast. Like overflowing milk, the white clouds poured between the tall fir trees along the River Lèze—the only firs in the entire Ariège—and crept up over the fields toward the Château. In the Château it was weirdly dark. A dull light burned in the hallway, and the children wandered around listlessly, shivering from the cold. A somber mood prevailed, with the hope of a beautiful Christmas the only saving grace.

When it wasn't raining, I took the Mickeys out for a walk into the gray landscape, usually along the county road, so as to prevent our sinking into the mud in our clogs. The exercise did us good. We warmed up, and returned to the Château with renewed energy. Sometimes the cold wind blew so ferociously around our ears (only Friedel, Peggy, Rose and Conchita had coats, but no one had a hat) that we immediately had to head back.

One day at the Château we had a huge surprise: a stove that burned, not smoked, and gave out real heat! It was wonderful—but also dangerous. It stood in the cellar across from the main entrance just behind the open cellar door. Up to that moment I hadn't laid eyes on it. Once more Egon tried his luck with this medieval iron monstrosity—but this time he succeeded! The children were tightly packed all around and wanted to get even closer. The ones in the back pushed against the ones in the front, and those in the front were getting burned on their knees, arms or hands. There were cries and shrieks of pain. Now in the evenings in the infirmary I had to deal with the burns alongside of the frostbite and boils. The worst were the burns that did not heal and became infected. Unfortunately, the burned children did not fear the fire!

On a brighter note, my lessons progressed at a good pace. The students had grown accustomed to the cold and were as hardened as people from Tierra del Fuego! My own capacity to adapt left something to be desired. Without my brown tweed coat I never would have survived. But even with that I suffered deeply under the cold conditions.

School was my daily source of joy. With Christmas not far off, we practiced some Christmas carols, among them a German carol that presented us with many difficulties. It was the song: "From Heaven high, Oh Angel come." ["*Vom Himmel hoch, o Englein, Kommt*"] The children just couldn't get it and constantly sang "*Vom Immel och*." Especially François! [Translator's note: In French, an 'h' at the beginning of a word is often silent, and thus native French speakers may have a tendency not to pronounce the 'h' at the beginning of a word in other languages as well.] I had François repeat twenty times "*Vom Himmel hoch*," and twenty times he sang "*Vom Immel och*." François was impishly enjoying my consternation, smiling from ear to ear, and then laughing with his eyes crinkling up, as only he can do.

Even after our schoolwork was finished, we usually stayed in the big classroom. For a few days now, the Mickeys had a project that fascinated them. We had received a packet from Switzerland filled with the tiny ends of colored crayons, only five to eight centimeters long. A former school colleague had sent them to me. (These were a teacher's "substandard articles"; whole crayons would never have made it across the border.) This present released an enormous wave of enthusiasm and creativity among the children. From now on everyone was drawing and coloring whatever they wished on the small leaves of paper the size of an envelope that my school chum had included in the packet. I was astonished by how little it takes to make my children happy. Swiss children would have turned up their noses at this gift!

Chapter 53
A Very Ugly Christmas Tree

Christmas was coming up quickly. Everyone was looking forward to the celebration. We teachers, however, had a difficult problem: where were we going to get a Christmas tree? We knew that apart from the giant firs along the Lèze River, there were absolutely no fir trees in all of the Ariège. What to do? We were quite disconcerted. Although it was a hopeless task, Eugen and I had resolved to search for a suitable tree. I asked Annelies to take over my pupils, and without further ado we set out on our way. It was raining incessantly. Since we were walking on waterlogged paths through the fields, our heavy wooden clogs would constantly get stuck in the mud. We wandered around in the area, keeping our eyes peeled for a tree. The rain gradually soaked through our coats. Finally we ended up in a forest thick with scrubby bushes. We were on a footpath along a sloping hillside, and to our right and left were bristly black thorn bushes about six or seven feet high.

Since it was quickly getting dark, we had to hurry! We were soaked through to the skin and terribly cold. What to do? Return home without a tree? Impossible! For lack of any better choice, we settled for one of these black thorn bushes.

Naturally we chose the best one—though they all looked exactly the same. Frankly, it looked like a dreadful, bristly, inverted wet broom! The lowest branches reached up to the top parallel to the trunk, and were partly dried up. The smaller "leaves" were indistinguishable from thorns. Taking turns, we worked very hard with just a pocketknife on the thick trunk—not an easy task! When we finally had cut it through and took some deep breaths, we realized that our hands and arms were horribly scratched and bleeding. But after all, we had succeeded and immediately started out with our incredible prize toward home. Not far from the Château we both suddenly stopped in our tracks, as if by a secret signal. We had simultaneously come to the same conclusion: No, we may not show up in front of our children with such a frightful bush! Right on the spot, we threw the thorn bush with all our might into the ditch by the side of the road.

Soaked through and freezing cold, we were soon back at the Château. It was the dead of night, and the rain had let up. In the workshop I changed my clothes as fast as I could—shaking like a wet dog—and headed for the kitchen to Mrs Schlesinger. Some kind of chestnut meal gruel was simmering on the stove. I got as close to it as I could, and slowly the warmth began to return to my body.

"Where's the Christmas tree?" inquired Mrs. Schlesinger. In the Château there were no secrets.

"Hidden!" I answered.

The children, especially the little ones, were looking forward to Christmas more and more each day—strangely enough, even the Jewish children. "I have never seen a real Christmas tree," Jojo confided to me one day during our lessons. "We always celebrate Chanukka!" Not all the pupils understood what she meant, so we invited Jojo to come to the front of the room and explain Chanukka to us. "At our house we have a menorah, a candelabra with eight candles. Every day we light another candle."

"For eight days," Friedel piped in, "until they are all burning."

"That's right," I said and added: "We will talk more about Chanukka later on. But tell me, how shall we celebrate Christmas in a few days? What do you think, Peggy?"

Peggy had wildly raised her hand to get my attention. Very excitedly she exclaimed: "We are going to have a Christmas tree decorated with candles, magnificent colored ornaments, and stars...." This caused an uproar.

"Quiet," I called out. It was silent immediately. "A Christmas tree can be really beautiful!" I affirmed. "But couldn't it also be ugly?" I was thinking of our thorn bush in the ditch.

A general protest ensued. "A Christmas tree is always beautiful!" cried Peggy, drowning out the voices of all the other Mickeys.

That night I had a terrible dream. I saw scraggly shrubs and tall blackthorn bushes transform themselves into dark, menacing monsters with innumerable arms, like a giant squid. Attacking me from all sides, the prickly arms wielded dangerous shining daggers. I wanted to flee, but I couldn't budge. In vain I tried to free my feet and my wooden clogs from the morass. The squid-like arms grabbed me and squeezed me; I felt my whole body being pricked by hundreds of daggers. I cried out wildly! Luckily I woke up in the nick of time; otherwise, the monstrous thorn bushes would have squeezed me to death.

The day after this nightmare, we returned to the subject of the Christmas tree during our lessons. My pupils wanted to convince me that a Christmas tree is beautiful and cannot under any circumstances be ugly. They spoke of gold and silver stars, glittering garlands, brilliantly colored balls and a thousand other heavenly decorations. Finally I interrupted this excited group of children blessedly carried away by their imaginations, and spoke in a serious tone that captured their attention.

"Listen up! Everything you say is true. The Christmas tree has to be a fir tree and has needles. The leaves on other sorts of trees would immediately wither and drop off. Think of an apple tree. Except for the giant fir trees along the Lèze, there is not one fir tree in the entire Ariège. Listen to that: not one fir tree! Where then are we supposed to get a real Christmas tree?"

Perplexed, the children fell silent. Then François blurted out triumphantly: "An angel will bring it!"

Sadly, no angel brought us a Christmas tree.

On December 24, it was high time for us to get our tree—the black thorn bush. Toward evening, Eugen and I set out to find it. It wasn't really cold and it wasn't raining. We soon came to the spot where we had left the thorn bush, but we didn't see it. Where could it have gone? We wandered around for a good hour but turned up nothing. Just as it was getting dark, we finally found it. We didn't even recognize it—it was even uglier than we had remembered! To avoid being pricked and scratched again, we carefully picked it up and carried it back to the Château as quickly as possible. It had gotten quite late. At the workshop we met up with Heiri. He was surprised: "What kind of broom have you got there?" he asked.

"A black thorn bush," I answered.

Heiri, who was an experienced botanist, looked more carefully at it and declared: "It's a juniper. A juniper doesn't have any thorns."

"But this thorn bush does have thorns!" I countered.

"Nope," answered Heiri. "Look more closely. It has only thin, tiny, pointy leaves that prick like thorns."

"You're right," I admitted. "I hadn't really noticed!"

"What are you going to do with this bush? Sweep the courtyard?" Heiri's question embarrassed us.

"No, Heiri," I responded. "We...It's our Christmas tree!"

Heiri had to grab hold of the water-pump. He was speechless.... We heard the dinner bell clang. Heiri slowly shook his head and went into the Château.

For a while longer I stood in the darkness—night had come on long before—and then I hid our wonderful "find" behind the haystack near the workshop.

Chapter 54
Christmas Eve

After dinner and my duties in the infirmary, I went to our room in the workshop. Heiri was not yet there. On the table was a package from Switzerland that I had received at noon. Sister Ida, a religious from my Protestant community back home, had sent it to me for Christmas. Incredibly, it had gotten safely across the border. The package contained a pinecone, three tiny pine sprigs, and four thin candles. This thoughtful present deeply moved me and brought me great joy.

I was tired and felt sticky and dirty. I definitely needed to bathe. But bathing here was always a real problem.

A short time ago Mrs. Schlesinger gave me a very old, small and defective electric heating plate, whose heating coil I had already repaired several times. She didn't want to use it any more because it was so dangerous. However, I put it to good use. At lunch we often had the tiniest piece of bread that I would save for the evening. I toasted it on my heating plate and ate it as if it were a piece of the world's finest cake.

At the moment, after pumping a bit of water into the old jug Mrs. Nadal had given me, I heated up the water on my "mini-cooker," undressed, and washed myself from top to bottom. With so little water, bathing became an art-form, and I was very proud of my accomplishment. Then I quickly got dressed and felt much better.

Heiri still hadn't come.

I took my package with the pinecone and tiny sprigs into the workroom next door. Mr. and Mrs. Nadal were there warming themselves by the fireplace. I said hello in their language and thus used up pretty much my entire Spanish vocabulary. Then I sat down next to them on a new bench that Mr. Nadal had just finished. He had made all the benches and tables in the classrooms and dining hall. It was amazing to see what this man was capable of creating. He must have been very old, and in any case looked like a dignified, ancient Indian chief. At one point he had been mayor of San Sebastian, but with the arrival of Franco and his troops Mr. Nadal and his wife quickly headed for France. How he ended up at Château de La Hille no one knew.

The fire crackled and flickered. We sat in silence near each other. We had no common language to converse in. Lost in our own thoughts we watched the darting flames. I enjoyed the warmth. It was the first time this winter that I had sat by a burning fireplace. All the other fireplaces in the Château were cold and dead. My thoughts gradually turned to another warmer world.

Suddenly Mrs. Nadal nudged me with her elbow and pointed to the package on my lap. I opened it and pulled out the pinecone, the tiny sprigs of pine and the miniature candles. Was Mrs. Nadal disappointed? It seemed so. But I artfully arranged the pine sprigs between the scales of the pinecone to create a mini Christmas tree. I turned it around in all directions to find its "best side," and wondered where I could set it up. Mr. Nadal had an idea. He took my pinecone/Christmas tree and carefully fastened it to the vice on the workbench.

Now all we needed were the candles. With droplets of hot wax I pressed the candles as best I could into the pinecone and the pine sprigs. The candles were about as long as the whole pinecone, so it looked rather funny. But still: we had a remarkable, once-in-a-life-time Christmas tree before us! It was adorable! I was thrilled. The Spaniards clapped their hands with joy, and then got ready to leave. I tried to urge them to stay, since I was still hoping Heiri would show up to join our Christmas celebration, but it was nearly 11pm. I went to get my Swiss Nescafe and gestured to the Nadals that I was going to make some coffee. Mrs. Nadal understood right away and while I was boiling the water she set out four tin cups on the workbench close to the Christmas tree. The coffee was ready in a jiffy, and a wonderful aroma filled the room. It was very festive, and I lit the candles.

Mr. Nadal put another log on the fire, and we sat down again, this time with our backs to the fireplace so that we could watch the candles burn on our tiny "tree." Quietly we enjoyed our good coffee and enjoyed the flickering light from the mini candles that threw funny silhouettes onto the ceiling.

I was plunged into my own thoughts—of former Christmas trees at home, decorated with red apples and red candles. I was homesick for our traditional Christmas Eve supper of delicious sandwiches and fresh orange juice. We didn't have any oranges here, of course. It was wartime. Nor did we have the sandwiches: there was no butter, no ham, no eggs. I wondered what we would have for Christmas dinner?

The candles quickly burned down and threatened to set fire to the pinecone.

Mr. Nadal got up to extinguish the candles—and brought me back to reality. Mrs. Nadal stood up also, and they took leave with a delighted smile: "*Muchas gracias!*"

I sat down again, as close as possible to the fire that was slowly smoldering.

Would Heiri finally show up?

Just past midnight he did finally show up. "Where were you?" I asked, with my annoyance so long held in check stirring me up. "I celebrated Christmas with the Nadals. What did you do?"

"I cleaned the dining hall. Gerti, Fanny, Rita, Onze and Egon volunteered to help."

I didn't understand. "But why?" I asked.

"It's Christmas Eve!"

"Yes—and tomorrow is Friday."

"Tomorrow is Christmas!"

"And also Friday! And according to the wishes of the Director, every Friday the dining hall has to be cleaned. Since I surely didn't want to do it tomorrow, I did it this evening."

I was so sorry; I didn't know what to say.

We quickly crawled into bed under our stiff straw "comforters" that somehow still gave us the illusion of warmth.

Chapter 55
The Feast of Christmas

Christmas! The whole Château vibrated with activity and impatience for the evening to begin. For me and Eugen, however, the situation was critical. Our thorn bush still lay hidden behind the haystack. The older girls who had prepared the Christmas celebration last year and the year before started pestering us since early morning. They wanted to have our tree in order to decorate it. "The Christmas tree has to remain a secret," I told them. "If the children were to see it now, it would ruin the surprise for later on. Just get everything else ready."

And so that is what they did. In the girls' dormitory, they shoved all the beds together to make room. They reserved a little table for the Christmas tree to stand on. Again the girls came running to find us. Since Eugen was nowhere to be found, they led me into the dormitory to show me how they had prepared. Even the worn out piano stood by the door. "And now we would like the tree!" they begged. "In a few hours everything must be ready."

"Don't we have any candlesticks? Couldn't we celebrate Chanukka?" I asked. "We want to celebrate Christmas!" responded pretty, dark-haired Gerti impatiently. "Most of the Mickeys and the Middles are Catholic and don't know anything about Chanukka. Please, just go fetch the tree now!"

"It's not particularly pretty," I warned them. "You are going to be disappointed."

"It doesn't matter," they all exclaimed. "We will make it pretty!"

At this point, I had no choice: I had to bite the bullet. Wrapped in a wool blanket, I carried the thorn bush inside. The girls were excitedly waiting. Even Miss Groth had joined them. Rita Kuhlberg closed the door behind me. No one else was allowed in. So that I wouldn't get scratched, I carefully unwrapped the prickly juniper bush. There it was at last: a pitiful sight! The girls let out a cry of horror.

Fanny called out: "Why, it's just a broom!"

Onze and Egon, who had been standing behind me, stepped up to get a better look. Onze's whole face grinned from ear to ear—always the Cheshire cat. He was always ready to poke fun at something, but I was in no mood to laugh. Fanny, Gerti, Rita, Cilly—they were in an uproar. I had to try to calm them down and offer some consolation. "It's not so bad," I said to appease them. "We can hang stones on the branches to make them come down, and then you can decorate them. Besides, it will be dark this evening and we won't be able to see the tree so clearly."

I wanted to leave with Onze and Egon, but Gerti took me by the arm and asked rather sadly: "Where shall we put the broom?" I didn't have the foggiest idea.

As we returned laden with stones, we met up with Mr. Nadal who had come to help with setting up the bush—which really did look like a broom!

We had a lot more trouble with the stones than we had imagined. The branches kept pricking us unmercifully, and as soon as we thought we had them weighted down, they would shoot up again. We needed heavier and heavier stones.

Luckily, Miss Groth had enough heavy string for us to use to tie them on. Finally, as our reward for our efforts, the branches managed to stay in an almost normal position. At least fifteen big pieces of stone were hanging like some weird surreal fruit on all the branches. It was an unbelievable sight. Onze was bent over with laughter and didn't stop laughing until the girls threw him out of the room.

For our Christmas feast, we had crepes. Marvelous! The whole day Guy and François had loudly announced the menu. And then we did indeed celebrate the long-awaited Christmas feast. My memory fails me on all the details, but some of them stand out in my mind so clearly as if this Christmas had happened only yesterday.

In the glow of the candles the Christmas tree really didn't look so ugly. Silver garlands and angel hair partially hid the stones. To begin the evening's celebration, my children sang some carols—and as usual got lost in "*Immel och.*" François's voice carried above the others, and he gaily sang on and on even after all the others had stopped. The children of Château de La Hille thoroughly enjoyed this joke.

Then Heiri and I played a flute duet. We started out pretty well, but I didn't get very far: I was suddenly overcome by a crazy, unstoppable urge to laugh. The whole scene—François's singing, the incredible, grotesque Christmas tree with its ridiculous hanging stones: it was too much! I had to stop playing and just laughed. Heiri played to the end— and then he burst out laughing too!

I forget exactly what the other festivities of the evening included. Surely Walter played the piano, for that was part of our tradition. Too bad that Edith was not there. I would have loved to hear her play too. Was she safely in Switzerland this evening, I wondered?

Chapter 56
Miss Tobler Disappears

M y detailed account of Christmas in 1943 at the Château de La Hille delayed me from reporting other events. One is that Miss Tobler unexpectedly disappeared in the middle of the night. As I already mentioned, our "*Schnitzelbank*" songs with the satirical verses poking fun at Miss Tobler deeply angered her. We had teased her waiting so very long for a visa to re-enter Switzerland. But in fact, she was in despair, barely speaking to us anymore, and rarely even showing up for events or meetings. She seemed unable to endure life in the cold Château any longer.

About seven or eight days after our St. Nicholas feast she disappeared, taking Toni Rosenblatt and Inge Bernhard with her. In her room she left this laconic message: "I've taken off for Switzerland with Toni and Inge."

At the beginning of January we received a letter with another short message: "We made it safely into Switzerland. The Germans aren't all like the way you have imagined them."

After that, we didn't hear anything from Miss Tobler—or from the two girls.

Until the year 1985!...

Forty-two years later, in 1985, I saw Toni and Inge again! There was an unbelievable, once-in-a-lifetime three-day reunion with the children from Château de La Hille in Lehavoth Habashan, a kibbutz in Northern Israel. Ruth Schütz and Peter Salz organized the reunion, and happily they invited us to attend. This event proved to be truly unforgettable. In 1943 Toni was a young girl. Today she is a lively, attractive woman who does not look her age. She and her husband live in Sicily, where they run a hotel. She told me the story of her escape into Switzerland with Miss Tobler in such a vivid, detailed way that I felt it had happened only yesterday.

Chapter 57
Toni Rosenblatt and the Barbed Wire Fence

The following is Toni's story:

Miss Tobler came to get Inge and me out of bed in the middle of the night. She left us little time to get dressed. We were still half asleep and totally disoriented. We had no idea of what was really happening. "We are going to Switzerland!" she said. We didn't understand. "Hurry up, hurry up!" she insisted. I don't remember that we even thought about taking our things with us. Everything happened so fast. I wanted to say goodbye to Edith Jankielewitz and all the other girls, but they were fast asleep, and Miss Tobler did not allow us to wake them up. Before we knew it we were on our way to the train station. It was a very long, long way, and I thought I would die. I wept, and so did Inge. We didn't want to go any further—in fact couldn't go on, but Miss Tobler was determined. She pushed us forward unmercifully. "Tomorrow we will be in Switzerland, and you will be saved," she said.

What happened next, I remember in only a general way: the overcrowded train, sleeping on the floor in the train's corridor, the flickering of the lights from the train stations and villages as we passed by... I was more dead than alive, and I slept most of the time.

At one point we had to get off the train. It was pitch dark. I was terribly cold. I had no coat, and wore only a summer dress with no stockings. I had practically no feeling in my legs except pain. Inge was freezing too. After all, it was the middle of December. As we stepped down onto the train platform, we immediately saw German soldiers coming toward us. Suddenly I was sweating, my heart nearly bursting, and my body trembling with fear. The German soldiers didn't pay any attention to us, however, and marched on by.

What I remember next is our arrival at the Swiss border, though I don't know exactly where. It was night, and we went along a barbed wire fence, looking for a good place to slip through to the other side. We came to a tiny hole. "Squeeze through there," Miss Tobler ordered me. "You are small and thin, you can do it!"

I wept and sobbed in despair. "I don't want to," I cried. "You can't follow me!"—"Be quiet!" hissed Miss Tobler. The Germans can show up at any moment and snatch us. Hurry up!" I had to obey. Without losing sight of Inge and Miss Tobler, I crawled backwards through the hole in the fence—and promptly got hung up by my dress. "Miss Tobler!" I called out despairingly. But Miss Tobler had taken Inge by the hand and was quickly dragging her away to find a place to hide. I called out in panic, screamed as loud as I could and tried to free my dress from the barbed wire. In vain! The pointy wires had buried themselves in my short skirt and my underwear, and were scratching me horribly. I was beside myself. I howled and cried for help. Suddenly I heard a dog barking! It was quiet for a moment, and then as I saw a German soldier with a giant wolfhound coming at me, my heart stopped... The dog raced toward me—and just as suddenly turned around and ran off! I lay immobilized under the barbed wire and struggled no more. After quite a while, Miss Tobler and Inge left their hiding place and came back to free me from my misery. I was hurting tremendously! The barbed wire had sunk deep into my flesh, but I couldn't cry any more. Fear had paralyzed my whole body.

Finally I managed to stand up. I was quite a sight! My dress was torn, my white underpants were red with blood that dripped down my legs. I was covered in mud and trembled with cold. I practically had nothing on. Inge was also freezing in her thin blue skirt. If only we had some leggings or just stockings! Naturally our socks didn't provide any warmth. Our feet were ice-cold in our miserable, wet, low shoes with the cardboard soles that had gradually fallen apart.

Where we spent the rest of this worst night of my life I don't really know. I only know that I was freezing terribly. The temperature was around zero degrees centigrade. My legs were like ice-cubes.

At dawn, we returned to the border and came again to this hole in the barbed wire fence. This time I absolutely refused to crawl through. Miss Tobler was angry. "Can't you understand that Switzerland is your only salvation?" she said exasperatedly. But I was filled with angst.

In contrast, Inge raised no objections. She lay down flat on the wet ground and slowly and carefully inched her way under the wires to the other side. I saw Inge run from there just as Miss Tobler drew me to her. "The Germans are coming!" she said and led me away.

We came to another promising place in the fence. I had to lie flat on the ground, like Inge, so that Miss Tobler could push me through the opening. I didn't resist any longer. Inge was gone, and I too wanted to be in Switzerland as quickly as possible.

Miss Tobler was right. Switzerland was my only hope. It was a matter of life and death. By myself I had a greater chance of not being sent back by the Swiss. I was such a small, dirty, half-frozen girl....

And so Miss Tobler shoved me under the barbed wire fence through to the other side. Arriving on the Swiss side, I didn't look back but ran ahead—and soon stood before a second fence! Without a moment's hesitation, I climbed over it and stood face to face—as I supposed—with German soldiers! I threw myself on the ground and cried: "I don't want to die!"

"That's not going to happen," said one of the soldiers. "You are in Switzerland now!" He picked me up and carried me to a car. I was taken to a transit camp where I was washed and bathed, my wounds dressed, and given new clothes. And there I met up with Inge! We fell into each other's arms. We were saved!

A good family in Reinach near Basel later took me in.

✳

That was the end of Toni Rosenblatt's story. Her account of her harrowing experiences moved me deeply. Unbelievable what this girl had to live through physically and emotionally: people wanted to kill her just because she was Jewish!

Chapter 58
Edith's Escape to Switzerland

At the same time as Toni Rosenblatt's and Inge Bernhard's dramatic border crossing, Edith Goldapper also managed an incredibly strenuous hike over the Jura peaks at Risoux to get to her "promised land," Switzerland.

Edith had the advantage of being well prepared and outfitted for her dangerous expedition over the border. From her friend and teacher Anne-Marie she received warm clothes and solid, watertight hiking boots. In contrast, that morning at 4am when they were roused out of their sleep, Toni and Inge had no idea of where they were going, were fully unprepared, and received no suitable clothes or gear. They barely had time to put on their thin summer dresses and had to set out quietly into the terribly cold December night.

Unlike Edith in the Jura mountains, Toni and Inge did not encounter any snow near the border. They would never have survived! Nevertheless, it was indeed a miracle that they made it into Switzerland relatively safe and sound.—"Not all the Germans are the way you have imagined."

In the final analysis, Miss Tobler had saved them.

Edith's journey to Switzerland was less dangerous, but it presented some almost insurmountable obstacles. Let's read what she wrote in her journal:

[Edith's journal: Part Six]

December 4, 1943: It was Inge's birthday. I wanted so much to make her happy, but what could I do? Then I had an idea: She always wanted a calendar where she could write notes every day. I bought her one that cost 25 francs, and I bought one for myself as well. So in a twinkling I had 50 francs less. I also gave her my photo, and so the birthday present was ready. She really enjoyed the gift even though it was so small. Hopefully next year we can celebrate our birthdays in better circumstances.

December 7: Victoria had a male guest. He had come from across the border in Switzerland and would return on Saturday. I was thinking to myself, if only I could go with him! Just at that moment Victoria suggested that this would be the best opportunity for me to go along with him. I was incredibly excited. I was ready to leave today, at any time of day or night! And so it was arranged: on Saturday December 12, we would set out.

December 11: Victoria explained to Inge that she was going to take me across the border into Switzerland. Inge fully agreed. In any case, I tried to see if Inge could come along with me, but Victoria said that it was already very difficult with me along to get through the snow. Inge completely understood that I should go without her. First of all, I had not found a position yet, and second, she had a good position where she was happy. She would come to meet me in April or May. Nevertheless I felt really bad to go without her. I said farewell to Inge but I felt downhearted to leave her there. Well, all I can do is hope she will follow soon. My backpack is already packed, and I could leave immediately if I had to. Tomorrow is the big day!

December 12: It's really funny but I am not at all anxious. I am fully convinced that I will make it over the border. One last time I inspect my bags. Around 10am Mr. Altweg arrives. At 11:30 we have lunch. Now I did begin to feel nervous, and I am not at all hungry. Victoria's mother is also there. She definitely wants to give me some goodies to eat, but I can't even swallow. The train leaves at 12:30pm for Chapelle de Bois. I put on my coat and strap on my backpack. Mrs. Cordier hastily slips some holy cards with sayings into the pocket for good luck. I put photos of Mama and Papa into my coat pocket. These above all should bring me luck!

The whole family comes to the train station. Sadly, I say goodbye. Now it's time to go and the train departs. From the window a beautiful green landscape unfolds before us, but soon the fields are blanketed with snow. My courage sinks, but I constantly repeat to myself: "Be courageous! Your life depends on it! Hang on!" We arrive at the biggest town and leave the train station. Presumably Victoria's uncle will meet us with a sleigh, but nothing of the sort is to be seen. We go to a café where he may be waiting for us. There is already a lot of snow. Since the streets are totally icy, one has to walk gingerly. I'm not really cold because walking with the pack on my back keeps me warm. Even here it's dangerous: we might meet up with Germans, but luckily we don't. Finally Victoria spots her uncle waiting for us with the sleigh. Mr. Altweg is already exhausted and can barely keep going. The uncle apparently knows about my situation, but I am very wary about this whole business and barely open my mouth.

Our slow ride begins. We are bundled in warm blankets, but my feet are hanging out and gradually get stiff with cold. I can barely feel them anymore. Now I'm beginning to get cold all over. I can hardly keep myself sitting upright. It's already 6pm and beginning to get dark. Now we are approaching the danger zone where there must obviously be Germans. If we get stopped I will present myself as Victoria's cousin. Strangers are not allowed into this region, only the Cordier family who have a "pass."

I try with all my might to control myself. Everything simply must go well! At this point we are not far from Victoria's uncle's house. Victoria gets off the sleigh to ski to Chapelle des Bois in order to check out whether the Germans are patrolling near her house. Meanwhile, Mr. Altweg and I get down from the sleigh at the uncle's house, for he knows what the answer is. I'm totally frozen and am invited to go in to warm myself by the lovely fireplace. Gradually my feet thaw out. It's now 9pm and in a few minutes Victoria will come back to fetch the two of us and take us to her house not far from the Germans' border control station.

As planned Victoria arrives and we are ready to leave for Chapelle des Bois immediately. While we hike across the snow-covered field as quickly as possible, I try not to think of anything other than "Onward!" We must be terribly careful not to meet up with any gendarme, but finally we reach the house. We go through the stable to get to the living quarters where Miss A., the eldest sister, has been waiting for us. She offers us buttered bread and hot cocoa to warm us up. Then we have to talk. Should Miss A. take me across the border tomorrow? Or should I go now with Mr. Altweg and Victoria? Either way is terribly dangerous. Finally it is decided that I will go along now. I probably wouldn't get very far in the shoes I am wearing, so they give me a pair of mountaineering boots—size 42. I swim in them! Since Addi Nussbaum wore these very boots safely to the other side, I feel they should bring me good luck also! We get ourselves ready. Despite my protests, Victoria takes my heavy backpack. In exchange, I carry a very light one. Once more Miss A. shouts that the coast is clear—and we're off! December 12, 1943. 10pm. The moon is shining so brightly one could swear it was daytime. With the photos of my parents in my coat pocket, I feel that Mutti and Papi will not abandon me in the next several hours. At least I am not at all cold. Besides my winter coat, I am wearing a ski-suit and under that a pullover. Now our task is all about paying attention. First of all, we must not leave any tracks in the snow, for otherwise others could easily see that we are coming from Victoria's house. For that reason we climb a fair distance up the mountain on large pointed rocks. For now the snow is not too deep and we can manage. But then I see that the Jura are very steep indeed. Victoria is in front, followed by Mr. Altweg, and I'm in the rear.

Now it begins to get more difficult. The snow is very deep and I sink in up to my knees. It's very unpleasant. When I take a step forward, I sink in. It's terrible—and of course very strenuous. Mr. Altweg is clearing the way for me by making "steps." I'm exhausted, and my courage is failing. The danger is really not so great; it's much more a question of effort and endurance.

It's midnight, and we are still on French soil. Now comes the greatest difficulty of all: we are confronting a glacial cliff as straight up as a wall. How can we possibly climb that? With great effort Victoria makes her way to the top. Granted, she has had a lot of practice! Mr. Altweg makes a very peculiar face, and I've already written my last will and testament! Victoria climbs down again to help Mr. Altweg. I wait. She comes down again and helps me to the top. I'm not really tired, just completely drained! But it was worth it—for now we have arrived in Switzerland!

Can that really be true? I can't grasp it because after all the forest has not changed at all. One tree is just like another—and yet I am in Switzerland! My guide Victoria explains that in a minute we will be at the "Hotel Italy." And indeed: just a stone's throw away we spot a hut where during the day woodcutters have their lunch. The door is closed, but Victoria unlatches a small window and climbs through the tiny opening. It's amazing, but I can't believe that I will be able to do it also. After Victoria has been in there a while, I manage to climb in too. Everything goes perfectly, and then Mr. Altweg joins us. I am rather exhausted but I try not to show it.

Victoria opens a small cabinet—and then I seem to be living in the fairytale about the table that can set itself with food! Inside the cabinet are milk, cheese, bread and cocoa powder. Victoria lights the stove and makes some cacao. In a few minutes we're sitting there all cozy having a meal. I'm thoroughly enjoying it and feel surprisingly well. Mr. Altweg promptly goes to sleep, and Victoria is ready to do the same. Although I am very tired, I can't seem to fall asleep. The same theme keeps running through my head: I'm in Switzerland! How many times we had spoken of this, and now it's a reality!

Meanwhile, time flies and it's 2am, time for Victoria and Mr. Altweg to wake up. We get ready to leave, again by way of the tiny window. But this time we had practice. Now it's much darker because the moon is no longer visible. Up to now Victoria had carried my backpack—and frankly, I had had enough trouble without it—but at this point I carry it myself. The path continues up a very steep incline between two groups of trees. I have to be careful. My studded mountain shoes are slippery, and I could easily fall and break some bones. Victoria and Mr. Altweg are talking, but I don't say one word. During the entire trip one could count on one hand the number of words I have uttered. My thoughts are elsewhere. My hands buried in my coat pockets hold tight to the photos of my beloved parents as I go on. Victoria often asks me how I am doing, and my answer is always the same: "Thank you, Miss Victoria, I'm doing very well. Don't worry about me." After an hour we take a little break and lie down in the soft snow. At this point the snow feels really good because we are sweating with all our efforts. We no longer have to talk about being cold!

We go on. In just another hour we will reach our goal. But our descent is terribly steep and icy. Now I've really had it! I can feel every bone in my body. I sit down on the ground, but to tell the truth, it is not pleasant. I can barely stand up again with my heavy pack. Victoria didn't notice any of this. I have fallen way behind and try to hurry to catch up.

Despite all that we have gone through on this trip, I decide that Mr. Altweg is a nasty person. When he presses two hundred *francs into my hand and tells me that we can still be easily nabbed, he scares me to death. In that moment I realize that I cannot count on them. Victoria and Mr. Altweg are pretending to be a married couple, but I will have to get through all this on my own. What a feeling, to be all alone! Victoria tries to calm me down.*

The first houses are visible—and a light comes on! It's the police! We hurriedly continue on our way and don't encounter a single person. It's great!

4am: We reach the camp. Victoria's friends are expecting us. Victoria throws pebbles at the open window so that we don't have to call out. After ten long minutes, the door finally opens. You can imagine the enthusiastic reunion. The whole family comes rushing out to greet us, and food is soon on the table. I don't trust my own eyes. They have everything—butter, cheese, bread, real coffee—I feel like I've gone to heaven.

After that, I tidy myself up a bit, change my clothes, give back the heavy mountain boots and put on my own shoes. Then I write to Inge and Anne-Marie that we have reached our goal. Victoria gives me the letters that I have brought along for Inge's mother and friends. Shortly after, I say goodbye to Victoria, who is immediately leaving for Lausanne with Mr. Altweg. She bids me a heartfelt goodbye, and I am deeply moved.

I can't stay here long. For the first time, I realize that I am a "poor refugee." Naturally, the people here are anxious about my presence, but they are also very kind. One of the daughters, Miss Madeleine, is ready to take me to the Piguet family, who live only ten minutes away. We arrive at their chalet at 6am. A young woman opens the door for us. I think I am not seeing right: it's Anne-Marie who welcomes us! At least she looks exactly like Anne-Marie but is in fact her younger sister. She is busy bathing her baby, and is completely astonished to see Miss Madeleine and me at her house. She was expecting me for over a month, but certainly not in this snowy season.

Miss Madeleine soon says goodbye, and I am led into the dining room to tell my story. But I am too exhausted; I fall asleep in the middle of a sentence. Meanwhile it's already 7:30, and Mr. and Mrs. Piguet come in for breakfast. They are very surprised to see me. I immediately give them the letter Anne-Marie had written a month ago, and they are overjoyed to hear from their daughter. We sit down to breakfast, and I am introduced to the son in the family.

Naturally I have to tell my story...

In the morning I help Mrs. Piguet wash vegetables and do other household tasks. In the afternoon I write to Miss Tännler. She will certainly be surprised. In the evening I am shown the room where I will sleep. The son is lending it to me. I notice a piano and next to it a music stand and a violin. I go up to the piano, and what do I see but the "Spring Song" sonata. What beautiful memories I have of that piece. For a long time I lie awake in bed. I still can't get over the fact that I am really in Switzerland.

The next morning, December 14, 1943, Mrs. Piguet wakes me up at 5am. Ah, I slept really well finally. Around 6am our train leaves for Lausanne, and Mrs. Piguet will accompany me on that trip. There is ice everywhere and it is really very cold. As always, I don't really feel free. I still watch out for the gendarmes and the border inspectors, for I am terribly afraid of being sent back. I am only twenty-five kilometers inside Switzerland, and at the Château we used to say that you had to be at least thirty kilometers inside the border to be really safe from being sent back.

In Lausanne I see many students with their colorful berets, and that helps me to believe I am really in Switzerland. We take yet another train, this time for Zürich. I'm beginning to feel happier and more relaxed. We pass several familiar towns, such as Aarau and Olten, and arrive in Zürich at 10am. Leaving my backpack at the baggage claim, I set out to find Peter Salz and Hans Garfunkel, who also made it safely into Switzerland. Mrs. Piguet points out many interesting sites in the city. Now we are walking along the street by the train station and I see a sign with the name "Türler." Well, that's the brand name of my watch. Interesting. Then we come to Parade Square and take a tram. For me Zürich seems comparable with the beautiful city of Vienna.

When we get to Manesse Street, I am very excited to see Peter and Hans again! But sadly they are not home. I'm so disappointed. Well, another time then. We go into a restaurant and order a midday meal, and after that we will look up Pastor Vogt on Streuli Street.

A woman opens the door for us. After Mrs. Piguet explains my situation to her, she refuses to let me in because I am not Protestant, but Mrs. Piguet reminds this woman of her daughter Anne-Marie as well as Edith Moser and Manfred Kammerer.

With that the woman shows us in to the office. An amiable

pastor greets us, and I think that now the questioning will begin. But that is not at all what follows—rather, something much worse! After this I must go register at the police station! I am so dreadfully afraid of being sent back that to reassure me the pastor phones the police station before my very eyes and ears to make sure that I will not be sent back. He says that he has a "little daughter" here. Would she be refused and sent back? On the other end of the line one solemnly promises that I will be able to stay. I am relieved.

The secretary Miss Saladin and Mrs. Piguet accompany me to the police station.

We are sent to the third floor, office 36. A very nice man welcomes us. I have already been registered, so my name is familiar. The kind man is charmed by my first name 'Edith.' He regrets that he has to send the two women away, and so I say goodbye to Mrs. Piguet. She gives me five Swiss francs and warmly wishes me well. For the first time, I cannot hide my emotions in front of strangers. Tears run down my cheeks.

Everyone tries to console me, even the police officer, but nothing works—I weep all the more. Miss Saladin promises to come back tomorrow, so I finally pull myself together. The women leave, leaving me to my own fate. As I sit down, the police officer feeds a piece of paper into the typewriter, and slowly begins to interrogate me. I have to be careful not to betray my guide or to mention the Château. I explain that I arrived in Switzerland on December 14, but exactly where I do not know. Four other police officers come into the office carrying piles of maps. I carefully look at the maps, but I can't recall the name of the town where I entered Switzerland. I try to keep calm and not show any sign of anxiety.

Meanwhile my backpack has been picked up from the baggage claim. All the contents of my handbag that I have with me must be inspected. They take my gold watch and my ring; in fact they take everything, even my handkerchief. Meanwhile it is already 8pm, and the officer has six sides of paper full of information about me. He reads it out to me, and I have to sign that I accept the truth of its contents. Then a guard shows up to take me to a cell. Terrible! I'm so unhappy! Am I some kind of criminal that I have to be stuck in such a place? In the cell there is a bed with a mattress and a small table with a bench attached to the wall. The key rattles in the iron door, and the guard announces in a gruff tone: "Here is your food!" I take a giant cup of coffee and a big piece of bread, but I can barely eat anything.

Now I have some time to reflect. What have I done and why am I here? I study the walls covered with graffiti. Often I see "Heil Hitler" or something similar. Later I lay down on the hard bed. Although I've gotten used to hard beds and I'm not particularly sensitive, after our incredibly strenuous trip I don't feel very well and experience some pain especially on the places where I have fallen. I stay awake the entire night. In the morning, the "friendly" guard comes by with more coffee and bread. Then my police officer comes to get me to ask more questions. At 9:30am. I get into a gray police car and am taken to a clinic. Then there is a medical examination—from top to bottom. I think the result is good, because the female doctors wink at me with a smile. Again, I get into the police car, and I am taken back to the police station and back to my cell. I have lunch in my cell, and around 3pm leave the police station to be transferred to a barracks somewhere in Zürich.

First, I am again thoroughly examined, and afterwards I have to fill out endless questionnaires. When that's over, I'm led to another lovely cell. But this one is actually far better: a nice bed with white sheets and a washbasin with hand-towels next to it.

But I don't stay alone for very long. A young man brings me five more questionnaires, each with six pages. Well, that keeps me busy! Later, a really nice female guard brings me some potatoes. I don't have my watch but I estimate that it is around 10pm, so I go to bed. This is the first time in a long while that I can actually sleep.

At the first sound of bells, I quickly jump out of bed and rush to straighten up the cell as best I can. On the door there is a set of rules that must be strictly followed: the blankets have to be neatly folded and the floor must be mopped. I think that everything is fine just as the guard enters my cell. She brings me some bread and coffee, looks around at the cell, and is satisfied. Then she leaves and locks the door.

Soon after I hear footsteps approaching my cell. I patiently wait.

Indeed, the door opens and some kind of officer comes in and looks around. At first he seems to find everything in order—but no! He shouts at me: "Lay the blankets neatly on top of each other!" and leaves. I'm befuddled and annoyed. I can't fold the blankets any better than I have. Oh well, we'll see. I sit on my bench—and weep. I feel terribly unhappy. What do they want of me? What crime have I committed that they treat me like this?

Again the door opens, and in comes my dear female guard who sometimes smiles at me. A man follows her. Now what? I think to myself. But I soon find out: he's a doctor! For the umpteenth time I am examined. He confirms that I am healthy, and leaves. The nice guard says that it is likely that I will be released later today.

December 14, 1943. My future looks a bit rosier.

In fact, I don't have to wait long. A soldier comes to get me and informs me that I am being taken to a transit camp. I put on my coat, and a man in civilian clothes straps on my backpack for me. Then we take a streetcar for about an hour, with a ten- minute walk after that. I see a row of tiny houses that looks like a little town. I notice a lot of soldiers, and indeed my chaperone hands me over to a soldier who once again asks me for my identity papers. Then I receive two blankets that I have to guard as if my life depended on it. Again accompanied by a soldier I am led in to one of the tiny houses, which are really wooden barracks. About fifty men and women, young and old, are seated at a long table having their lunch. It's very noisy. In comparison our Mickeys at La Hille are quiet as mice! I hear many foreign languages: Italian, Russian, Polish and also German. I have no appetite. After the meal, I constantly ask where I am. The answer is: in a transit camp in Ringlikon, near Zürich. I am shown where I will sleep—not as nice a bed as in the former barracks. In fact, it is a bed of straw, and the place is very dirty too!

It is uncanny. I sit down to write to Peter, the Piguets, and Mrs. Goldschmidt. My first thought is to write to the Château, but I am told that it is forbidden to write to anyone outside Switzerland. That's quite a blow. As long as I am in this camp, I may not write!— I'm only one day in the camp and I get mail—but from whom? It is the Israeli Refugee Aid Society that learns through Mrs. Schragenheim that I am in Switzerland.

[End of Edith Goldapper's journal, Part Six.]

Chapter 59
Onze in Switzerland

Egon had a giant boil on the calf of his left leg. During my hour in the infirmary I didn't have enough time to take care of him and the other children, so I arranged to see him during the ten o'clock morning break.

With all my successful treatments of boils up to now—that they would dry up like cow plops after having ripened—this was not at all the case with Egon's. First of all, his boil kept getting bigger, more colorful and more horrible to look at. When it finally ripened, after a few days it opened out like a wound which took me at least twenty minutes a day to treat.

Egon and Onze were good friends, and Onze frequently came with Egon to the infirmary. While I was busy with Egon, Onze would tell all kinds of stories, grinning from ear to ear as usual. One time we were talking about Switzerland, and Onze wanted to know where I had come from. He totally surprised me with his remark: "I was in Switzerland once, but only for a few hours." He then described those frightful hours in Switzerland. Egon, whom I wanted to send away with a nice surgical dressing, chose to stay to hear Onze's tale once more, even if he already knew it by heart. Onze had told this story so many times! For him it was the experience of his lifetime.

At the end of December 1943, Onze and Kurt Moser set out for Switzerland. Eugen Lyrer had given each of them 2000 old francs [$100]. They walked, as did the others before them, from the Château toward St. Jean de Verges by way of Foix. Then they took the train to Toulouse, and from Toulouse to Lyon and then on to Annemasse.

Near St. Cergues, northeast of Annemasse, they intended to cross the border. Right at the border there was a Red Cross Children's Aid colony, which served as a jumping off point for their escape. Hans Garfunkel, Peter Salz and others before them had already passed through this spot. They were all lucky, so why wouldn't Kurt and Onze also be lucky? At this point they couldn't have heard from Walter Kammerer about the tragic fate that awaited the group of five.

Let's listen to Onze's story:

✳

"At the Red Cross colony we were given explicit directions on how to get to the Swiss border. We were told we couldn't miss it. Waiting for nightfall, we traveled along a small forest until we got to the border fence. We climbed over, and then to our astonishment we came to a second fence, this one made of barbed wire." Onze grinned like the Chesire cat, although in truth he had nothing to be grinning about. Then he continued:

"We stood clueless in front of this second fence and didn't know if France was on the other side of it. Kurt figured out that the first fence must be French, and this second one Swiss. His conjecture seemed so right to us that without another thought we climbed over the second fence and were congratulating ourselves on how easy it was for us to get into Switzerland. Now we only had to travel at least thirty kilometers further into Switzerland in order not to be sent back if we were caught. At least that was the going wisdom at the Château. We set out confidently, covering good ground. The terrible anxiety that had nearly thwarted us at the beginning disappeared. We wanted to burst into song, we were so happy. But suddenly we could scarcely believe our eyes: we were surrounded by soldiers shining their flashlights directly at us. We were scared to death!

"What are you doing here?" shouted one of the soldiers. Paralyzed with fear we couldn't respond. Only when they explained that we would have to go back to France were we relieved. We were indeed in Switzerland and these were Swiss soldiers!

"We are Jews," I cried out.

"Let us into Switzerland! Back in France the Germans will kill us. I am only fourteen years old. We have already traveled over a thousand kilometers to get here. Let us stay!" we begged.

"If only! All our begging and pleading didn't help. The Swiss

soldiers were unmoved. 'We have orders from Bern that all Jewish refugees must be sent back,' they explained. As criminals caught in the act, they led us to a nearby covered truck. They shoved us inside and set off, back across the border. At a sharp curve in the road, we jumped out."

Here Onze paused. He seemed very downhearted.

"Unfortunately the soldiers noticed us. They stopped, got out of the truck and ran after us. They fired once into the air and shouted like madmen…"

"But in the dark," interrupted Egon, "you might have been able to get away!"

"They had powerful headlights," Onze answered. "They caught us like runaway rabbits and dragged us back to the truck. One of the soldiers sat in the back of the truck with us. He pointed his rifle at Kurt and said: 'The next attempt to flee and I'll shoot.'

"Along the border we had to get out. They knew there was a tiny opening in the barbed wire fence that they used to send back the refugees threatened with death. 'Go back to France!' they said—as if they were merely saying 'good morning.' They kept their rifles pitilessly pointed at us.

"I cried out: "The Germans are killing us!"

"Kurt threw himself at the feet of the soldiers and howled: "They are killing us over there. Let us stay here!" Again, it didn't help. They showed no mercy. We had to go back, through the hole in the fence. To a sure death, it seemed to me."

Onze looked around, lost in his own thoughts. I had never seen him so downhearted before. After a few moments of silence I asked: "And then, what happened next?"

"I had had it," he answered irritably. "I realized that a border crossing was hopeless, indeed completely absurd. I gave it up and wanted only one thing—to be back at the Château as quickly as possible. Where else could I go?"

"What about Kurt?" I asked.

"Kurt wanted to try again. I tried to dissuade him, but he was adamant. So we parted ways. On his second attempt to get into Switzerland, he was arrested by the French, about the same time as Walter Strauss. After fourteen days in jail, they met up and both came back to the Château."

"And then the police came," Egon elaborated, "and hauled off

Walter, Elkan and Mr. Schlesinger."

"Yeah, that's what happened. That was horrible for us! After that, Kurt decided to escape to Spain along with Charles, Werner, Addi, Edgar and Fritz. That terrible story you already know."

We remained silent. Then I asserted: "Actually it was the Swiss soldiers who sent Kurt to his death..."

"Almost me too!" Onze seemed to be reliving that scene on the Swiss border.

His face was unusually serious. Lost in our thoughts, we remained silent a while longer until Egon abruptly asked a question: "Onze, why didn't you go with Kurt, Werner and all the others to Spain?"

Onze jumped. "Borders!" he said, almost shouting. "Since Switzerland, borders are my deadliest fear."

"How did you get back from Switzerland to the Château?"

"I ran as fast as I could back to St. Cergues, and from there to Annemasse. It was an uncannily dark night, and I felt that bad luck was coming my way. Suddenly two SS guys were standing in front of me, blocking my way. Without saying a word, they picked me up and took me to the Gestapo headquarters. Then the cross- examination began.

"What are you doing on the street so late?

"I am going to the train station to meet an uncle."

"What's your name?"

"Jean Petit."

"How old are you?"

"Fourteen."

"Let me see your papers."—I was waiting for that one; I didn't have any papers...

I was lost! I ruffled through my pants pocket and finally said: "I either lost them or forgot them at home." I was in a really bad predicament.

One of the SS guys asked: "Where do you live?"

"39 Market Street," I answered. Then they left me alone. After about a half hour—I already had given up on living—these figures dressed in black came in with three new victims. And they sent me home! At first I couldn't understand what was happening. It was a miracle! I was saved!

"After a bad night in an overcrowded waiting room, I was on a train to Lyon, where the Germans nabbed me again. This time I had some experience in dealing with them. Again I went through the story of picking up an uncle and so on. Luckily they spoke little French (just like the SS men in Annemasse), and had a worse accent than I do. They didn't even notice my poor pronunciation. Again I had good luck—they let me go! I finally got to the Château completely famished but still alive. I slept for about forty-eight hours. A few months later, Kurt did not understand why I did not want to go along with them. But the truth is, if I had not had this bad experience at the Swiss border, I would have fallen into the hands of the Gestapo at the Spanish border, along with Kurt, Werner, Charles and Fritz. And after that, Drancy and deportation!"

Chapter 60
Everyday Life at the Château

The Midi in southern France is not at all like Switzerland! Incredibly, it suddenly turned much warmer. Toward the end of January one could catch some sun out in the courtyard in shirtsleeves without a pullover. I was in the process of recovering from a nasty intestinal flu that had left me quite weak. It was so pleasant in the sun—and I remember precisely it was January 26—that we dragged out all the tables and benches from the dining hall to have lunch outdoors.

Luckily for us the winter was short, and the temperature didn't get below freezing. We had very little snow; the little snow we did have would melt by the afternoon. We were lucky in another way too. Despite living in an unheated Château, none of our children became seriously sick. Of course, there were always injuries, boils, or scrapes of one kind or another to be treated in the infirmary. The issue of bed-wetting was gradually resolved. My pupils were working hard. The first-graders—Conchita, Rose, Guy and Josette—learned how to read and were as proud as if they had completed their high-school diplomas.

One thing had changed. Miss Tobler's replacement arrived from Toulouse.

She was withdrawn and solitary, and we had almost no contact with her. She didn't get along well with the Mickeys and didn't last long in that job. Heiri's finançée Annelies arrived just in the nick of time to replace her.

The political situation seemed to run as follows: Hard-fought battles continued on all fronts. So far the Allies had not broken through in any significant way. The war could continue for a long time....

The good weather held. With everything turning green and blooming, spring was heralding its triumph over the cold of winter. The most beautiful was the Marimons' magnolia tree in their flower garden on the south side of the Château.

Never in my life had I seen such a gorgeous tree in bloom.

Once again I was able to take the Mickeys outdoors into the beautiful countryside—but now without their wooden clogs that we gladly left behind in the Château! We went to look at the "train" that the Middles and I had constructed, but we did not try riding it; it had become entirely too dangerous, especially for the younger ones.

Heiri had been teaching the Middles in the small classroom the entire winter, and he and the students were glad to be out hiking in the beautiful weather.

Two new middle-schoolers had arrived at the Château: Jean Pedrini, an Italian, and Daniel Reingold. Daniel was a sort of "little savant." He didn't tell stories to his friends but lectured to them like a professor. One time in the kitchen he was going on about "the weaker sex," but the girls were certainly not happy about this. One of them picked up a tin plate, hit Daniel over the head with it, and said calmly and coolly: "So much for the weaker sex!"

Together with all the other Middles, Daniel sat in the dining room next to me. That dining hall! I still shiver when I think of how we ate from ice-cold plates and sat on glacial benches all winter long. Thank goodness that was now a thing of the past!

One evening Daniel showed up late for dinner. He came in limping and holding a magnolia blossom that he laid carefully by his place at the table. During the entire meal he kept sniffing it without saying a word. The sweet odor was overpowering. The boys complained and rebelled. Pierre wanted to snatch the flower from him, but Daniel defiantly defended it. "Leave me alone!" he cried.

"Let him be," I said to quiet them down. "We would like to eat in peace." But then I asked Daniel: "What are you going to do with the flower?"

"I'm going to sleep with it!" he replied. He paused and then explained hesitatingly: "I have to go see you in the infirmary. I have a sore on my foot and can barely walk! I know that you will hurt me, so I have to go to sleep beforehand." Having said this, he deeply inhaled the intoxicating magnolia perfume.

Chapter 61

Mr. Kempf's Death

The flowers on the magnolia tree had faded, but everything else had turned bright green. All around the Château Nature was displaying its infinite wonders. In the midst of this gorgeous springtime Mr. Kempf showed up. He brought me the suitcase I had left with him in Montluel, and visited his wife's grave in Gabre. He stayed only a short time. Only a few weeks after his departure, we learned that he had been killed.

In the Haute Savoie region of France, there were many more resistance fighters than in our area of Ariège. The *Maquisards* attacked German soldiers wherever they encountered them. They cut telephone wires, blew up rail lines, derailed trains, and so on. In short, they caused havoc everywhere they could. To counterattack, the Germans initiated even more deadly raids and mass arrests, while the Gestapo captured, tortured and shot untold numbers of resistance fighters.

Following an attack by the Resistance against the Germans in Montluel, all the men seventeen and over were ordered to gather in the town square—the very place that stocky, gruff collaborator had rifled through my suitcases on my way to La Hille. Since Mr. Kempf was part of the Swiss Red Cross colony in Montluel, he believed he was safe. After all, there was a huge red cross against a white background on the entrance to the "Colony of the Swiss Red Cross." The Germans had to respect that!

Unfortunately, on this fateful day, when all the men were already assembled on the town square, Mr. Kempf was accompanying a lady visitor to the exit of the park. He had opened the iron door and was just showing her the way out, taking two or three steps into the street, when the bullets shattered the stillness. Mr. Kempf fell to the ground, dead. Now François had lost his father. Another Jew had lost his life in this senseless, barbaric war.

Chapter 62
The Wedding

Heiri was lucky to have Annelies at the Château. Just a few days after Christmas he spoke of their upcoming wedding, and by the end of January they had set the date for March 22.

The rest of us engaged in a lot of secret planning and discussion. We wanted to surprise Heiri and Annelies with a momentous marriage celebration, an evening filled with numerous activities: theater, a piano recital, dances and so forth. We worked out a wonderful program, and every day we practiced and rehearsed, and were very careful that Heiri and Annelies not notice anything unusual. The Château was filled with feverish activity, and we could barely wait for the Big Day!

A few days before the wedding, the official civil union took place at the "Town Hall," which was the mayor's office in the schoolhouse in Montégut- Plantaurel. Since the witnesses had to be French, the schoolmaster and schoolmistress filled that role.

The wedding day, a few days later, was an extraordinary event. Farmers from the region, who had up to then not paid any attention to us, generously loaned us their high wagons with the two giant wheels. The farmers accompanied us to drive the horses. Heiri in his dark suit, looked tall and stately; Annelies in a dark dress with a white lace collar, appeared small and lovely. They sat in the first wagon beaming with joy. In the next wagon sat Luise Groth and Anne-Marie Piguet, with Mrs. Marimon, Mrs. Palau and Mrs. Nadal. Their husbands were dressed in their Sunday best and walked alongside. Dressed in my best suit, I followed the first wagon along with Walter Kammerer who uncharacteristically wore a tie. The older teenagers along with some of the middle-schoolers rounded out the procession.

The Protestant ceremony took place in the tiny village of Gabre, in a small, undecorated room that held only a few wooden benches and a table. Although the setting was simple and spare, the service was extremely moving, especially under the circumstances.

Heiri and Annelies sat facing the rest of us. Even in the blossoming of their own happiness during their engagement, they were dedicated to alleviating the suffering of the children in France. I admired them for that, and felt lucky that they had come here to this forlorn corner of the Ariège.

After their exchange of vows, the minister gave them the rings, said a prayer, and bade us farewell.

What a varied group of people we were, thrown together in extreme circumstances, but ready for a hearty celebration nonetheless. We included the Spaniards, victims of a bloody civil war; the Jewish children and young people from Germany and Austria, victims of the deadly persecution by the Nazis; the French, victims of the German occupation; and finally the few of us Swiss, the only ones not directly victims of war or persecution.

The Château was brimming over with festivities. Mrs. Schlesinger had prepared a special meal, and after that came the celebration. Everything had been set up in the girls' dormitory on the second floor. Walter Kammerer began by playing a Beethoven sonata. That was followed by an act from Bernard Shaw's "Joan of Arc," with Anne-Marie playing the leading role. Then, the older girls presented a dance they had carefully choreographed and rehearsed. Their delightful costumes were fashioned from bed sheets. After some other presentations, we concluded the evening's entertainment with a second theater piece. I took the role of a swindler, while Anne-Marie was my worried mother, and Walter Kammerer the victim. Onze also had an important part in the piece, but unfortunately as soon as he made his entrance, words failed him. Since he knew no one could help him, he simply grinned his usual grin out of sheer embarrassment until he was hauled off the stage. And so our drama was concluded.

After the wedding, Heiri and Annelies headed for Nice to look for Monique Evrard, an extremely pretty twelve-year-old whom Heiri had gotten to know at his parents' house in Zürich. At that time, a convoy of young war-victims organized by the Red Cross, had already carried Monique and the others safely into Switzerland.

Chapter 63
The New Mill

In May the sun shone nearly every day. It was so lovely and warm that we just had to get out of our classroom in the afternoons. So after lunch and a short siesta, we headed for our favorite swimming spot, the New Mill. Passing by the hamlet of Borda Blanca, we were soon on the White Road that led us in less than twenty minutes to the Lord's Spring that you will recall from my stories about the Middles when I first arrived at the Château. By the Lord's Spring the kids quickly undressed, and like the "Piped Piper of Hamelin" I cut through the tiny forest to the rocks, with the entire throng of children following along behind me.

Arriving at our spot, I threw pebbles in all directions to disturb any vipers that might be sunning themselves on the rocks. Then the children were free as birds under the blue sky. Their spirit of discovery and play knew no bounds. Their favorite game, at least for the boys, involved looking for snails in their shells. I don't know where they found them, but in a rather short time they had an impressive pile of snails. The game was this: the boys would lie down on the flat rocks and place snails along their own chests and stomachs. Then they would lie there absolutely still, with their eyes shut, and softly sing their monotonous refrain: "Mr. Snail, Mr. Snail, show me your horns." The game required great patience, but after some time the snails would slowly and hesitantly leave their shells and creep along the boys' bodies, sometime even their faces. The boys got such a kick out of this game! Even the girls would laugh and clap their hands with enthusiasm, although they themselves would certainly not let a snail touch their bodies: the snails were "disgusting!" The girls preferred either sunbathing on the rocks or swimming in the natural water holes carved out by glaciers eons ago.

Chapter 64
A Bolt from the Blue

April 24 was a day like every other. As usual, I had my lessons with my pupils: reading, writing, and 'rithmetic. At ten o'clock I saw Miss Groth cross the yard on her way to Montégut to fetch the mail. At twelve noon Mrs. Schlesinger rang the bell in the courtyard to summon us to lunch. After we finished eating, Miss Groth as nonchalantly and indifferently as always distributed the mail. Our older teenagers never received any mail. They did not know where their parents were or if they were still alive. But on this day, before she returned to the table to give the signal for being dismissed, she handed Walter a letter. The Mickeys and the Middles immediately left the dining-hall, but the older ones remained seated, frozen with anxiety or at least curiosity. Bearing the emblematic Nazi cross, the letter came from the Gestapo in Pamiers! It was a summons: "Pamiers, April 19. Present yourself on Friday, April 26 at 5pm regarding a matter concerning you. Gestapo Toulouse, Pamiers Division."

We were terrified, as if literally hit by a bolt from the blue! We already imagined the Germans with their machine guns advancing on us. Panic spread among the older ones at the Château.

We went to Miss Groth to have a discussion about the case. But as usual with Miss Groth, she didn't offer much to discuss. Finally she declared: "Walter has to go to Pamiers. Nothing else can be done." Without batting an eyelid, she could have handed over any one of us! Out of ignorance? She didn't see reality, only duty. She lived her own life in an impermeable shell. We didn't have any choice; we had to handle this situation without her. Heiri tried one last time to speak to Miss

Groth in her tiny office. But she remained adamant in her decision: "Walter has to go," she said. "Otherwise the Germans will come to get him—and all the older ones with him!"

We were at a loss.

Behind Miss Groth's back, we formed a tight circle of conspirators: Heiri, Eugen, Anne-Marie and myself. From the beginning it was crystal clear to us that we could not relinquish Walter. We had to hide him, but we couldn't do that at the Château.

Luckily, Eugen was well acquainted with the farmers in our area. Perhaps he would find a solution! Eugen went from one farm to another, and finally hiked over the high mountain ridge that stretched into the east. There in a tiny, alpine valley, he found a farmer who was willing to take Walter in. His farm was called "La Coste," and in the future we often went there to visit.

One problem was solved. But the issue of the rest of the older Jewish teenagers was not thereby eliminated. There was no way that they could remain at the Château, for the Germans would surely come for them.

Onze, Egon Berlin, Ruedi Oelbaum, Joseph Dortort and Georges Herz decided to build themselves a tiny hut in the forest near the New Mill.

That dreaded, fateful Friday was all too soon upon us. Miss Groth had directed Eugen to accompany Walter to Pamiers after breakfast. After Walter said his goodbyes to the remaining teenagers, his best friends, he and Eugen set off on their way around 10am. carrying a large backpack. Miss Groth was not to be seen.

The day unfolded peacefully. In the morning I had my usual lessons with the younger ones. In the afternoon we took a walk toward the New Mill. That night, around 11pm, I was busy sharpening my pupils' pencils when Egon appeared on tiptoe in my classroom. He was terribly excited, "We're going!" he whispered and anxiously looked around. "We have a little hut on the mountain to the right side of the New Mill." He wanted to disappear instantly, but I held him back:

"I'll visit you and bring you food," I said quietly. "But how will I find you?" I thought about it for a moment and then had an idea. "When you hear an owl late at night, then answer—it will be me."

Egon nodded—and left as quietly as he had come. Miss Groth's light was still burning in her office.

Very early the next morning Heiri left the Château with Mrs. Schlesinger and her son Pauli in the direction of Tambouret. At 8am.

Annelies rang the breakfast bell, for she had taken over the kitchen duties. The director didn't suspect a thing. Miss Groth was the last to arrive in the dining hall. She looked around and realized that the teenagers' table was half empty. "Where are the older ones?" she asked.

The older girls were all still there. If the Germans were to come, they counted on hiding in the *Zwiebelkeller*. But for now no one answered the director.

"Irma, where are the others?" Miss Groth repeated.

"They left," Irma Seelenfreund responded hesitatingly. Miss Groth showed no reaction. Had she not noticed that Heiri was missing as well?

She took her place at the table with the usual: "Bon appétit!"

Chapter 65

The Boccerini Minuet and the Owl's Call

So far, so good. Let the Germans come! Mrs. Schlesinger and Pauli, along with Walter and the older boys were safe, and the older girls—Imra Seelenfreund, Gerti Lind, Trude Dessauer, Rosa Goldmark, Martha Storosum, Irene and Guita Kokotek—were ready at a moment's notice to disappear into the *Zwiebelkeller*.

The mood in the Château was weirdly strained. On Saturday, the whole day, we were on the lookout, listening for the slightest noise, quiet but on edge, like soldiers awaiting an enemy attack. I don't know why we were so convinced that the barbarians were interested in sacrificing us. As all those who have suffered under an occupation, we greatly overestimated their strength. We were immediately overcome with fear and angst whenever we saw any German soldiers, armed to the teeth, deployed on the streets of Toulouse or Pamiers. We waited the whole livelong day—but they didn't come. Miss Groth, looking grim, appeared at mealtime, but disappeared afterwards without saying a word. We avoided her. That we were supposed to hand Walter over to the Gestapo we could not easily forget. At the same time, we did grant that her argument was to a certain extent understandable. She wanted to obey the Red Cross mandate that "nothing illegal" or contrary to the German regulations was to be done. Otherwise, the SS could come in the next few days and take the rest of the Jewish children: Friedel Kriegstein, Isi Bravermann, Mane and Gustav Manasse, Pierre Bergmann and many others. But did that justify sacrificing Walter?

And if the murderers did not show up? From our point of view, that would amount to sending Walter to his death for nothing. For Miss Groth it was right to hand over Walter to the Germans because in her mind that would save all the rest of the children at the Château. She could not explain, however, why Mrs. Schlesinger and her son Pauli had disappeared and why so many of the older teenagers had apparently fled. For her, there was nothing more to fear, since Walter had—she thought—dutifully registered at the Gestapo in Pamiers. Therefore, she had not the slightest inkling that we were utterly panicked, expecting the arrival of the Gestapo at any moment.

Basically it was good that Miss Groth knew nothing of our plans made behind her back. In case the Germans did actually show up, she could speak freely and openly, in complete good faith, and answer their questions without having to lie.

Had she known the truth, it might have led to fatal consequences.

On Sunday everything remained relatively calm on the surface. Even the Mickeys, who had no idea of what was going on, were uncharacteristically quiet and kept indoors rather than playing out in the yard. Although Annelies had so much work to do in the kitchen, she offered to take my kids for the afternoon so that I could go off to visit Walter. "You simply keep climbing over the mountain," explained Eugen, "You can't miss the La Coste farm.

The climb was strenuous. There had been a path, but it was overgrown by the thickets and scrub growing in the region. It was tough going, as I had to fight my way through almost impenetrable hedges and thorny bushes. "How easy this mountain climbing would be in a Swiss forest," I thought to myself. "Here in the Pyrénées it seems almost impossible!"

At the crest of the mountain I came across a small path that led directly to La Coste. Walter was not there.

"He's in the forest," said the farmer. Where exactly he didn't know. Luckily Walter and I had agreed on a signal: I whistled the famous theme from Boccerini's minuet as I looked for him in the farm's surroundings. Totally unexpectedly Walter suddenly jumped out of a bush. He was happy to see me.

"Did they come?" was his first question. He was in deep despair, hopeless and depressed. He couldn't see any way out, and believed himself lost. He refused to hear anything about going to Switzerland.

"Too dangerous," he said. "I have no papers, no clothes and no provisions. Just take a look at my pants." He stood up—and I was dumbfounded! I had never seen anything like it. They were patched with all kinds of multicolored materials. If he were a beggar on the streets of Toulouse, only his dark, well-groomed hair would have clashed with the impoverished situation. His thick glasses with the dark frames only underscored the salient traits of the hungry student fallen on hard times.

I tried to offer our pianist some hope. "Clothes are not a problem," I told him. "For example, mine would fit you just fine. We are about the same size...We can get you some fake papers. Anne-Marie can get you some in Switzerland, it's really that easy!"

But right away Walter saw insurmountable difficulties. "But the papers..." he objected.

"No problem," I interrupted. "What would you say about using my green identity card with your picture?" Walter fell silent. Gradually he seemed to feel a little better, more confident, and finally admitted that Switzerland was his only chance for safety.

That evening I arrived just in time for dinner. The Germans still had not come. After my duties in the infirmary, we had a discussion in the classroom—without the director who had different views from ours. Anne-Marie was ready to take Walter Kammerer, Mrs. Schlesinger and Pauli to Switzerland. My suggestion to falsify my green identity card for Walter was acceptable to the group. The question now was whether Mrs. Schmutz, a farmer from Tambouret would be willing to let Mrs. Schlesinger have her identity card. That remained to be seen.

On Monday the Germans still hadn't come. The day remained quiet.

Nevertheless, we were convinced that they would come at any moment.

Our boys up in the hut desperately needed food and wool blankets. The nights were still cold.

The director's light was off, as Heiri and I slipped off in the direction of the New Mill. As usual we went past Borda Blanca and then onto the White Road. The night was pitch black, with no moon. The road was barely visible against the dark landscape. The thickly forested mountains where we were heading were hardly distinguishable from the blackened sky.

To Heiri's question as to where the boys were hiding, I answered with a vague gesture toward the long mountain ridge that ran to the right of the New Mill. "Someplace on that mountain," I said.

Our footsteps uncannily resonated in the silence of the night—as in the song we often sang: "Only the tempo of our footsteps finds the holes in the silence." We were making good time. Soon we recognized the high rocks that overhang our swimming hole. We found the path that turns right and cuts through the shrubs before climbing and then abruptly stops at the edge of the *Maquis*. It was impossible to go further because of the prickly thickets.

How I cursed these woods! After looking for a passable way, we soon came to a large clearing. The woodcutters had cleared a forty-meter wide strip in the forest that ran from here to the summit. On the right and left the branches and unusable wood formed two big piles along the clearing. In the center were logs about a meter long that the charcoal workers are able transform into charcoal. Larger trees are left on the ground. These cuttings, or clearings, take place every twelve years and transform the forests into thickets, the so-called *Maquis*, the ideal place for resistance fighters to hide!

Given that we absolutely had to climb to the summit, we had no other choice but to use the fallen logs as stepping-stones as we climbed. In the dark we couldn't see where we were going. The logs kept rolling under our feet, and we were constantly falling. As soon as we got back on our feet we would fall again. It was a miracle that we didn't break any bones! After a strenuous and slippery climb we finally reached the summit and a field with groups of trees. The moment had arrived. I had warned Heiri beforehand, and then let out a long, loud "hoot" that echoed in the darkness. We waited and listened—no answer. I hooted again and again—and then suddenly, very close by, was a loud hiss.

We stood paralyzed with fear, and listened for more sounds in the night. Nothing moved. "Don't hoot anymore," begged Heiri, after we had not moved a muscle for several minutes. "It gives me the shivers!"

I hooted no more and softly asked: "What was that noise, that hissing?"

He didn't answer.

"There must be someone here somewhere," I reflected. "I'm going to hoot one last time!" My make-believe owl hooting, magnified with my hands, rang out deep into the night, ricocheted off the rocks, and returned as a frightening echo. The hissing sounded again from very close. A black shadow detached itself from one of the groups of trees and was approaching us.

"Be quiet," it said softly, and cursed, only a few steps away from us. It was Egon! We recognized his voice.

When he was by our side, he whispered: "We have to be very quiet.

The charcoal workers sleep here."

Egon led us to their hut close by.

They were all there: Ruedi Oelbaum, Joseph Dortort, Georges Herz and Onze. With Egon there were five of them. They stood by their little hut they had made with branches, an ideal hiding place because they could crawl inside. They happily greeted us with a silent handshake. We could barely make them out: the thin crescent of the new moon was hidden behind the clouds. We gave them the wool blankets and the food we had brought along: bread, potatoes to grill and tomatoes.

The dark night's stillness was uncanny. We stood there for a few moments without saying anything. In the distance I saw a flare rising above the forest. What could it mean? How many people hunted down by the Germans or collaborators are hiding here in the *Maquis*? Certainly quite a few, like our older boys, living hundreds of kilometers from their homes, facing an uncertain destiny.

The way home was extremely difficult. The descent on the freshly cut logs was even more of an adventure, rather like skiing without skis! The thick logs and short branches kept rolling as if invisible hands were continually moving them beneath our feet. We kept falling and rolling, but eventually made our way down the mountainside.

We arrived back at the Château around 2am. I was incredibly hungry, and hoped I could find a crust of bread in the kitchen. I went through the little door in the west wall of the Château and made my way into the inner courtyard. From there it was only a few steps from the entrance to the tower, formerly reserved for the staff. I had a little trouble opening the creaky door with its rusty lock, but then found myself in the narrow anteroom of the kitchen. It was pitch black. Right away I smelled smoke, and saw on my right small flames leaping up. I groped for the light switch and finally found it. Two wooden crates must have caught fire from the smoldering ashes under our enormous cooking pots—and these flaming crates were about to set fire to the entire Château! I had shown up in the nick of time! Using the water in the big kitchen kettle, I quickly doused the fire. To be on the safe side, I broke down the two crates and poured water all over them. That produced a soggy mess of ashes all over the floor—quite an unpleasant surprise for Annelies at six o'clock in the morning! For a while I stayed to make sure the fire was completely out, and then searched unsuccessfully for something to eat. I finally gave up. Dead tired but satisfied, I let myself crawl into bed. (I had moved back into the attic. Since their wedding Annelies was living with Heiri in the "workshop.")

Chapter 66
Fried Eggs

The following day we were tired and worn out. Listlessly I taught my classes, but the day dragged on and on. The Germans did not show up.

In the late afternoon, after school, I suddenly remembered that I had to have a photo for my identity card for our plan to get Walter some false papers. I looked for Heiri to tell him about the photo, but unfortunately, his response made me rather anxious. He said he couldn't take portraits with his camera because he didn't have the proper lens.

The next day I got up at 4am to catch the 5am bus from Pailhès to Toulouse. I had unexpected good luck: by midmorning I found the right lens and was back at the Château by early evening.

I don't recall how we arranged to photograph Mrs. Schlesinger, who was staying out on the farm in Tambouret with the Schmutz family. In contrast, I remember the exact details of the expedition I made with Heiri to visit Walter Kammerer on the La Coste farm. It was mealtime when we arrived at La Coste. We were warmly welcomed and led into the kitchen. We were invited to sit down on a small bench near the door where we had a good view of the fire burning in the fireplace under an enormous chimney. A very large, steaming pot hung on chains over the fire. On our right was a large table set for a meal. A hearty, crusty brown loaf of bread caught my eye, and my stomach rumbled.

All the family members, including Walter—who greeted us only briefly—gradually gathered and sat down at the table. Little John arrived last; he ran up to the fire, planted his little legs wide apart, and promptly peed into the fire, which made it hiss and smoke. I was astonished to see that no one paid him the slightest attention. Just at that moment, the kitchen door opened and in came platters of fried eggs. My mouth was watering! Since we had arrived in France we hadn't seen a single egg. We were completely famished. With our eyes fixed on the platter, we watched the farmer's wife dish out the fried eggs one after another. I had high hopes that a fried egg would be left for us too. But there wasn't anything for us, not even a piece of bread! I was deeply frustrated, and looked around in utter torment as the others heartily devoured the wonderful food.

After this deep disappointment about the meal, Walter came over to us, and we arranged ourselves in front of the house. Luckily it was light enough for Heiri to take the photos so important to Walter and to us.

We didn't linger, but said our goodbyes and told Walter that we would be back soon to get him.

Chapter 67
We Bring Walter Back to the Château

On Tuesday, as usual, Miss Groth took the bus to Pamiers to do the food shopping. We gave her our film with the all-important photos, and requested that she take them to our photographer that had always given us special service. (This photographer regularly received photographic materials slotted for the German soldiers—and we were able to take advantage of what he had to offer.)

A week later, just to be on the safe side, Heiri accompanied Miss Groth to Pamiers, to help her with the grocery shopping and to pick up the passport pictures from the photographer.

A lot had happened in that week. Walter was back at the Château, but only a few of us knew about it. Meanwhile, the older boys in the hut joined the *Maquisards*—a risky decision that would lead to tragic consequences.

But I need to back-track a bit. First, Anne-Marie Piguet went to Toulouse in order to find the tiny rivets we would need to attach the passport picture to the identity card on the required spot. Eugen Lyrer and I met Anne-Marie at the bus- stop in front of the National Police Headquarters in Pailhès. From there we could go directly to La Coste by way of another valley. We had the crazy idea of bringing Walter that very night to the boys' hut only recently unoccupied.

After a long, strenuous hike in pouring rain we made it to the La Coste farm.

The farmer's friends—two gendarmes from Pailhès—were luckily not around. During our previous visit, the two policemen were in fact there and posed a potentially serious danger for us. With the help of a ladder, the farmer had to get Walter out of the living quarters on the first floor, while the farmer's wife chatted up the two policemen in the kitchen. The fairly frequent presence of these gendarmes was the main reason we wanted to get Walter away from La Coste.

This time the coast was clear. We explained to the good farmers that we wanted to take Walter with us and that we had found him another hiding place. We heartily thanked them for their kind help and departed.

It was still pouring down in buckets. One could barely see one's own hand in front of one's face. We climbed up to the mountain ridge, but then lost our way, wandering around aimlessly. Just as Eugen and I discovered what we took to be the correct path, we were surprised to hear Anne-Marie calling out that the path we had found would take us directly back to La Coste! We didn't believe her, but she was totally confident about where we were, even though we could barely see a thing. In any case, Anne-Marie led the way, and we followed. She found a switch-back trail that indeed took us safely through the thickets and back down to our side of the mountain.

Except for being soaked to the skin, we arrived back at the Château without more difficulties. We had only a little more than an hour now to get Walter to the abandoned hut above the New Mill. But with this pouring rain it would be impossible. We gave up. Besides, it was late, almost midnight.

We headed for the workshop. Usually I just slip through the window, but because of the rain, it was shut fast. I threw pebbles at Heiri's window. When he finally responded, we explained that we wanted Walter to spend the night in Mr. Nadal's work-room, and Heiri immediately agreed. We quickly said our goodbyes. Given that we were soaked, hungry and half frozen, we hurried to our beds.

Chapter 68
The Forgery: Big Worries, Small Rivets

What luck that Annelies was in charge of the kitchen! During our meals, she could discreetly take food to Walter without anyone's noticing. Absolutely nobody was to know that he was here at the Château. We soon abandoned the plan to take him to the older boys' hut because it was too impractical. In the end we decided to keep him at the Château until his trip to Switzerland. That, of course, was a tremendous risk for us. In the daytime, he stayed in Heiri and Annelies's room. Miss Groth would not unexpectedly find him there. At night, he had the workshop at his disposal.

Still the Germans had not come. The whole time, however, we were under tremendous psychological stress from continually awaiting their arrival. Our stress was somewhat lessened by our daily activities. We just couldn't think about the constant threat facing all of us. Nevertheless, every time we thought of Walter who was living in our very midst, our stomachs would sink. In fact, we experienced a deep-seated angst. We knew very well that if the Germans came to get Walter, they would find him right away. That would be a catastrophe with horrendous consequences: the arrest of the director, the staff, and the Jewish children, as well as the shutting down of this Red Cross colony.

In any case, it was absolutely necessary that we get Walter to Switzerland as soon as possible. On the surface, the first day with Walter back at the Château went like every other day. I had my lessons with the Mickeys morning and afternoon. It was still constantly raining. After the evening meal, I took care of the children who came to the infirmary as I had been doing for several months. While I was in the infirmary, Edgar came to see me to bring us Mrs. Schmutz's identity card. We had been impatiently waiting for this card ever since Ruedi Schmutz had promised it to us a while back. Having the identity card was the key for deciding if and when Anne-Marie could venture the risky trip to Switzerland with Mrs. Schlesinger, her son Pauli, and Walter. Without papers it would be impossible because of the many inspection stations along the way—and the way was over a thousand kilometers!

I was delighted to see Edgar, but after giving me the card, he quickly departed. He no longer felt safe at the Château.

As soon as I took care of the last child and gave him a "Sunday band-aid"—a tiny band-aid decorated with a miniscule star, which was really super special treatment—he happily trotted off and I was free to go find Heiri to work on our project for forging the new identity cards. Now we had Mrs. Schmutz's and my green cards, so all we needed to do was change the photos! I found Heiri in the kitchen with Annelies who was preparing tomorrow's breakfast. I showed Heiri the identity cards and we resolved to work on the forgeries that very night. We already had the photos.

At eleven o'clock, when we no longer had anything to worry about from Miss Groth, we met in the big classroom. Heiri brought all the "necessary tools," or at least the ones we had at our disposal: a pocket-knife, pencil, ruler, and sewing needle to imitate the official stamp.

The insufficient lighting was a problem, but we had to make do with it.

Taking turns, we had to remove the miniscule rivets that were holding Mrs. Schmutz's photo in place. We had already spent a lot of time on this, and had to be extremely careful. Finally we decided to stop for now and continue tomorrow evening.

The next day the weather was beautiful. I had spent the afternoon with my kids at the New Mill, and upon returning to the Château met up with Mrs. Schlesinger wildly waving her arms and crying out despairingly: "It's all over! It's all over! Miss Groth has gone over to the workshop." I was shocked! In the workshop she must certainly have discovered Walter!

Very, very worried, I went back down the steps to the courtyard, just as Miss Groth was heading in my direction. She nodded her head at me, as usual, and went on without saying a word! At that point, I headed straight for Nadal's workshop. In Heiri and Annelies's room I met up with Walter. "I was unbelievably lucky," he responded to my worried questions. "I had to go out to pee, and was outside behind the straw pile when totally by chance I saw the director coming toward the workshop. I waited until she went away again, and then scurried back to my room." Whew! Everything had gone well. If Miss Groth had found Walter, that could have led to disastrous consequences.

Later that evening after my infirmary duties—one of the children had 'impetigo,' a nasty, contagious skin disease—Heiri and I once again sat in the big classroom with the identity cards. We had a lot of trouble extracting the rivets and then straightening them out, in order to take out Mrs. Schmutz's photo and replace it with Mrs. Schlesinger's. Replacing the rivets would be another long story, but we somehow managed to succeed. While Heiri was busy copying the imprint of the official stamp by using Annelies's sewing needle, I took out my identity card. I was going to detach my passport photo when I heard footsteps in the hallway. We were enormously frightened and immediately made the green cards disappear. We were well aware that falsifying identity papers was liable to the punishment of "forced labor in perpetuity." The door opens, and who comes in but Edgar with Rosa Goldmark!

"I picked her up near Pailhès," he said, pointing to the frightened girl in the gray skirt. She seemed to be drawn into herself like a hedgehog. From behind her thick round glasses she stared at us wide-eyed and confused.

We said a few gentle, kind words to her, and then Edgar led her to the girls' dormitory. He returned to us immediately. I invited him to sit down, and asked: "How are things at Tambouret?"

"At the moment not so good," he answered. "Today two policemen came and wanted to see Mrs. Schmutz's identity card. Hans and Ruedi pretended to look all over for it. The two of them acted as if they were furious, grumbling and swearing about this 'insolence,' until the Vichymen said they would come again tomorrow, and departed."

"And now you need Mrs. Schmutz's card that we just finished forging?" asked Heiri. Edgar nodded.

There was nothing to do but to exchange the photos again. We used a new set of rivets from Anne-Marie, but the result was bad. With some special pliers we might have had no problem. In any case, Edgar returned to Tambouret with a clearly forged identity card.

Already the following evening Edgar came back once again and returned the green card. "How did it go with the police, what did they say?" I asked excitedly and couldn't wait to hear the response.

"They showed up before noon, " he answered, and sat down on the bench across from us, worn out from the strenuous bicycle ride. He pointed to the identity card lying on the table and said: "We couldn't possibly show them this identity card.

But Ruedi masterfully helped us out with an act of sheer bravado. He received the unwelcome guests by taking the identity card from the kitchen table, furiously waving it in the air, and shouting: 'We looked for this for an entire hour. My mother was terribly upset. We finally found the card in her small suitcase. It is unbelievable that three times you would trouble an old woman for nothing, absolutely nothing!' You should have seen the look on the faces of those policemen! They were so shaken by Ruedi's angry outburst that they didn't even dare inspect the identity card that was being thrust in front of their noses. 'Okay, okay,' they said, raising their arms, and then they left. We laughed until the tears rolled down our faces!"

Heiri and I admired Ruedi's clever act. Once again things turned out well.

Edgar stood up to go. "I have a long way home ahead of me," he said. We would have offered him something, but alas, we had nothing to offer. He said goodbye, and we went back to our interrupted project. Everything depended on our being able to forge the green cards without any noticeable error and to exchange the photos without a trace. Mrs. Schlesinger's and Walter's lives depended on it!

On the basis of our bad experience with Mrs. Schmutz's identity card and our attempts with the odious rivets, we realized that we couldn't touch the rivets. The solution was to cut a tiny round hole in the left-hand corner of the passport-photo in such a way that it would fit perfectly around the rivet and that one could then glue it on. This was a delicate but satisfying operation that we managed to carry out perfectly.

We still had Mrs. Schmutz's damaged green card to deal with. We racked our brains for a solution. We had already spoiled innumerable tiny rivets that were virtually unusable without special pliers. Despite all our efforts, we ended up with only a rather poorly executed forgery. We had a bad feeling about it all, when two days later we handed over our faulty specimen to Mrs. Schlesinger. Both she and we were running a high risk with that card. As I already stated: the penalty for forgery of identity papers was life-long hard labor!

One consolation for us was that at least Walter was running no risk. All that he had to do was learn by heart the details of my life!

Chapter 69
Anne-Marie's Second Illegal Trip to Switzerland

Two days after our illegal forgeries, everything was set for the departure. That Mrs. Schlesinger came to visit us at the Château—especially with her son Pauli—puzzled Miss Groth. She must have surmised that something was brewing behind her back, but her pride prevented her from asking any of us what was going on. Of course, she was still unaware of Walter's presence at the Château. She never asked about him, which was just as well.

In every respect, the director was not implicated in any of our plans. Should the Germans or the French gendarmes from Pailhès show up at the Château, she could speak and respond with a clear conscience. Had she known anything about our plans, she would never have allowed such a dangerous, illegal expedition to happen. The Red Cross had unconditionally submitted to the occupying force.

Anne-Marie's first trip to Switzerland with Addi Nussbaum was already difficult enough for the directors in Toulouse, Mr. Gilg and Mr. Parera, a Spaniard. (I will tell you more about them later on.) At the time, Anne-Marie had to beg on her knees for forgiveness and solemnly swear she would never do anything like that again. And now once again we were going behind the backs of these men to do the very same thing as before.

Around midnight Anne-Marie's group was ready to set out. Heiri had decided to serve as their "pathfinder" on the strenuous and difficult way to Saint-Jean-de-Verges. This was the way that all the La Hille children had taken who wanted to be saved by entering Switzerland. It was a strenuous hike of about five hours.

We set out on tiptoe—I was along for the beginning. Walter joined us in front of the Château. In silence, lost in our own thoughts, we walked on next to each other as far as Montégut, where we turned left onto a narrow, unpaved country road leading into the hills. It was a dark, moonless night. Heiri carried Mrs. Schlesinger's backpack and went in front. He knew the road well, and had an excellent sense of direction.

As we neared a farm, a dog started barking ferociously. We were very fearful of dogs in this region because they were allegedly dangerous. We made a large detour around the farm before taking a break.

I had to get back to the Château. I said my goodbyes to Anne-Marie, Mrs. Schlesinger, Pauli and Walter, and wished them good luck. In opposite directions we set out again on the path. They still had another good three hours ahead of them.

Their train to Toulouse departed at 5am. From there on they faced a thousand life-threatening kilometers to the Swiss border, at the mercy of inspections and roundups brutally executed by the German soldiers in their black leather boots.

In the morning, Heiri was on time for breakfast back at the Château. The last one in to the dining hall, he sat down at his place with the teens—and promptly fell asleep!

He had accomplished an admirable mission!

Chapter 70
A Dangerous Life Without Papers

few days after Anne-Marie and her charges left on their risky trip to Switzerland, I received a summons from the Director of the National Police in Pamiers: "You are hereby summoned to appear with your identity papers on May 20, 1944, at 4pm at the National Police Headquarters in Pamiers." Had I been betrayed by someone who knew that I had given away my identity card? That was inconceivable! Who knew it anyway? What should I do now? There was no way that I would actually show up at the National Police Headquarters, for they could immediately hand me over to the Gestapo.

To my surprise, Ruedi appeared at the Château just by chance. When I showed him the police summons, he thought about it for only a short time, and said: "Let me do it! I will go to the Gendarmerie and tell the police that you are very sick and cannot show up. Besides, you are Swiss, and they can't do anything to you."

"And what do you say when they explain that I have been hiding Jews and that our whole house is full of Jews?"

Ruedi was visibly shaken, thought about this for a bit, and then answered with less conviction: "I will say that that is not true, and that the house which is run by the Swiss Red Cross is caring for French and Spanish children."

Ruedi kept his word. He successfully made his case, and the National Police left me alone. In any case, the Allied invasion followed soon after, and the police had other, more pressing concerns.

But then it became absolutely vital for me to secure a new identity card. For several days I had a raging toothache, and I really had no alternative but to see the dentist in Pamiers.

I decided to take the Tuesday bus to our shopping market. It must have been toward the end of May. I was walking peacefully along the streets, looking for a dentist, when suddenly I saw three policemen coming toward me. I suddenly remembered I had no papers. I was gripped by fear, almost to the point that I wanted to run. No hunted-down criminal could fear the police more than I did! I thought I looked terribly suspicious, but the dreaded men in khaki with their cocky kepis went by without even noticing me. I was congratulating myself on my good fortune when I spied two more of these khaki-clad guys in front of me. "This time I've had it!" I thought to myself, expecting the worst. But these two also walked right on by. I crossed over to the other sidewalk, and there encountered two more of these hateful uniforms! I didn't understand what was going on. The city was jinxed. Police everywhere!

Luckily I found myself right in front of the photography shop we used for our passport photos. Salvation! I was still shaking as I quickly ducked inside. The photographer recognized me immediately and brought me the copies we had ordered. I also bought three rolls of film, and before I left I asked him why the city was overrun with police.

"The police academy is not far from here," he answered, "and they have the day off."

I breathed a sigh of relief as I stepped out into the street, but then quickly retraced my steps and asked the helpful photographer for a dentist's office.

Mr. Dupont, the dentist, was very kind and forthcoming. As an emergency, he took care of my abscessed tooth without making me wait, and told me to return in a week. As I headed back out into the street, it was a wonderful feeling to have the toothache suddenly gone.

On a bench in a small, run-down park, I ate my piece of bread and Swiss cheese that Annelies had prepared for me to take along. The afternoon seemed to me terribly long. I felt lost here in town and longed to be back at the Château with my children. That evening I was glad to be sitting on the bus—without guessing that I was soon to be facing another enormous fright.

The bus was overcrowded and departed late. After passing the larger town of Varilhes, we were stopped by a German military truck. On the platform of the truck sat a circle of soldiers with their submachine guns on their knees. A huge machine gun was fixed on the driver's cabin, and another was set up among the soldiers. The whole scene seemed extremely threatening. We feared the worst! At the command of the officer the soldiers jumped down to the street. We tried to pull ourselves together. "Now comes the inspection," I thought. "Without an identity card I will be immediately shot as a 'terrorist' (what the Germans called the resistance fighters)."

Two officers were inspecting the bus-driver's papers, while the rest of the soldiers carrying submachine guns were standing around looking on. Paralyzed with terror, we waited for the order to get off. It didn't come...The soldiers marched off in two single files on either side of the street heading back into town. We all let out a sigh of relief; no one said a word. A man wiped the sweat from his brow.

Later on we heard that in Varilhes five people—resistance fighters—had been dragged from their homes and shot dead in an open field.

Chapter 71

Poor Rosa

It's already been two weeks since Anne-Marie left for Switzerland with her little group. Have they arrived safely? We hadn't received any word—and presumably will not hear anything more since the postal connections with Switzerland have been interrupted for quite some time.

About our five teens in the abandoned hut on the mountain ridge, we heard that they had joined the *Maquis*. That was a shock for us, because life with the *Maquis* was extremely dangerous. Traitors lurked everywhere....But what other choice did they have?

Gradually our everyday life at the Château ostensibly returned to normal, and we went to bed at a halfway decent hour. At this point we had nothing more we could do for Walter. Inexplicably, the Gestapo from Pamiers did not pay us a visit at the Château. All the better! (Nevertheless, should they come, we were ready to receive them.)

I avoided Miss Groth. She gave the impression that she was very busy with something. Did she really not know anything about what we had so carefully planned and carried out behind her back? She had every right to be puzzled about Mrs. Schlesinger's unexpected visit and Anne-Marie's sudden disappearance.

One morning a note lay on the staff table with this short message: "This morning I have gone to Toulouse with Rosa Goldmark. L. G."

We weren't particularly surprised. The director sometimes had to travel to Toulouse. But why had she taken Rosa with her? Something wasn't right.

And indeed, that was true. The director returned without Rosa!

To our questions about that she simply replied: "Rosa could no longer remain with us. I took her to Lannemezan."

"And where is she in Lannemezan? With a family?" I asked innocently. "No," she responded. "In Lannemezan there is a large psychiatric clinic."

That took our breath away! That could not be true—Rosa in a mental institution! "You have taken her..." I stammered.

"I had no other alternative!" she interrupted and left us standing there speechless.

We had never had a discussion with the director. We had never sat down together to hash out some problem, whether pedagogical or organizational. So there had never been a word spoken about Rosa Goldmark. But that was not only Miss Groth's mistake. We could easily have requested such a discussion—but we hadn't done so! What a shame! That was a mistake that cannot be undone. We all bore the responsibility for that omission.

For us Rosa was not a particularly difficult problem. She behaved well and bothered no one. No one complained about her. Granted, from time to time—perhaps every two or three weeks—she would run off. But we could easily deal with that problem since she would be fairly quickly found.

We had not the slightest idea what the director had had in mind for Rosa.

Otherwise we would have sat down together and figured out some plan, as we had done for Walter Kammerer. Everything could have come out differently. During my duties in the infirmary that evening, I was still trembling with rage. How could Miss Groth have come to the idea of committing Rosa Goldmark to a psychiatric clinic?

In Vienna, Rosa had lost her parents, her brothers and sisters, and her home.

After years of living in constant danger, traveling through Germany, Belgium and France, she finally landed at the Château de La Hille. Many of her comrades, both girls and boys, had left the Château as if it were a burning house. But Rosa stayed behind and could no longer cope with the outside world. No one had any time for her—myself included. Under some pretext or other, she was awakened at 4am by Miss Groth and taken to Toulouse and left at a psychiatric clinic in Lannemezan.

Now she had lost everything! After my time in the infirmary I looked high and low for Miss Groth, but couldn't find her. I sat down in the salon with the Spaniards and listened with one ear to the BBC news report from London. On the entire Russian front, the Germans were retreating; they had lost one position after another. The Allies were also advancing in Italy. But about the long-anticipated Allied invasion there was not a word.

Later that night, I accidentally encountered Miss Groth on the steps leading down from the salon. She was going to pass by me without saying a word. That was so troubling to me that I could barely contain myself. I stopped her and asked in a loud, harsh tone without even being aware of the fact that I was shouting: "Can I visit Rosa Goldmark Monday morning? She knows no one in the clinic. We can't simply abandon her like that. She belongs to us!"

Miss Groth simply nodded her head in agreement and slipped into the girls' dormitory. I slowly climbed back to my room in the attic. Since Heiri's marriage I again lived in the attic close to my first tiny cubbyhole, but my new abode at least had a real window. While I was getting ready for bed and contemplating my trip to Lannemezan the next morning, I was suddenly filled with angst: I still had no identity card! If I valued my life, I could not and should not undertake any trip without papers.

The next day, after school I walked along the dreaded road to the Police Headquarters in Pailhès. Upon my arrival, I encountered all the scary policemen in a bare room, painted white. My heart was in my throat. The police always scared me to death. For me they were the embodiment of evil.

The policemen in their khaki uniforms were idly sitting around a table and looked at me with curiosity. No one from Château de La Hille had ever shown up at their headquarters. From all the stories that I had made up, I chose the shortest: "I do not have an identity card anymore," I said. "I lost it during a walk with my school children."

"Explain that!" demanded one of them, perhaps the officer in charge. "We were making a fire in the rocks above the New Mill," I said. "As I was bending down, my green card fell out of my shirt pocket into the fire." Now I was really scared! This story sounded so unlikely that I was afraid the entire group would burst out laughing. That didn't happen, although it was obvious that not one of them believed a word of my story. They sat there, rubbing their hands together, and said nothing. For a while it was totally quiet. Finally, one of them, thickset and unpleasant looking, leaned back in his chair, pushed back his cap, and asked sarcastically: "Didn't you at least try to fish out the green card from the fire? At least you should have brought along the partially burned card to show us."

I was embarrassed. "I...I didn't fish it out..."

The policeman laughed. Then they all laughed—except me. They conferred with one another for a bit and came to the conclusion that this situation had to be investigated. "You will receive a summons," said the man morosely. Totally unexpectedly, they said I could get a provisional identity card in Montégut.

Greatly relieved, I headed back home to the Château. The very next afternoon I took my children on a walk to Montégut-Plantaurel. This "village" boasted less than one hundred inhabitants but, as we were aware, the long-abandoned Château officially belonged to it. Oddly enough, this was the first time I was in Montégut-Plantaurel. In the village shop set up on a farm, there wasn't much to buy except paper ribbon and old, yellowed postcards. I introduced myself and asked to see the "mayor." He lived in the house next door and welcomed me. He said hello to the children and invited me in. Over a glass of wine, I explained my request and—wonder of wonders!—he immediately issued me the all-important document, which would serve as a temporary identity card.

He knew that we Swiss were taking care of Spanish and French refugee children. One assumes he also knew something about our young Jewish refugees from Germany and Austria. It would have been interesting to learn what the people in Montégut really thought and said about us. For what reasons did the farmers never bring us any food from their harvests? Why didn't they ever (as far as I knew) give us any of their fruit? Was it simply indifference? I didn't know then, and I do not know now the answers to these questions.

In any case, I had my official "temporary card." I was saved. Now there was nothing standing in my way of visiting Rosa Goldmark.

Chapter 72

My Visit to the Psychiatric Clinic

A few days later, toward the end of May, I got up at 4am on a Monday morning, and struggled through heavy wind and rain to get to Pailhès, where I had to wait in front of the dreaded Police Headquarters to catch a bus. The bus finally arrived at 6am but by then I was already soaked through from the rain and shivered from the cold. Besides, I had a long bus ride ahead of me.

Around noon I arrived half frozen at the Swiss Aid office on Taur Street in Toulouse. A Swiss woman welcomed me into the Red Cross office. Mr. Gilg, the director who had replaced Mr. Dubois, no longer worked at this office. Luckily, Mr. Parera, an extremely corpulent and unpleasant man who enjoyed controlling and harassing his employees, especially his fellow countrymen, was also no longer there, or at least not today. I was introduced to Mr. Salvide, a Spaniard who unlike Mr. Parera was very nice. Mr. Salvide drove the Red Cross truck that brought new children to the Château and also certain supplies from the Red Cross, such as powdered milk and packaged cheese. He greeted me warmly and saw right away that I was soaked to the skin. He loaned me his blue workpants and a pullover, while my clothes were hung on an electric heater to dry. A Swiss woman whose name I forget brought us a little lunch.

In the early afternoon I was lucky to catch the only train to Lannemezan. But my joy was short-lived: the train did not budge for quite a while, and then stopped for a half hour or more at each station.

Some other passengers on the train explained to me that there was no longer any grease for the train's wheels and at each stop they had to wait for the wheels to cool down.

I was standing in the train's corridor with many people, among them two German soldiers. During a long stopover, a group of Germans got on, with an officer at their head. He looked at his fellow Germans and said: "Follow me! We will quickly get some places to sit!" He entered the next compartment and shouted: "Get out!" All the people, including some elderly, quickly abandoned the compartment. The two German soldiers in the corridor, however, didn't move and didn't choose to sit down. Had they become aware that their cruel war could not be won with such brutish methods? In any case, I was glad to see an example of "other kinds of Germans." But even so: decent, respectful Germans were few and far between in France.

It was not until 7:30pm that the train arrived in Lannemezan. Since it was too late to pay a visit to the clinic, I remained on the train as far as Tarbes. Close to Tarbes I had a cousin who lived in Laloubère with his wife and children. Three years ago with the German occupation of Alsace they had fled to southern France.

On a very dark night the train pulled in to the almost unlighted station of Tarbes. We were met by German soldiers. Something didn't seem right. A voice announced on the loudspeaker that the city was under curfew and that anyone who did not have a "pass" would be shot. One of my fellow passengers explained to me that presumably a German had recently been shot in Tarbes.

On the train platform two policemen were issuing these "passes" which were valid for only a measly half hour. After what seemed like hours of waiting—a huge line had formed—I eventually got my all-important "pass."

I left the train station and stood in the impenetrable darkness. There was virtually no light visible anywhere. On top of all that it was still raining. Luckily, from a previous visit, I recalled that to get to Laloubère, I simply had to cross the station plaza and then head straight through the city. Luckily I found the street I wanted. I couldn't really see, but I oriented myself by the bit of light from the sky that outlined the houses. When I found the middle of the street—of course there was no traffic!—I set out running, irrationally thinking that by running I would get less wet. Suddenly I literally ran up against a chain link fence that barricaded the street. I was stunned!

I groped along the chain links, looking for an opening. Obviously this fence closed the road, but why? Confused and despairing, I began to wander around in the darkness of this ghostly town. Finally I had an idea that might save me. Behind these shuttered windows presumably there would be a light. I searched—and I found! But when I knocked at a door, the light went out. Understandably, the inhabitants were afraid. So I continued to run, wetter than before and even more desperate. All I heard was the sound of my own footsteps and the pounding of the rain. I didn't know how to get out of this situation.

Just then I heard the marching cadence of a German patrol, at first in the distance, but then drawing closer. These steps were utterly terrifying in the deserted streets. Was this my lucky chance? Or my most unlucky one? I couldn't stay out in the pouring rain all night. But my "pass" had expired!

I approached the German patrol and stood there without moving. Their powerful flashlight shone on me, and I waved my "pass" like a flag. "Halt!" shouted an officer, and with a stomp of their studded boots, the Germans stood still. Two soldiers left the patrol and approached me. One of them pointed his strong flashlight on me, the other his machinegun. As they came toward me, I said in French that I had gotten off the train in Tarbes and was completely lost. They understood me and pointed out the way to Laloubère: "Two streets straight ahead, then right, and again straight ahead."

While I could still hear the echoes of the soldiers' boots, I came to the second street, and then turned right. Always in the middle of the street, I began to run as if a shot had been fired, signaling the start of a race. But not for long! With all my might I again crashed into the bloody chain-link fence. I let out a wail. A kind of craziness took hold of me, and without thinking I began running wildly in no particular direction. I would stop from time to time to catch my breath and listen for sounds in the night. When I heard footsteps far off, I followed the sound and met up with a couple taking shelter under an umbrella. They had just come from the train station and knew the city pretty well. Thanks to their directions, I was able to leave Tarbes and get to Laloubère.

At an inn at the entrance to the town, I reserved a room and then set off to see my cousin Hans. It was very late. Given that I was dripping wet, I stayed in the entrance way of their house for only a few minutes, and then quickly retraced my steps back to the inn. All of a sudden I couldn't see a thing! Perhaps due to a vitamin deficiency, I experienced night blindness. I missed the right way and fell into a small canal. Here I must insert that Laloubère is a mini Venice. All over town, on both sides of the streets, are small channels or canals for constantly flowing water. I fell a second time into one of these canals and injured myself on a stone kilometer marker. I was furious and whined like a nasty little dog. There was nothing left to do but to return to my cousin's house. Thanks to a light in the window I was easily able to find it. My cousin showed me the correct way to go, and once again right in front of the inn I fell into some water. Despite the late hour, the innkeepers who had been expecting me were very kind. The woman brought me a nice towel, and her husband loaned me some clothes to change into.

The next morning I felt I had been beat up and could barely move. With my many falls everything hurt. Like an old man I tottered to my cousin's house, and decided to take a day off before visiting Rosa in the clinic.

The following day it must have been around 11am when I arrived in Lannemezan and asked for directions to the clinic. The clinic turned out to be a very modern complex with many pavilions connected by covered walkways. The main building was in the center. I was asked to wait in a comfortable waiting room. Rosa soon appeared. She was wearing a long black dress, similar to a pilgrim's robe, and looked very much like a nun. Her small face has become thin and pretty, especially without her former thick, old fashioned glasses. She threw herself on me, crying; "Mr. Steiger! Mr. Steiger! You've come to get me!"

Startled and bewildered, I was rendered speechless. Her cry of despair touched me to my core. Yes, I should bring her back to the Château. I somehow felt that that was crucial for her....A thousand thoughts rushed through my mind, but I reproached myself for not having given a thought to bringing her back with me. But now, what seemed so cold and unfeeling, I had to tell her that I could not take her with me, for I had no right to do so.

"But can't I..." She pulled at her dress. "Can't I go with you?" she asked, looking at me pleadingly.

My situation felt wretched. If only I could have said: "Yes, of course, you can come back with me to the Château." But I was powerless. "Dear Rosa," I tried to explain. "I cannot take you with me right now...." She looked at me with her eyes wide open, but not comprehending.

"But you are coming for me, right?" she repeated pitifully, in almost a whisper. Then like a sudden storm she started shouting: "It's a mistake that I'm here. They threw me into the wrong bus like a bundle of rags. Then instead of driving me to the Château, he brought me to the insane asylum. I am not crazy," she cried out in despair. "Get me out of here, please, please, please!" She broke down into tears. My heart was heavy. I was also in despair—and angry. Why was this poor girl brought here?

"Please take me with you," she sobbed. "I am so hungry..." She hid her face in her hands and her whole body trembled. To add to all her misery she was famished!

Then I had an idea: "Look, Rosa," I said and opened my briefcase. "Look what they sent you from the Château!" I took out a can of condensed milk and a package of cheese and set them on the table. I also had a piece of cooking chocolate.

With tears still in her eyes, she glanced at these strange delicacies as if transfixed. Then she immediately began ripping at their wrappings and feasting on them. She was really hungry! She devoured the cheese and half the chocolate, and then gulped down the whole can of milk.

After I had a modest lunch in a nearby-restaurant—thanks to a meal coupon—I returned to the clinic around 2pm. I found Rosa's pavilion without any trouble. I came to a glass door and peeked inside to a large room. I was so frightened by what I saw that my heart stood still: it was a glimpse into hell! Women with ugly, disfigured faces wandered around, gesticulating and crying out. One of them stood on a table with a tin plate in her hand, bellowing and waving it around. She looked like a dreadful creature from another world. Everyone was crying, raving, swinging their arms wildly about, running aimlessly as if possessed, climbing on the tables and benches... and in the midst of this hellish chaos was Rosa pacing up and down. I didn't want to venture into this place, truly a crazy house. I went looking for the director. When I explained Rosa's situation, he apologized and said: "You know, we have far too many patients here. A psychiatric treatment is no longer even in question. Only a few weeks ago we received more than 50 severely-injured children. We had to clear out an entire pavilion for them. Come along, see for yourself what an impossible situation we are in."

He led me to Pavillion 5, not far from the main building. We entered a large room perhaps formerly used as a training room or gym. We were greeted by a terrible din: searing screams, bizarre and terrifying sounds, scraps of inarticulate languages. What I saw was horrible. These children too seemed to come from another planet. I had never seen such misshapen creatures, either emaciated or bloated, with grotesque heads either too tiny or too large. They ran here and there emitting sounds like wild animals. Some were dirtied with their own excrement or had urine dripping down their legs; others lay motionless in their beds.

"You see how filthy everything is," said the director. "The stink is unbearable.

We face insoluble problems. We have too few staff members to clean things up. Besides, we don't even have any cleaning materials. We are lacking in everything, including space and food. We have so many sick children and patients that we don't know what to do."

Upon leaving this stinking pavilion, I took a deep breath. I felt sick to my stomach. The director promised to change Rosa's place, and apologized for having assigned her to the wrong pavilion due to a mistake or a misunderstanding. He had an aide fetch Rosa and said goodbye to me.

In the visiting room, I again met with our young woman condemned to this hellish asylum. We spoke for a long time. At this time Rosa seemed to me perfectly normal. But she kept returning to one point—that she had been mistakenly sent to the "crazy house," that she had been thrown like a bundle of rags onto the wrong bus....She also returned to the issue of eating and remarked that she was so hungry and that the "food was so good." That she had vomited up all my food offerings because she had gobbled them down so quickly she didn't say a word. I heard about that when I was talking with one of the nurses' aides. This aide told me that Rosa never spoke, not with anyone—and so she was astonished to see Rosa talking with me for such a long time.

Chapter 73

François and the Police

Teaching was a real joy for me. The children were so sweet and worked so hard. The first-graders—Guy, Rosa Marimon, Conchita and Josette—had learned to read very well with the aid of my printed letters on cardboard cartons. Violette, Renée and François had more difficulties. The fourth-graders, in contrast—especially Peggy and Friedel—had developed into outstanding students. We still used the slates for writing because paper was nowhere to be found, not even in The Capitol department store in Toulouse.

The days were becoming sunnier and warmer. We often took walks in the beautiful countryside. It seemed that the whole magical landscape belonged to us because we never met anyone on our walks. Only one time we accidentally encountered two *Maquisards*—but more about that in the next chapter.

You can easily understand why we often spent time at the New Mill. The children would happily swim and play there for hours. On the way home, however, going down from Borda Blanca to the narrow footpath through the thorny underbrush, a child would often be injured. Thorns would penetrate the skin on their bare feet. We called these nasty thorns *"picots,"* or sticklers. Sometimes the children would try to extract the sticklers themselves, or they would come see me in the infirmary. Only François, so highly sensitive to pain, was afraid to come. One day his brother André alerted me to the fact that François had an enormous infected blister on his foot.

"This evening you must let yourself be taken care of!" I ordered François.

So that evening François showed up, the very last one, and as I was taking care of him he screamed at the top of his lungs: "Help! Help! Police!"

"But there aren't any police here," I tried to convince him.

"Yes, yes, there are," he insisted.

The next evening, François was first in line at the infirmary. Again he screamed: "Help! Help! Police!"

At that moment someone knocked on the door and in came André. He came over to me, put his hand on my shoulder, and said: "Mr.Steiger, I arrest you."

François smiled triumphantly. "You see, Mr. Steiger, there is a policeman here!"

Chapter 74
The Walk from Hell

Everything began well. Annelies had put together a nice picnic for us. Each of us would have a piece of bread and a bit of nearly over-ripe package cheese. With that we were going to prepare an instant package soup, and so we schlepped along the big, heavy cooking pot that had served us well.

We were enjoying our walk, barefoot as usual, and had traveled a good distance. Gradually it was getting so warm that we took off our shirts. I had in mind to take the kids on a long roundabout route to climb the high, jagged peaks above the New Mill that commanded the entire region. After a long hike on a narrow path that led us through the forest—an almost impenetrable thicket—we gradually climbed to the mountain ridge. Towards noon we reached our rocks that we had seen only from beneath. The children were thrilled! We had a fabulous view over the entire region, toward Pailhès and Montégut, all the way to the Pyrénées still dusted with snow on their peaks. To the left of the houses in Borda Blanca, we caught a glimpse of the Château.

After a long rest at our magnificent viewpoint, we began the descent to the New Mill. We were hungry and looked forward to our soup and snacks. At the fork in the path that I surmised would lead us to our swimming spot, we unexpectedly encountered two terribly unsettling figures: two wild-looking, unshaven men barred the path. One of them had a rifle slung over his shoulder, the other waved a shabby, paper-covered book as if it were a weapon. "Send the children away!" ordered the man with the gun. Shaking with fear, I shooed my children away.

"They say," angrily hissed the man with the book, "that the

Germans regularly send teachers with their pupils into the forest to hunt us out. You are obviously one of them. Show me your papers!"

I didn't have anything on me except my pants and shirt. What should I say? I explained to him that I was Swiss, worked for the Red Cross, and had nothing to do with the Germans. They didn't believe me. "And the children? What about them?"

"They are poor war-victims from the Red Cross, refugees from Spain... We are on an outing."

"Liar! Dirty liar!" The *Maquisard* with the book was trembling in every limb. "You had this answer all prepared!"

His comrade pointed his gun at me and said in a low voice: "If it weren't for the children I would shoot you on the spot!"

"But I'm Swiss. I work for the Swiss Red Cross Children's Aid!"

"OK," said the man with the book who was calming down a bit. "Let's suppose you aren't lying and we let you go. The children go home and talk about us. Then for a lot of money someone will be dead certain to betray us to the Germans."

"The children have no home to go back to," I answered. "They all live in the Château de La Hille near Montégut. Should I show you the Château from the rocks?"

They didn't want to see it. I don't know anymore how long I argued with these rough resistance fighters, but gradually they calmed down. I promised them that none of the children would talk to anyone about this encounter. Before they would let me go, I had to write my name and address on the filthy cover of their book. "If something happens to us," threatened the book owner, "if we are betrayed, then you will be shot!"

They didn't allow us to use the little footpath that led down to the New Mill because that would run into their den. They forced us to go down on the other side, through the thickets.

The men disappeared, and I went to fetch my children. Friedel was trembling with fright. She was afraid I would be shot. I made every child solemnly swear not to tell a single person anything about this experience. It was a serious, almost sacred moment: each child solemnly promised and gave me his or her hand.

The ensuing descent was an almost impossible undertaking. The impenetrable forest could have come straight out of "The Sleeping Beauty." Like a snowplow driving through deep snow, every meter of the way I had to clear a path through the woods, to disentangle and tamp down the branches and thorny underbrush. Don't forget—we were all barefoot! In single file the children followed me over the relatively passable stretch of the forest. My backpack containing the picnic for all the children I had to leave behind and go back for later on. Only with great effort did we make even a little progress, for we were always getting hung up on the thorns. The terrible forest seemed to go on to infinity! When the little girls were exhausted and couldn't go a step further, we took a break in a fairly favorable, less overgrown spot. I let Friedel and Peggy distribute the bread and cheese. We had to do without the soup: we had no water and no place to make a fire. While the children ate and rested a bit, I climbed up one of the lower trees to get the lay of the land. Disappointed, I realized we still had a very long way to go. I rested for a short time myself. Friedel brought me some bread and cheese.

Around 4pm after a three-hour battle against the tangled branches and thorns, we reached sunlight. Finally we were released from the forest's evil spell! What a celebration! Although we were all exhausted, the girls rejoiced, and the boys threw themselves on the grass. How did we look? Totally scratched up, as if we had been playing with a hundred wild cats.

At the New Mill we had time to recover. Everyone jumped into the water, and forgot for a while what we had just been through.

Later on the children would call this excursion "the walk from hell." They kept their word and told no one about the terrifying encounter with the *Maquisards*. But I had nightmares! On the way to the New Mill a man with a rifle jumped out of the bushes and shot me. Night after night, I would be shot dead. This trauma remained with me for a very long time.

Chapter 75
The Cry for Help

After my luck in Toulouse finding the proper lens for Heiri's camera for taking portraits, from time to time I would photograph the neighboring farmers. In payment, I would receive a few eggs, which I did not eat myself but handed over to Annelies in the kitchen. One time, however, quite by chance, I came to enjoy half an egg all by myself. How this came about you will find out in the following story.

René Baumgart had mange, a skin disease caused by parasitic mites that leads to severe itching, hair loss, scabs and lesions. His hair was totally tangled and his skin all crusty. My medicinal products so far had done nothing to get rid of the tough parasitic mites that cause this skin condition. I decided that I had to shave René's head in order to try a more efficacious treatment.

While I was busy with the haircut, someone knocked at the door, and Mr. Palau entered. "Have you heard?" he asked. "Someone called for help down by the Lèze. I'm going to see what's happening. Will you come along?"

"Go ahead. I'll be right there!" I answered. After Conchita's father had closed the door behind him, I released René with the strictest orders not to scratch his newly shaven head.

Pierrette had a similar ailment to René's: hers was impetigo, a streptococcus infection. Her entire chest and stomach were covered with a nasty wound. My disinfectant products and salves did little to help Pierrette as well. Dr. Pic would certainly be helpful. After Miss Groth called him, I had to wait for an entire week for this unpleasant man to arrive.

I dismissed Pierrette, and promised that tomorrow morning I would have some new medicine that I would give her before school. Then I took off my doctor's coat and ran out of the infirmary, leaving everything behind. At the entrance I met up with Mr. Palau accompanied by a small thin man. We led this strange visitor into the dining hall. He said he had come to visit his children—Josette and Daniel. He hadn't found the Château and didn't see the bridge over the Léze.

I knew from the children's personal files that Josette and Daniel's father was an astronomer—and he certainly looked like one: thin, haggard, bent-over, and so near-sighted that he moved only by groping ahead of him with a stick.

As Annelies brought a fired egg on a tin plate from the kitchen, Heiri also appeared in the dining-hall. Annelies set the dish on the table in front of our guest and wished him "bon appétit."

My mouth was watering. Such a beautiful fired egg! I also wished our guest "bon appétit" but he did not move. Something extraordinary happened: he showed no interest in eating the egg! I was astounded, and looked over at Heiri. "Please, help yourself, you must be very hungry," we insisted. The astronomer shook his head.

There was nothing to do; he didn't want the egg!

"I'll take it back to the kitchen," I said, and hurried off. Quite unnecessarily, Heiri accompanied me. Scarcely had the kitchen door closed behind us when the egg disappeared. I put the empty plate down on the unused stove, where once Heiri had killed twenty-seven flies with one swat. Together we headed back into the dining hall looking as innocent as lambs to the slaughter.

Chapter 76
The Invasion

For three or four months I hadn't received any news from home. I was not terribly worried because Heiri and Eugen had also not received any mail from Switzerland. It had been forecast that Germany would cut its lines across the border.

The situation of the German army became increasingly dire. After the Allies arrived in Rome, a bitter struggle for control of the capital ensued. Things were also going very badly for the Germans in Russia: retreat and desperate flight.

Eagerly waiting the Allied invasion, we listened to the BBC London every evening. The bizarre personal news went on longer and longer, in more detail. One evening, in early June, it went on interminably: 'the apple is red,' 'Grandpa is sick' (two times),' 'the chocolate is good (three times),' ' the boy plays with the balloon (two times).' And so on and on, perhaps for a quarter of an hour. I said to Heiri, "You know, I think they're coming. It's the invasion!" The next day, at 5am the Allies landed in Normandy with an armada of four thousand ships. It was June 6, 1944. Heiri had won the bet: *patisserie* and cookies of his choice!

After the landing in Normandy, nothing much changed for us at the Château. Although life went on pretty much as before, we were indeed really happy! Finally the Allies had arrived. The biggest change, of course, was that our Jewish children who had stayed behind at the Château no longer had anything to worry about!

A few days later our director came into the dining hall with a package. I couldn't remember a single child receiving a package by mail. Who was the lucky recipient? Everyone was anxious to find out.

After the meal Miss Groth stood up and carried the package to the Mickeys' table. Friedel was the lucky one. Her parents had sent it from Nice where they were hiding. Trembling with excitement, Friedel examined the package from all sides, and in front of the curious Mickeys gathered around to see, Fiedel unpacked a beautiful light blue bathing suit! Friedel was thrilled. She was the only one to have a bathing suit. All the children admired it, as did the staff, the Spaniards and the Swiss. I saw right away that the bathing suit needed to be tried out as soon as possible. The weather was sunny and warm, so I gave my students the afternoon off and we headed for the New Mill.

Friedel could hardly wait, and ran ahead like a puppy and then had to stand and wait for the rest of us to catch up. When we got to the Lord's Pool, we made our usual stop. The Mickeys took off their clothes and laid them neatly on the rocks by the edge of the spring. Friedel slipped into her blue bathing suit. It was a bit tight, but it fit well enough. She danced around and let all the other children admire her.

We went together through the bit of forest to the stream that thousands of years ago had cut through the rocks and left a deep pool of water. The reader may recall how the initially troublesome Middles dived from the rocks into this pool on our first excursion to the New Mill. For now, we bypassed this spot that was too dangerous for my young pupils. I went ahead as usual to throw pebbles at the rocks to scare away any vipers that might be sunning themselves. The boys and girls followed me and then plunged happily into the stream of the Lèze, splashing each other, shrieking, laughing and generally having a wonderful time.

And then it happened. I was distracted for only a moment by André who wanted to show me a handful of snails he had collected. That's all it took for the blue of Friedel's bathing suit to disappear from my field of vision. I jumped up, and scanned the whole area. There wasn't any trace of the bright blue.

"Where's Friedel?" I called out worriedly. And then there she was, naked, carrying her wet bathing suit in her hand.

"I was looking for you," I gently reproached her. I didn't see you because you had taken off your bathing suit. Is it too tight?"

"No, but I have to wash it because it got dirty," she responded. She ran toward the stream, bent over, and swished her suit in the water. Then she cried out: "Oh no! My bathing suit is swimming away!" She ran toward it and then it was suddenly gone. I came to help her, but I couldn't see it anywhere. The bathing suit had totally disappeared. I searched the entire stretch of the stream up to the pool.

For nothing! And that was the end of Friedel's happiness too.

I went back to my rock and wanted to fetch François for a haircut. But then I spied Friedel, totally alone, heading toward the forbidden place, the deep pool. I didn't believe my eyes, and stood up. Yes, it was Friedel on her way to the dangerous pool! What was she thinking? Had the loss of her bathing suit taken away her good sense as well? "Friedel, Friedel!" I shouted.

She turned around for a second and replied: "I'm going swimming!"

"But you can't swim! Stay there!"

Defiantly she continued on—Friedel the sweetest, most obedient student.

Now I had to run! I dashed over stones and rocks—and arrived too late! Friedel sank quietly into the deep water.

Luckily, I knew my way around here very well. At the edge of the deep basin there was a rock formation that allowed me to slip into the pool where the water was only about a meter's deep. I had just gotten to that rock under the water when Friedel resurfaced right next to me. I grabbed her by the arm and pulled her toward me. She clasped onto me, and with all my strength—for Friedel was ten years old, and quite a big girl—I rose out of the water with Friedel in my arms. I carried her to the large flat rock—Pierrette's favorite spot—and gently laid her on the rock, knelt down next to her, and brushed the dark wet hair off her face. Although she was still breathing, she was deathly pale and paralyzed with fear. She looked at me and whispered, "You saved me!"

Then Guy came running with all the others. "Is she dead?" he cried.

"No, she's moving," observed Peggy drily.

The whole throng of children gathered round. "There's nothing to see," I said angrily. "Get away!"

I got up and they all went off.

Peggy stayed to care for Friedel, who recovered quickly. Luckily, she hadn't gulped any water. I returned to my rock and called François a second time to come for a haircut. He showed up with René. In all seriousness, René offered me two fish to eat that were still wriggling between his fingers. I thanked him and said: "You know, they aren't very tasty."

"Oh yes they are," he replied beaming. He shoved the two

squirming fish into his mouth, and proceeded to eat them with obvious pleasure, as if they were made of chocolate.

Chapter 77
Onze and Egon Are Dead

I don't know how this dreadful news reached the Château. In any case, one evening we heard it: "Onze and Egon are dead!" We couldn't believe it, couldn't grasp it.

"They died in the *Maquis.*"

It was as easy to say as it was horrible to hear. It was simply inconceivable that we would never see these two familiar faces again: Onze with his broad smile and Egon, my stove specialist, with his dark hair in his face....They just couldn't be dead!

We saw them so often, almost daily at the Château, and we knew their every gesture and movement. I see Onze in my mind's eye—like that first time in Pailhès when I had my heavy suitcases and he came to pick me up with his old bicycle. And I see Egon as if it were only yesterday, as he sat at the table in my classroom with his eyes ablaze and told me his story about surviving *Kristallnacht.* And now these two young men, so full of life, with their futures ahead of them—dead? No, that may not, cannot be true!

Chapter 78
Miss Groth Saves Mrs. Weinberg

During the time we were coping with the dreadful news that Onze and Egon were dead, Mrs. Weinberg came to visit her three children at the Château: little Percy, high-spirited Peggy, and loyal Robert, my former champion fly-swatter. After an extended stay in a hospital in Toulouse, Mrs. Weinberg pulled herself together to come to Château de La Hille. I welcomed her in the courtyard and invited her to sit down at one of the tables there. Exhausted from her long walk to get here, she happily sat down and asked me immediately if she could stay overnight at the Château. She wanted so much to be able to wish her children "good night." I recommended that she ask the director, Miss Groth, who was the only one who had the right to decide such things. We certainly had enough room in the Château, that I knew!

Percy, who was playing with Mireille, was the first to see his mother and dashed to her. Peggy and Robert soon followed. What a lovely reunion after such a long separation!

I had assumed that Mrs. Weinberg's request to stay overnight would certainly be approved—especially since it was already evening. But in fact I was mistaken: Miss Groth rejected Mrs. Weinberg's request. Once again, our director was strictly adhering to the rules of the Red Cross: No one—no parents, no strangers, and especially no one from the resistance—was allowed to stay at the Château.

Heiri had also advised Mrs. Weinberg to speak with our director. We were horror struck when we heard the decision. What could we do?

Where could the sick, overburdened woman spend the night? Robert came up with a solution. He found a stall at a neighboring farm that would suffice for a place to sleep for his mother.

Later that evening, in time for the 9pm news, we all came together in the salon. Miss Groth and Mrs. Weinberg were already there when I arrived from the infirmary. The two women sat on the rickety sofa and were conversing with each other. The Spaniards, as usual, had made themselves comfortable on the old chairs by the window. Eugen was also there this evening. Heiri with Annelies came in right after me. I turned on the radio, which crackled terribly until I was able to tune in the correct station. We heard the last of the three gongs announcing the BBC news.

Naturally, we were anxious to hear more about the Normandy beach landing. Unfortunately, the Allies were not able to advance as quickly as we had supposed.

The Germans were stubbornly defending themselves, and a vicious battle was taking place in Caen. Given the enormous Allied supremacy, however, the Germans could not hold out for very long, especially without airplanes.

After the news report we sat in silence for quite a while, each of us lost in our own thoughts. As I looked around, I noticed Mrs. Weinberg in particular. She looked terrible, so drawn and fragile. Had she been able to hug and kiss her children "good-night?" I went over to her to see how she was doing.

"Yes, the three of them got their hugs and kisses," she said happily. She asked me if they got on well with the other children in the community. I disarmed any fears she may have had, and praised Peggy especially as being one of my best students. I realized this was an opportune moment to learn more about the Weinberg family. "We really love your children," I said, "but we don't know very much about them." As if she had anticipated this remark, she began to recount their story, at first quite hesitatingly and then more confidently, speaking in a French heavily accented by her German. Everyone was paying attention as this frail woman began to tell her poignant tale, which I can reproduce here only partially.

Mrs. Weinberg's story:

"I grew up with my family in Vienna. My mother was a Scottish

Protestant and my father a Polish Jew. At first, we didn't have any troubles. I could study at any of the schools I wanted. When I was twenty, I was hired as a secretary in a law office. A lawyer named Dr. Weinberg had often come to visit us. He was very nice to me and asked for my hand in marriage. That he was Jewish didn't bother me in the least. After all, my father was a Jew also. Soon after Robert and Peggy were born.

"Then Jews began to be persecuted. Suddenly, swastikas were appearing everywhere. Enthusiasm for the German Führer animated the city. Percy was born in March 1938 at the time of the German annexation of Austria. That was a catastrophe for us, but Austria as a whole was overjoyed. Soon they came looking for my father. He died in an atrocious manner: confined to the back of a small truck, he was asphyxiated by the gas emissions that had been redirected to the interior of the truck. My mother managed to escape to England. We knew we had to escape also, and for us the time was right: my husband was the lawyer for Schuschnigg, the chancellor of Austria. Leaving all but the most necessary items behind, we bundled up the children and headed for Switzerland. We had good luck at the border, but that didn't last long because only a few days later we were expelled. You can imagine our desperation: after struggling with three small children on such a long, strenuous trip into a foreign country, we succeeded in entering only to be expelled almost immediately!"

The Weinberg family left for Athens, where Mr. Weinberg had a relative who could help them. They were able to rent a lovely apartment and lived a peaceful life in Athens. I don't know why they left after only a year—perhaps because of financial reasons. In any case, they left Athens and arrived in Paris. Their arrival in Paris unhappily coincided with the triumphal entry of the Germans on June 14, 1940!

"Scarcely had we arrived in Paris," Mrs. Weinberg continued, "when we had once more to pack up our belongings, and we headed to Marseille. With the last of our money we rented a shabby attic room in a dilapidated apartment building.

When it rained the water dripped from the ceiling onto the bed, where my husband slept with the three children. I myself slept on two chairs. Now we were living in extreme poverty. On top of all that, we had a large dog that, like us, was always hungry and often whimpered. My husband loved the dog more than anything. On the Cannebière, a well-known street in Marseille, every day I stood on line with the other beggars for some soup to save my children from dying of starvation. But my husband would follow me. As I headed home with the soup, he took it from me and gave it to the dog. 'Rex eats first,' he shouted, 'and then the children.' Our miserable conditions had driven my husband mad."

Mrs. Weinberg continued her story of those sad times "on the two chairs." A beggar offered her his favorable spot on a busy street. Robert and Peggy were in school and had their lunch there. That was one less worry; at least they had one decent meal a day. In autumn things looked up. Mrs. Weinberg was hired at the Berlitz Language School as an English teacher. While her employment helped them out of their most extreme misery, the winter was extremely cold and their attic dwelling was not heated. The family was freezing.

I'm going to skip over a large part of Mrs. Weinberg's distressing story. It would take us too long to go into the details of what she and her family had to go through. I will jump to the conclusion of her narrative:

"In November 1942 the Germans arrived in Marseille—another catastrophe for us! My husband just barely escaped on a ferry. Soon after, the dog that he had to leave behind simply fell down and died.

"Robert, Peggy and Percy were not in good health. They were pale and very thin. I was afraid that they too could fall down dead. I looked for help, and found that a co-worker from the Berlitz School knew a woman from the Swiss Red Cross Children's Aid Society that had an office in Marseille. I went to see her, and she told me about the Château de La Hille and the children they take in. On her recommendation Robert and Peggy were accepted at the Château. I was so happy. The Swiss Red Cross also offered me a position in their Toulouse office on Taur Street, and I moved with Percy to Castelnaudry."

Margaret Weinberg fell silent, and we did too. We were deeply moved by this woman's fate—especially to have to live so far from her children.

As tears rolled down her cheeks, she again addressed us and thanked us for everything we had done for her family. In the hallway, the clock struck twelve. We got up and quietly said good night. Mrs. Weinberg went off to her farmer's stall, and Miss Groth accompanied her. I watched them go off into the night. In despair, I wearily climbed to my attic room and wept bitterly.

When I finally recovered a bit and lay down in my bed, some ghastly screams suddenly shattered the stillness of the Château. I jumped out of bed and stood there a moment as if paralyzed. Then I ran as quickly as possible down the steps toward the salon. I opened the door and turned on the light. There was Mrs. Weinberg lying on the sofa, apparently grasping for her last breath. In a panic I turned to get help from the director. On the steps I nearly ran into her. "She's dying!" I cried, my voice breaking. Miss Groth didn't answer and disappeared into the salon.

Her screams again reverberated through the Château and then gradually became less frequent. It was a good thing that Miss Groth had taken Mrs. Weinberg back into the Château. In a stall, on the straw, she probably would have died a terrible death. Miss Groth had saved Mrs. Weinberg's life!

In the morning after this horrendous night, Mrs. Weinberg looked more dead than alive, but she seemed to have survived the worst of it. Miss Groth had her taken to the "Holy Chambers," a secret room behind her office that no one was allowed to enter. All kinds of objects—huge vases, tables, cupboards, beds, chairs and all sorts of bric-a-brac from the former owners of the Château—were stored in that space.

Now we had a sick woman staying at the Château, but according to the strict rules of the Red Cross even a sick woman was not allowed to be sheltered there—that was made clear to us in no uncertain terms by Miss Groth the following morning after breakfast. We were dumbfounded. "A seriously ill woman cannot be sent away!" we rebelled.

"A rule is a rule," she replied.

What should we do? We sat down together, Heiri, Eugen and I, and drafted a letter to the Red Cross office in Toulouse. We explained to our superiors that we would quit our jobs if this sick woman was not allowed to stay at the Château until she had sufficiently recovered. Without knowing the contents of our letter, Miss Groth took it to the post office. Two days later the men from Toulouse arrived in their white truck from the Red Cross: Mr. Salvide, a Swiss, was the driver; Mr. Parera, the fearsome Spaniard who harassed and dominated all his coworkers; and Mr. Gilg, a Swiss who was actually the current director. They entered the Château without any greeting. Mr. Parera, the "little Franco," looked around at everything and finally said to me sarcastically: "Tell me, are there many sick women at the Château?"

I nearly exploded with anger, but managed not to reply.

Mrs. Weinberg stayed until she had recovered. Then she returned to Castelnaudary. Her children accompanied her as far as Pailhès, the exuberant Peggy as always in the lead.

My heart breaks when I think about them. Six years later, in a narrow street in Castelnaudary, Peggy was hit by a truck. I can still see the telegram from Mrs. Weinberg: "Peggy is dead."

Chapter 79
Rosa Goldmark's Death

It was several weeks since my first visit to Rosa Goldmark in the clinic. What's become of her? I really had to visit her again in Lannemezan.

This time, as I set out at 4am to catch the bus in Pailhès it was a beautiful, cloudless day. Everything went smoothly. In Toulouse I even managed to catch an earlier train so that by 2pm I was already in Lannemezan. I headed straight for the clinic where I was asked to wait for Rosa in the visitors' room. I was very anxious to see her. Had she changed much in the interim? I had a long wait—but she didn't come. Finally, instead of Rosa a nurses' aide came to get me. "Rosa is doing very poorly," she said. "She can no longer get up out of bed and for several days now she has eaten nothing."

The aide led me through a long corridor to a dormitory. Rosa lay alone in one of the many white iron beds. I barely recognized her. Pale and hollow-cheeked, she looked at me with her dark, sunken eyes. When I said hello, her pale, expressionless face lit up. "Mr. Steiger... You have finally come to get me!" she said in a weak voice. She tried to raise herself up but sank back into her pillow.

Despairingly, she raised her eyes toward me. That flash of light had disappeared from her face, and she again seemed utterly sad and hopeless. Resignedly, she struggled to say: "You have come too late!" and closed her eyes. As if she were dead, she lay there like a little bundle of sorrow.

Deeply frightened, I stood there by her bed feeling dizzy and then sat on the edge of the bed.

Poor, poor Rosa!

"At least she has spoken," I heard the voice of the aide who had led me to Rosa's bed. "Up to now she has not said a word to anyone."

"I know," I answered softly without looking up. Then after a while I said: "She comes from Vienna and doesn't have anyone."

Rosa again opened her eyes and looked at me for a long time, almost reproachfully: "How are things at Château de La Hille?" she asked in a whisper.

I moved closer to her and told her about the Château. "Do you remember Mrs. Schlesinger?"

She nodded.

"And her son Pauli, and Walter Kammerer, our piano player?" She nodded again.

"Also Miss Anne-Marie? Anne-Marie took Mrs. Schlesinger, Pauli and Walter Kammerer to Switzerland. The Germans wanted to arrest them at the Château."

I don't know if she understood me. Barely intelligible, she asked: "And who is left at Château de La Hille?"

I listed those who immediately came to mind: "Irma, Trude, Eva Fernanbuk, Gerti Lind, Cilly Stückler, the little Friedel, Pierre Bergmann, Mane and Gustav Manasse…"

"And I'm here in this insane asylum…" she buried her head in the pillow and wept.

"Rose, don't cry!" I begged her and handed her my clean handkerchief. She took it and again stared at me for a long time. It broke my heart to see her so miserable, so pale and emaciated.

"Papa and Mama simply sent me off like a package for the post office," she said slowly, her voice breaking.

"They wanted to save your life."

"They never wrote to me. The Germans killed them, and I want to die also. I no longer eat…"

What should I say? I looked at this girl wasting away who long, long ago in Vienna was once a happy child beloved by her parents.

Rosa again closed her eyes. I took her cold, tiny hand in mine and asked: "Do you hear me, Rosa?" She opened her eyes and nodded. "Dear Rosa, please eat, and then you will be healthy again, and I can come to take you back to the Château. I promise you that!"

Rosa reflected for a long time and then asked: "Why did they throw me into the wrong bus like a mail package? I even said to Miss Groth, it's the wrong bus."

"Now listen carefully, dear Rosa," I tried to explain. "At the Château you were always running off. That was very dangerous. Something could have happened to you. That's why Miss Groth brought you to this clinic, this hospital. Here you are safe, like in the Zwieblekeller at the Château. Here the Germans will not find you."

"Are they looking for me, the Germans?"

"Just like gold-diggers looking for gold, the Germans are always looking for Jews."

"I know, they want to kill all the Jews, like they killed my parents. Many children from the Château were also killed—Inge Helft, Adele Hochberger, Walter Strauss—many. Why do they kill the Jews?"

I thought back to that discussion I had with the Middles at the Château ruins in Foix. What I really wanted to do again was simply cry out: "It's crazy! It's crazy what they are doing!"

Rosa again closed her eyes. She seemed totally exhausted. There was a long pause. She seemed to be sleeping. The aide had left us alone for a good long time. In despair, I was still holding Rosa's hand. I was overcome by a profound sadness mixed with anger and revolt. Tears rolled down my cheeks. Rosa again opened her eyes. I took her tiny, emaciated hand in both of my hands and pleaded: "Dear Rosa, I implore you, eat again! You may not die—for that would make the Germans happy. 'One less Jew' they would say. Please, don't let them have that satisfaction! Eat again!"

The slightest suggestion of a smile passed over her sunken cheeks, and she again closed her eyes. I believe she understood me. She lay there deadly pale. I could no long bear the sorrowful sight. I laid her hand gently on the bed-sheets and stood up. "Goodbye, Rosa!" She didn't hear me anymore. Profoundly troubled, I left the depressing atmosphere of this dark room.

Out in the fresh air, sitting on a bench in the park next to the clinic, I tried to regain my equilibrium. Little by little I was able to give some semblance of order to my thoughts. I was overcome with rage—rage against our indifference at the Château to Rosa's plight and rage against the director for her unilateral decision to secretly take Rosa to this horrible place.

On my way to the train station I bought myself a handful of cherries. While I was washing them at a public hydrant, I saw a policeman coming towards me. I still could not bear the sight of policemen! My anger was deep within me. "These impossible policemen," I hissed through my teeth. "These cowardly flunkies of the

Gestapo!" I continued washing my cherries but bent further over the hydrant in hopes that the chap in his khakis would go on by. Suddenly I heard his rough voice behind me: "Your papers!"

If that's all he wants, ok, I thought. I stood up, laid the cherries carefully on the bench beside me, and pulled out my temporary identity card. He took the paper and studied it. "Fourteen days in jail!" he said. "Follow me!"

Incredulously, I followed him to the police station where I had to wait in the corridor at a small table. I overheard my policeman telephoning. "We have here an individual by the name of..." He spelled out my name. At that moment someone slammed the door. After quite a while the policeman returned and asked: "Have you read what's on your temporary card?" I responded that I hadn't. "Read it!" He gave my paper back to me and I began to read it aloud: "It is forbidden, with a penalty of fourteen days in jail, to leave the county with this 'receipt.'" I was indeed aware of that, but I had figured it was worth taking the risk. My visit to Rosa was too important.

"You have left the Ariège, so that earns you fourteen days in jail!" he said calmly. My heart nearly stopped beating. Really? Fourteen days?

"That's impossible!" I cried out with alarm. I imagined the Château, the children—what would they think when I didn't return? So many thoughts ran through my mind. I already imagined being in my cell.

"You are Swiss and work for the Swiss Red Cross?" inquired the police officer.

His question brought me back to reality. I nodded mechanically.

"I will give you the gift of the fourteen days in jail," he said. "You are free to go." I was so deeply frightened that I couldn't move a muscle. He repeated: "You can go, you are free!" Finally I understood—and left! I was so relieved that for a short moment I felt almost happy.

When I arrived at the train station, I just made my train. This time there was no curfew in Tarbes, and I crossed the city in daylight with no problem. In Laloubère I managed not to fall into any canals, and was warmly welcomed by my cousin and his family.

One or two weeks after my visit in Lannemezan Rosa died. The news came from the director of the psychiatric clinic in Lannemezan. Miss Groth did not show us the letter with the sad news.

Poor Rosa! Why couldn't we have helped you?

Chapter 80
Saved by the Violin

Mr. and Mrs. Kriegstein lived in Cologne with their daughter Friedel. They ran a small boutique that sold blouses, shirts, ties, scarves and various other articles. Heinz Storosum, Mr. Kriegstein's nephew, lived with them. Heinz was a gifted violinist and studied at the conservatory.

The persecution of the Jews was becoming more and more extreme, which very much unsettled the Kriegstein parents. They worried about their only daughter and their nephew for whom they were responsible. Mr. Kriegstein was a Polish immigrant. One day all the Polish Jews in Cologne were arrested and sent to a camp, but Mr. Kriegstein was lucky enough to be able to escape to Belgium. At the border town of Spa he found accommodations in a hotel. He wrote to his wife urging her to follow him to Spa with Friedel and Heinz.

And so a long, complicated story of their escape began. Mrs. Kriegstein, speaking German with a heavy Polish accent interspersed with many Yiddish words and expressions, recounted their story to me in great detail. I often had trouble understanding what she was saying, especially when she would get caught up in minute details.

Here I will present only the highlights of their four-year exodus that ended in Nice where they found a secure hiding place.

The first step was to have their four-year-old daughter Friedel join her father in Belgium. Mrs. Kriegstein benefited by a happy coincidence of circumstances. She had a Christian neighbor with two children whose husband, a Jew, was arrested just a short time before. Worried that she and her children would share the same fate, the neighbor decided to flee to Belgium. Mrs. Kriegstein asked the neighbor if she would be able to take Friedel along with her own children into Belgium and leave Friedel with her father in Spa. The good woman agreed. A few days later, this woman along with the children safely arrived in Spa.

The situation, however, became ever more dangerous. *Kristallnacht* took place on November 9, 1938. Heinz Storosum also left Germany, after visiting his mother, his sister Martha and brother Willi. Martha, who was eleven, was able to join a group of children that was being taken to Belgium. According to Mrs. Kriegstein's account, the leaders of the group—people from a Jewish aid organization—attempted to smuggle them across the border into Belgium. But during this attempt they were surprised by vicious dogs. That was a tremendous shock for little Martha. This trauma along with the tensions of the escape and her sudden separation from her parents proved to be too much for this sweet little girl. Martha never recovered from the trauma, not even at the General Bernheim Home where she was warmly received. (The reader may recall that Edith Goldapper also stayed at this Home with the other girls who eventually came to Château de La Hille.) Later, at Château de La Hille, Martha remained noticeably withdrawn. She acted strangely, often unintelligibly, and no one wanted to be near her. Fortunately, she did not run off, like Rosa Goldmark, but most of the time she just sat quietly in her corner, or she helped Mrs. Schlesinger who always found little jobs for her to do in the kitchen.

Heinz Storosum's brother Willi remained with his parents. Shortly after, the three of them were deported and killed. Heinz, in contrast, engaged in a risky escape into Belgium. To the great joy of his uncle and Friedel, Heinz showed up one day in Spa, safe and sound. Mrs. Kriegstein received this good news from her husband. By then threatening round-ups were occurring everywhere. From one day to the next she had to find hiding places with neighbors. After a few weeks, Mrs. Kriegstein, carrying only one small suitcase, miraculously crossed the border into Belgium.

In Spa she met up with her husband, her daughter Friedel, and her nephew Heinz Storosum. They remained in Spa for almost a year. However, because of the proximity of the border, on the advice of friends they moved into a hotel in Antwerp and then soon after moved to Brussels where they stayed with friends.

On May 1, 1940, the Germans invaded Belgium. With luck—and without luck one would not survive—the Kriegstein family caught the last train to France that coincidentally was transporting the hundred

Jewish children, including Martha, who a year later ended up at Château de La Hille.

The four-day trip in the boxcars was dreadful. Edith also spoke of this lamentable experience in her journal. Mrs. Kriegstein gave a detailed account. Six- year-old Friedel was usually sitting on the dirty floor of the boxcar with Heinz crouched next to her. In the larger cities where the train stopped, they received some soup and sometimes a little bread. Because the rail lines had been destroyed in some places, they often had to make long detours. One time they were even bombed. The train often stopped for several hours. That provided the opportunity for the passengers to get out and go to the bathroom, since there were no sanitary facilities in the cars themselves. Finally, on their fourth day of travel they arrived in Toulouse. The children bound for La Hille got off one stop further on. The doors of the boxcars remained shut. (The Kriegsteins heard the children's voices but had no way of knowing that Martha was among them and that Friedel would also one day belong to this group of children.) Soon after they arrived at the end station, Ax-les-Thermes where they would find accommodations in a hotel.

For more than a year they stayed in this beautiful town with its thermal baths and springs. They would take walks with Friedel in the magnificent countryside. They were left in peace; it seemed that they had been happily forgotten.

Then fully unexpectedly, they were awakened early one morning by the sound of drum rolls. The whole place was overrun with police. All the Jews, wherever they were, had to gather in the street for immediate transport. The police combed through all the houses and hotels, looking for Jews. The Kriegsteins were arrested. Although they didn't have any time to get together even their most necessary belongings, Heinz was fortunate in being allowed to take along his violin. They were packed into buses and brought to a camp by the sea, near Agde. That was October 1941.

At the camp the family was separated. Friedel was assigned with her mother to the women's side, Heinz with his uncle to the men's. "It was a terribly primitive camp," Mrs. Kriegstein said. "Everyone was given only one thin wool blanket and had to sleep on the damp ground. During the night rats prowled everywhere. There was very little to eat, and we suffered from hunger and cold. At that time Heinz became very sick. I was in despair, and sent Friedel with some soup for him. But she didn't come back! I lost my head and ran screaming into the men's section. I found Friedel standing against the barracks wall with her hands in the air. A guard with a gun stood next to her. "Let me have my child," I shrieked, and grabbed Friedel and ran back with her to the women's section.

Here I'm going to interrupt Mrs. Kriegstein's account and present a summary of what happened next. The most important thing was that Heinz recovered! A miracle! He took up his violin and played, much to the delight of his fellow camp inmates who, during his illness, had taken good care of him and had really saved his life. He played every day. The camp director got wind of this. As he himself was a passionate lover of music, he summoned Heinz, had him play, and soon organized a concert with him. The director called Heinz 'Henri' and provided him with many favors. In short, he was Heinz's savior. The Commander, as he was called in the camp, again summoned Heinz and made him an offer. In the next few days the Jews were to be taken to Drancy and from there deported. Heinz, however, had nothing to fear because the commander would give him the necessary papers in order to be able to leave the camp. Heinz explained to his benefactor that his aunt, his uncle and his young cousin were also in the camp and that he would not leave without them.

At that point, the commander drafted a "pass" for all four of them. In addition, he gave his violinist the address of a friend in Agde who could be of further assistance.

The Kriegstein family packed up whatever they had, on the women's side and the men's, and were able to leave the camp without any difficulty. The violin had saved them!

The commander's friend, a high-ranking police officer, welcomed them into his home and advised Mr. Kriegstein to take his family to Cannes. He even provided them with their tickets. After what seemed to them a fairytale evening in the home of this French host, the Kriegsteins set out for Cannes and arrived the next day. In Cannet, a suburb of Cannes, they found a modest hotel where they settled in. Finally they could breathe! They had the feeling that everything was so wonderful that it couldn't really be true.

All around everything was peaceful; the sun shone bright and warm. Nothing bad could happen here. They felt secure. But Henri Storosum—he called himself 'Henri' now—worried about his family. Why hadn't his parents and brother escaped? And what had happened to Martha? He wrote to his old address in Cologne and to the General Bernheim Home in Belgium. He didn't receive any response from Cologne, but he did receive joyful news from the colony where Martha had been staying—his sister's new address in France: Martha Storosum, Colony of the Swiss Red Cross, Château de La Hille, Montégut-Plantaurel, Ariège. A few days after receiving this news, Henri went to see his sister at Château de La Hille.

After several changes of location, the Kriegstein family finally ended up in Nice. Mr. Kriegstein came into contact with the Resistance that found the family a secure hiding place on "Paris Street."

Henri wrote to them as soon as they were settled in Nice. He told them about Martha, about the children and about the Château de La Hille. "Send Friedel to La Hille!" he wrote. "She will be safe here with the Swiss Red Cross." The Kriegsteins were ready to send her there, but it was a very long trip. Who could take Friedel to Montégut?

Through the Resistance networks, they located a Catholic nun who took Friedel, now eight years old, to Foix where she stayed for the time being in a cloister school. "Apparently they were on summer vacation," Friedel recalled. "I slept alone in a huge dormitory with many empty beds. I spent a whole week there until someone brought me to the Château de La Hille."

"Under the Italian occupation it was peaceful in Nice," Mrs. Kriegstein recounted. "They left the Jews in peace. We thought it would remain that way, and had Friedel come back to Nice. But that was a mistake that could have cost us our lives. Suddenly the Italians moved out, and the Germans moved in. In a flash the persecution of the Jews began again. Today it seems impossible to believe everything that happened. The Germans rounded up the Jews wherever they could find them. They dragged the sick Jews out of hospitals, the old Jews out of old people's homes, the young ones—still in bathing suits—off the beaches. They arrested people on the streets and in the hotels. No Jew could feel safe. We were dreadfully afraid for Friedel. Thanks to the fact that my husband was working for the Resistance we were able to send Friedel back to the Château de La Hille where she was safe."

Chapter 81
Edith Moser

I've reached chapter 81 of my work on *The Children of Château de La Hille*, but there is still so much more to tell! There were so many children there, and each of them had his or her own sad story of leaving their families and homes, arriving at Château de La Hille, and from there fleeing to Spain or Switzerland, or joining the Resistance and encountering death.

Many, many children from the Château de La Hille will not find their stories in this book. I hope they will forgive me. But it would be impossible to present all of them. Many paths and many destinies were similar. Most of the children were very lucky, but almost a fifth of the original one hundred lost their lives. This was true, for example, of Kurt Moser whose unlucky attempt to escape to Spain I have written about earlier in the book. His sister Edith chose not to go along with him and remained at the Château, which as it turned out saved her life. After Kurt was arrested, Walter Kammerer took Edith under his wing. He gave her piano lessons and introduced her to the history of literature. They became very close. That was back in 1943, when I was still in charge of the Middles and we built the little train near the New Mill.

At the time of my recovery from my long bout with jaundice, Edith Moser planned to flee to Switzerland with the help of Anne-Marie Piguet. According to the regulations of the Red Cross, everything that happens in the Château must be "legal," that is, acceptable to the Germans. An escape was clearly "illegal." According to our director Miss Groth, an escape would be "legal" only on the condition that a young woman or young man find a position with a family—for example, local farmers—and officially register as such. Once the young woman or man leaves the Red Cross Colony to go live with the farmer or family, then they are "free" to escape, with no blame or responsibility falling on the Château.

With this condition in mind, Miss Groth had found a post for Ilse Brünell with Mrs. Authier, a person who had a high position with the police in Foix, but about whom we were not entirely confident. As for Edith, she was sent to work for the Roubichou family in Varilhes.

All these years I have been in correspondence with Edith, and I asked her to write about her escape from Germany into France with her brother Kurt.

Edith Moser's response:

As conditions worsened in Germany, on February 22, 1939 our parents put Kurt and me on a children's transport run by the Belgian Red Cross. [At the time Edith was fifteen, and Kurt seventeen.] That's how we got to Brussels. Our parents then went to England. When they secured the necessary papers for us to join them, the war had already broken out and no more ships were crossing the English Channel. We escaped into France on May 18 with the children from the boys' home and some others. We traveled for four days in boxcars all across France until we arrived half dead in Toulouse and then were sent to a small colony in Seyre. In Seyre we were allowed to settle in a couple of dilapidated barns, and for a year we lived there under terrible conditions. Some Polish soldiers were also living there. In fear of the soldiers we girls would go to the toilet at night brandishing sticks. We had very little to eat. Most of our bread was eaten by the rats. I remember stealing grapes and ears of corn from the fields; otherwise we would have starved. All of us had diarrhea, and since there were only four toilets for a hundred children plus the soldiers, we sometimes had to go in our underwear. Besides all this, we had brought along a Belgian director from Brussels who made our already miserable lives into hell. For example, if we spoke German to one another, he would lock us up or beat us.

After just a few weeks in France, all those over sixteen were interned and sent to St. Cyprien, a camp further south in France. My brother Kurt, Walter Kammerer and Ilse Brünell were in that group. Meanwhile, we had to be vaccinated, often in unhygienic conditions. In any case, we all came down with jaundice at the same time and nearly died of it. Our Belgian directors suddenly returned to Belgium, but not before taking all our "valuables"— anything we had that might have some value. In addition, we had to sign a paper that we freely gave them everything we had left behind in Belgium. Only Mr. and Mrs. Frank remained with us, and they contacted the Swiss Red Cross to send us Rösli Näf who arranged for our moving to Château de La Hille. All that, you already know. When the over-sixteens returned from Camp St. Cyprien, I almost didn't recognize my brother who had become so thin and badly sunburned.

We were in the first group to go to the Château de La Hille— to clean, install lights, dig a well and sew mattresses filled with horsehair. I remember all the dust from the horsehair and our constant sneezing. Kurt demolished a part of the west tower that was in danger of collapsing. Later when he was working on a farm, he used to bring me a sausage now and then..."

During my visit to San Francisco in 1986, Edith Moser gave me a copy of her journal. Like Edith Goldapper, she described her escape to Switzerland. In order to keep my book from bursting at its seams, I will include here only an excerpt from her 63-page journal:

Edith Moser's Journal (excerpt):

Fribourg, Switzerland, December 29, 1943

The morning of October 27, 1943, Ilse Brünell telephoned me: "Edith, you have to come right away. Geier is here!" "Geier?"— "Yes, the brother of your friend!" Now I understood. She wanted to say Manfred Kammerer, whom the police had been hunting for several weeks. Since I had to take some medicines to Foix for Mr. Roubichou, I had a good excuse for leaving. Despite pouring rain, I jumped on my bicycle and arrived dripping wet at Mr. Perry's (the father of Mireille, Guy and Raoul). I rang the doorbell, and guess who opened the door for me—Manfred Kammerer wearing a big smile! He told me how he had to move from one place to another. No one would take him in; he had no money, no food coupons and no work. It occurred to me that Mrs. Roubichou had spoken of a tailor in Varilhes who needed a helper.

Manfred followed my suggestion and came along with me to Varilhes. Since no one should see him, I hid him in my room and brought him food. Just as I was finishing clearing the table and straightening up the kitchen, the doorbell rang. I opened the door and there was Anne-Marie Piguet, our teacher from the Château. The last time I was at the Château and had spoken with Anne-Marie, she had promised me that when my turn came up to go to Switzerland, she would personally come to tell me. Since here she was in person, I realized that perhaps she had come to fetch me. I led her to my room where she was surprised to see Manfred. "Before I tell you anything," she began, "first sit down." I followed her direction and was very excited to hear her plan. She also sat down and began to explain the details. "Now, don't be alarmed and don't get too excited about what I am about to tell you. We have decided that you should leave for Switzerland today because the others are not ready. They don't have a position yet and may not leave directly from the Château.

Manfred volunteered right away that he would accompany me at least as far as Toulouse, where I probably would find someone else to go further. Meanwhile Miss Anne-Marie had gone to speak with Mrs. Roubichou, my employer, who began to complain that she couldn't do without me and that Anne-Marie would cause trouble for her with the police. If I were to go, Mrs. Roubichou did not want to be implicated in any way. Anne-Marie calmed her down and explained that she had arranged everything so that Mrs. Roubichou would have nothing to do with my departure. Anne-Marie had already gone to the police headquarters to obtain a four-day "pass" so that I could visit the Château. Mrs. Roubichou could say that I had indeed gone off to the Château and had not returned.

I had to hurriedly get my things together. I took all my photos where there wasn't anything German in the background. Other photos and my journal I gave to Miss Anne-Marie for safekeeping. Anne-Marie was writing a letter to Madeleine, my future guide at the Swiss border. Since she wasn't quite finished with the letter, I went to the train station by myself. I was so nervous! I was already sitting in the train, and it was one minute to departure. Anne-Marie still hadn't shown up with the all-important letter! I was on *edge, and ran from one window to the next. As the train already began to move, Anne-Marie came running. "Anne-Marie! I'm here!" I called from the window. She handed me the letter, wished me good luck—and disappeared into the night.*

Foix was the third stop. I got off and hurried with my heavy backpack to Mr. Perry's where I was to meet up with Manfred. It was a lovely evening: Ilse joined us and we ate roasted chestnuts. I wrote a long letter to Walter. Who knows, I thought to myself, if this might be the last one. If we are taken by the Germans, we wouldn't be allowed to write.

I spent the night at Mr. Perry's house. The next morning at 5am Manfred and I set off for the train station. Manfred had only a small briefcase with a change of underwear and such. Around 8am we arrived in Toulouse. The train station was blocked off by the anti-riot police. They were inspecting everyone's papers and baggage to counter any black market activity. I felt sick to my stomach. Manfred had a false identity card with the name Désiré Hermet, but I had nothing! "Don't worry," said Manfred. "No one would think you are nineteen years old, so I'm going to say that you are my little sister. You should call me Dédé from now on!"

It was our turn to be inspected. I tried to look innocent. Manfred showed his card, took me by the hand, and pulled me along. Whew! We were through! We let out a deep breath as we left the train station. We went to the Taur Street office of the Swiss Red Cross to speak with Lucy Farny who had already helped others reach Switzerland. Unfortunately she did not have time to take me to the border. She telephoned a co-worker from the "Union Général Israeli-Française" [UGIF, or the Israeli-French Union] to procure a false identity card for me. That afternoon I went to get my photo taken for my identity card, and at 4pm we had a meeting with René from the UGIF. As he greeted me, he took my hand and discreetly pressed a stamp-pad and my new card into my palm. Carefully and inconspicuously I slipped them into my pocket. We were sitting in a café. When I was sure no one was looking in my direction, I took the two precious items out of my pocket and held them under the table where I pressed my fingerprint onto the card, signed it, and quickly put the card away again. I didn't even look at it out of fear that there might be some Gestapo hanging around. So I didn't know what name René had given me, or where I was supposed to have been born, in what year....

The organization still hadn't located someone to accompany me, so Manfred decided to come along. In order to avoid another stop at the train station, we bought our tickets to Lyon at a travel agency. The train departed at 6pm. I settled down in a corner next to a window and tried to sleep, but in this overcrowded compartment it was next to impossible. The train traveled through Bézier, Montpellier, Nîmes, Avignon and Orange.

Meanwhile I carefully studied my new identity card so that if I were questioned, I would have the correct answers. Since I was supposed to be Manfred's sister, I had the same last name: 'Monique Hermet. Born December 28, 1927 in Dieuze. Current address: Orange, Rue de la Poste.' I carefully imprinted this information on my brain!

Suddenly there was a loud cry. In the corridor filled with farmers and their wares—baskets full of chickens, eggs, geese, rabbits and such—a chicken had gotten free from its cage and was now clucking and flying about in the corridor. The entire car was in an uproar—all because of a chicken! Suddenly I tensed up for a much more serious reason: some Germans got on the train. I slouched even further into my seat, pretending to be asleep. "Ladies and Gentlemen, your papers, please!" I didn't budge.

"Monique, wake up!" Manfred touched me on the arm. Dramatically, I rubbed my eyes and slowly fished out my identity card from my pocket. My heart was beating like mad! I noticed that my face felt alternately flushed and pale. It's a good thing it was dark!

The German nonchalantly looked at my card with his flashlight and gave it back to me. I breathed a sigh of relief. Then I got up and walked down the aisle to an open window, looked out at the starry night, and tried to recover from my fears.

The train went on through Valence and Vienne, and at 7am we arrived in Lyon. At the last minute we were able to jump on the train for Bourg-en-Bresse that was sitting on the opposite platform. Luckily we didn't encounter any inspector. At the gate in Bourg we validated our tickets. We went to the station restaurant to get something to eat, but our snack did little to satisfy our hunger. The bus for Lons-le- Saunier in the Jura came at 4pm. It was a bus intended for forty people, but a hundred got on. There was no air. Exhausted, we arrived in Lons-le-Saunier at 8pm. Following the explicit directions we had been given, we easily found the home of our guide, a pretty twenty-two-year-old woman named Madeleine who opened the door for us. We gave her Anne-Marie's letter. I was so tired that I immediately sat down on a chair.

When Madeleine had finished reading the letter, Manfred explained to her that he had come along to accompany me, but now that he was here he really wanted to go to Switzerland if that was okay with her. She agreed, and I was not unhappy with that decision either. I hadn't really eaten anything, but I had one overpowering wish: to go to bed! I needed some sleep to get ready for our strenuous hike tomorrow. A bed was set up for Manfred in the kitchen, and I slept with Madeleine, our guide."

I'm going to interrupt Edith Moser's journal at this point to avoid a repetition.

Edith Goldapper already wrote in her journal about Anne-Marie's way to get into Switzerland.

Under the guidance of the two sisters—Victoria and Madeleine Cordier—Edith Moser and Manfred Kammerer successfully climbed the long, steep Mount Risoux into their "promised land," where Mr. Piguet, Anne-Marie's father awaited them and had prepared a warm welcome.

A long stretch still lay ahead of them to the forest chalet, where they would again be warmly welcomed.

Actually, Edith could have concluded her journal here with the joyful celebration of attaining her dream that she had pursued for years and was able finally to achieve. She was finally saved!

However, she goes on to write pages and pages about her difficult voyage across Switzerland, full of tears, endless interrogations and examinations. She describes the tiny cells where she was kept prisoner. Always the same question comes up for her: what have I done that I should be treated like a criminal? She is consoled by the words of her dearest friend Walter Kammerer who said: "Whatever troubles and pains may come your way in Switzerland, remember that you are saved!" Edith held fast to this thought and it made her stronger. She also visited friends. (Many children from La Hille had "sponsors" in Switzerland—Mrs. Kaehr, for example, or Mr. Einstein). Those contacts renewed her spirits and gave her courage to persist in her endeavors. When she was released from the various jails, one of which was an army barracks, she was sent to a transit camp in Adliswil, and from there to another camp in a cloister in Fribourg. Mrs. Kaehr was finally able to get her out.

Manfred Kammerer was sent to a work camp...

[Three years after my visit with Edith Moser in San Francisco in 1986, she died of cancer.]

Chapter 82
Notes from Kurt Moser's Diary

W hile I was visiting Edith Moser in San Francisco, she also gave me two small notebooks from the years 1942 and 1943. Inside I found unbelievably miniscule but nevertheless very legible writing. These were Kurt Moser's notes from his daily diary. I am citing his entries concerning three different events.

August 26, 1942: Transfer to a camp.

Tuesday, August 25: I clear away the brambles at Serre, the farm where I work. Wednesday, August 26: At 7 o'clock two policemen pick me up in a car. From Serre we drive toward the Château. All those over sixteen years old were taken by bus to Camp Vernet, also the Schlesingers and Mrs. Frank Junior....Where is Edith?

Thurday, August 27: Adequate food supply. Twice a day we get soup made from bouillion cubes, onions, potatoes, grapes and bread. Afternoons peeling potatoes and onions in the kitchen. Wrote to Melanie [a farmer in Borda Blanca who took in many of the older kids] so that she could keep Mom up-to-date with our news.

Friday, August 28: Miss Näf shows up. She stays with us. Mr. Dubois goes to Vichy to plead our case. Miss Näf thinks we will be freed.

Saturday, August 29: Mr. Dubois accompanies the Colonel [the camp officer]. We need to be patient. Next time we will be in La Hille. We stuffed mattresses and set up barracks.

Sunday, August 30: Werner, the camp cook, makes us delicious meatballs for Sunday Monday, August 31: Mattresses stuffed. Eat again in the kitchen after almost every meal. Evenings we have a concert.

Tuesday, September 1: in the morning they tell us: You must be packed up in half an hour. OK then! When the names are read out, ours are not included. What I saw that morning I had never seen before. Heartbreaking scenes. We help where we can. Then our barrack is almost empty. That afternoon the Colonel arrived. We were driven back to the Château the next afternoon. That evening Mr. Lyrer arrived loaded down with packages.

Wednesday, September 2: Morning help a bit in the kitchen. 11am we leave Camp Vernet by train over Pamiers and Varilhes toward St. Jean de Verges. Farmers wait there for us with wagons. Around 5pm we are back at the Château. It was all like a bad dream. Dining-hall festively decorated.

A few months later: Kurt Moser's Trip to Switzerland with Onze

Thursday, December 31, 1942: 2am: Leave the Château with Onze. Each of us has 2,000 Francs, some bread, cheese and chocolate. As baggage Edith's briefcase. Walter Strauss, Inge Joseph, Manfred Vos, Adele Hochberger and Inge Helft also leave.

5:30am: Bus from Sabayat to Carbonne. Train to Toulouse. There validate tickets. Spend the day in waiting room. The others were there also. In the evening Miss Näf comes.

7:25pm: Departure. Between Narbonne and Béziers Onze sits between two policemen and a German soldier. Good luck in the New Year!

Friday, January 1: Arrive in Lyon in the morning.

Saturday, January 2: Noon departure from Lyon. Ducked the control officers on the train. Arrived around 7pm in St. Cergues. Dark. Immediately head for the border. At first didn't find the barbed wire fence. Then: we are in Switzerland! But border patrol saw us and take us to a small town. Had to stand before a border patrol officer, then taken to police station. Since we are over 16-years-old, without relatives and without papers, we must go back. I run away, but am immediately caught. Taken to border in truck. Go through the barbed wire fence. Back in France.

Sunday, January 3: Onze does not want to try again. We split up. I climb over the high barbed wire fence and rip open my hand. Swirling snow. I can't get oriented. I lay down from 10:30pm to

5:30am. Ice cold. More snow.—Start running. Mountains recede more and more. Always stayed on small path. After going about 10 kilometers, see a small village. Patrols in gray-green: Germans. The border control officer calls me into his office. I was in France! They record my information. Spent the day at the border patrol office. Ate well. My hand was taken care of. In the evening took a sled to the police station in Douvaine. I was searched. They took my money, watch, knife and briefcase. Then they put me into a dark cellar. Later a policeman gave me something to eat.

Monday, January 4: Morning in Douvaine, ate something. Then bus to Thonon-les-Bains. Brought before the examining magistrate. Did I want a lawyer? Yes. Do you want to make a statement now or in the presence of your lawyer?—The latter. Taken to police headquarters. First the office, then again the black cellar.

Tuesday, January 5: Morning in the train to Annecy. In front of the entrance to the prison another policeman with Walter Strauss! He had fallen into the hands of the French, the others were taken by the Germans. Inge Joseph had managed to escape, the others put on a train for Drancy.—They completely undressed me in the prison. The guards were disgusting. They put me into a cell for adolescents with Walter and others, two of them Jews.

Wednesday, January 6: Prison rations. For Jews 400 grams of bread. At 8:30am "café au lait." At 9am and 11am "beetsoup" = hot water with some slices of beets. At 4pm soup. Every Wednesday two pieces of cheese.—Get up at 7am, go to bed at 6pm.

Thursday, January 7: Sixteen of us transferred by bus to Thonon. Paired up two by two with handcuffs. Came before the examining magistrate. In the evening sent back.

Because Kurt, like Walter Strauss, had tried to cross the border illegally, they both were sentenced to fourteen days in prison. After completion of this sentence they returned to Château de La Hille.

A Half Year Later: Delivered to the Gestapo

Sunday, June 6, 1943: What about Spain? Those born in 1920, 21 and 22 were rounded up and sent to Germany for hard labor. Since many escaped, the borders were under even stricter surveillance. That can't last too much longer. I will still end up in Poland. Sunday, June 13: There are official "ads" warning the Jews: 'Disappear in three weeks. New deportations are planned!' I have never heard of such injustice!

Monday, June 14: In the morning driven again to Mr. A's. Before one or two weeks, nothing can be done. He already has so many hidden at his place. In the afternoon again spoke with F. He thinks 30,000 Fr would cover all ten of us. Go ahead and bring me the answer tomorrow.

Tuesday June 15: thirty kilometers by foot to Mrs. G. The 'smuggler' is back. Looks like it won't work since a crossing is virtually impossible. Because of the mobilization of workers the border is incredibly well guarded. Talked to F. that evening. It's on.

Departure: Friday night.

Tuesday evening. I'm finished with this book. It will go with all my other things (photos, diaries and papers) to Melanie for safekeeping. Hopefully we will get through to our dear Mother [Kurt and Edith's mother was very lucky to get to safety in England.] *Hopefully we can pay off our debt of gratitude to Mr. Dubois.*

Friday, June 18, 1943 [last entry]: *We meet up during the night. We: Edith, Werner, Edgar, Charles, Addi, Fritz, Mr. Meyer, two young Frenchmen and myself. That night F. will bring us to the 'smuggler,' who will set out immediately. Partly on foot, partly in a small truck.*

[Kurt had a bad feeling. He noted on the last page:] *"Perhaps we are already nabbed and en route to Poland! But one has to try. Poland one week more or less doesn't matter. But maybe I should have left my little Edith at the Château?"*

Luckily Edith did stay at the Château! Addi and Edgar, overcome with fear, turned around before getting to the meeting place and returned to the Château. Mr. Meyer did not show up at the meeting point.

In Kurt's diary I found one final remark written by Walter Kammerer:
"Yes, my dear Kurt, unfortunately it did go badly. We received the bad news yesterday evening, and the few of us who knew about it are with you in all our thoughts. I hope from the bottom of my heart that we will see each other again or that at least you will find this little book again in happier times. As long as I can think and wish, my thoughts and wishes go with you. I thank you profoundly for your friendship. Will we once again be able to celebrate our friendship?—Take care, my dear Kurt. As long as I live, I will remain your faithful friend.—Walter

Chapter 83
Kurt Moser's Death

Of the twelve children from Château de La Hille who were deported, Werner Eppstein is the only survivor. When he came back from the concentration camp, he wrote Edith Moser the following letter:

Viroflay, October 2, 1945

My dear little Edith! Thank you so much for your dear letter that brought me such joy. I see that although you were able to await the end of the war in relative peace and enjoy rather normal relationships, you never forgot us. When one lives in filth and sorrow and is condemned to death, it helps to know that one's friends are thinking about them. It was a life that one cannot even imagine, let alone forget. I was a miner. I worked in a coalmine two hundred meters deep, standing up to my belly in water. I shoveled coal for twelve hours straight, constantly driven by blows and kicks delivered by the SS, who had the honorable task of gradually finishing us off. After these excruciating twelve hours when one could only stagger, as if drunk, to the hoisting-cage, hardly able to stand up from exhaustion, we still had to march four kilometers back to the camp. In winter, that glacial Polish winter, soaked to the skin, they would treat us in the camp like wild animals. We always held out the hope that when we got back to the camp we could sink into bed. In order not to feel hunger, we tried forgetting about it. In these conditions, most of the time they still made us exercise, and the SS would throw pails of warm water over us. The SS knew their job! And all of this took place in winter.

That's just a little sketch of what went on, my dear Edith. I will not tell you more because you would not even be able to believe it, or suppose it was even possible. It's better this way.

Well, dear Edith, you write that I was a lucky one. But I must tell you that at this moment I am the unluckiest person because you have asked me to tell you about your dear brother Kurt. Do you really want to hear the bare truth? Well, then, here it is: Kurt worked with me in the coal mine Rudolf in Jadvizna for roughly four or five months. One fine day he came down with diarrhea. For three weeks I was not allowed to visit him. You have to know that even a father was not allowed to visit his son in the sick ward. Nevertheless, I managed to see him.

Dear Edith, you cannot even imagine how shaken I was to see that my sweet Moser, my good friend, had become a skeleton, weighing only about fifty pounds. He laughed and was in a good mood, even happy, that he would not have to suffer much longer. What he said to me, I will never forget. "My dear Eppelstein, you will and you must survive. Above all, you must look up my dear sister and tell her that I thought about her all the time and that Mama must never learn what became of me. I simply went missing, do you hear, Eppelstein? That is very important! And don't forget to send my greetings to Ilse Wulf and all my friends." Two days later he was sent by car to Auschwitz. To my question the doctor in charge said: "Crematorium!"

There you have the accursed truth that today still shatters my nerves. I have learned to hate this truth.

Yours, Werner

Chapter 84
We Are Free!

ugen Lyrer was always better informed than the rest of us about what was going on. One morning he showed up at my classroom by surprise, stood in the doorway, and said to me in Swiss-German: "Take off your shoes! I have a secret for you!" I went over to him but didn't take off my shoes. I was used to his practical joking. But this time, with a meaningful look, he pointed to a letter—the 'secret.' "And besides," he said, his voice quivering with excitement, his face glowing and his eyes beaming—"We are free! The Maquis have driven out the Germans from Pamiers and Foix!"

I was speechless with surprise and joy. Eugen went on with more details about his amazing news: "The Maquis captured the SS living in Foix, and made them march through the whole city before they took them to the Gestapo headquarters and hanged them there." I stood as if rooted to the ground and couldn't quite comprehend what he was saying. "Now the murderers have received their wages!" he said and went off. I closed the door after him. The children sat dumbstruck at their places. They understood that something special had happened.

I slowly went up to the blackboard. The children watched me carefully, and couldn't wait to hear what I was going to say. I couldn't hold it in any longer: "We're free!" I cried with excitement "The Maquis have driven out the Germans from Foix and Pamiers!"

The children didn't seem to understand. "Do you remember 'the walk from hell,' that terrible outing and your promise?"

The children nodded. "One may not say a word about it," Guy called out. "That's right. But now everything has changed. We are free!

The Maquisards,

the resistance fighters, no longer have to hide. They have driven the Germans out! It's marvelous news! Do you know what that means?"

Friedel was the first to get it: "The police in Pailhès will no longer be hunting for Jews!"

"Right! You are saved, Friedel! The gendarmes will no longer come to get Jews for the Germans. The Germans are gone, finished. They can't hurt us anymore. Let's take a break. Afterwards we will talk some more, and you can ask questions."

In the courtyard I met up with Heiri, Eugen and the Spaniards. We were all excited to talk about our liberation. It was at the post-office in Montégut that Eugen heard this almost unbelievable report. "It was pretty gruesome," he explained. "Mainly it was Spanish resistance fighters that liberated Foix. There was a lot of shooting but the Gestapo could not hold out for very long. The resistance fighters had the upper hand because the German troops had pulled out just before the attack." Eugen recounted to us everything that took place. The French collaborators were also shot. The women who had affairs with the Germans had their heads shaved and were paraded around in the streets.

While I was returning to my class after this lengthy break, I thought of Egon and Onze who had lost their lives in the Maquis. "If they had stayed at the Château, they would still be alive!" But who could have known that? We were so convinced that the Germans would come to get Walter, and that if they had come, they would take all the Jews, the little ones as well as the older ones.

Chapter 85
Onze Resurrected!

O ne morning in mid-August, two or three weeks after our liberation, I was sitting in the courtyard in front of the kitchen window, my right leg resting on a stool. Furunculosis had gotten me too! With the boils on my leg, I could barely stand and walk, and teaching was out of the question. So I was cutting the children's hair. Guy was next up when we heard a surprising sound we hadn't heard in a very long time. It startled us. A motorcycle drove past the east side of the Château, then turned around and drove with ear-splitting noise through our entrance right into the courtyard. It braked not far from me and two men jumped off.

I couldn't believe my eyes, couldn't grasp what I was seeing, but there right in front of us stood Onze and Ruedi Oelbaum! They stood next to the motorcycle and looked around, laughing and beaming, soldiers returning home after winning the battle. My school children who had been playing close by were surprised and frightened. I too was speechless. I knew that Onze was dead, and now he was standing there, grinning from ear to ear! Despite the pain, I quickly got up and rushed towards them. "Onze!" I cried. "Ruedi!" Beside myself with joy, I shook their hands and clapped Onze on the shoulder. "You're alive! Fantastic! You're alive! We thought you were dead!"

Then Heiri, Eugen, Annelies and the Spaniards all came out and warmly greeted our two resistance fighters. I couldn't take my eyes off Onze. "Onze is alive!" I kept repeating to myself. I was overwhelmed by a kind of joy I had never before experienced. Even though I could barely stand, I no longer paid any attention to my boils. Ruedi was wearing the khaki uniform of the newly formed French army—the FFI, "the French Forces of the Interior"—and showed us his belt. The belt had belonged to a German soldier and had carved on the metal buckle "God is with us!" We were enraged by this shameless blasphemy! That the German soldiers, their collaborators, the SS and Gestapo were mercilessly murdering all over Europe and still invoked God's blessing was beyond comprehension. In the face of such hateful impudence, we could only shake our heads.

Then the two of them began to tell us their stories. Until just the day before, Onze had been sitting in St. Michel's prison in Toulouse. He was set free at the same time as the liberation of the city. He immediately set out for Château de La Hille.

Where else could he go? Between Pailhès and Montégut Ruedi picked him up on a borrowed motorcycle. Up until a few days before, Ruedi had been in charge of a prisoner-of-war camp with a few hundred German soldiers. He along with his resistance fighter comrades had captured most of these German soldiers himself under very risky conditions.

Rita Kuhlberg, one of the few older girls who had remained at the Château, interrupted Ruedi's engrossing story by ringing the bell for lunch. After lunch we all met up again in the salon to hear more about Onze's and Ruedi's adventures.

Soon after that time that Heiri and I had brought food and blankets to Onze, Egon, Ruedi, Joseph and Georges in their "hut" about the New Mill, they joined the Maquis, as we had heard. Ruedi told us about their surprise attacks on German convoys. "We always worked in pairs," he explained. "One of us would throw a hand- grenade, the other would fire the machine gun, then we would disappear. When we attacked, we were always well positioned to be able to retreat into the *Maquis* where the Germans had no chance of capturing us. The English furnished our weapons. Each of our larger fighting groups had a small radio transmitter, dropped by parachute into our region, that was operated by an English expert. We gave our orders always under the same code words. Our own code for the BBC Personal News was: 'The sun warms the rock.' Every hour we would listen to the news report on the BBC. If we heard our code—'the sun warms the rock'—we knew that on an agreed upon spot that we would signal by fire, the necessary materials (food, weapons and ammunition) would be dropped, always between midnight and 1am."

Intrigued by his account, we now had the solution to our puzzling over the meaning of the 'personal news' portion of the BBC broadcast. But we were still eager to know what had happened to Egon, Joseph and Georges. Were they still alive? We had believed that Onze and Egon were dead. But now that we had Onze alive and breathing right in front of us, the report of the death of the two boys we knew to be false. Eugen couldn't hold back any longer. "Onze, Ruedi, tell us what's happened to Egon. Where is he?"

This question hung in the air for what seemed like an eternity. It made me shiver with the presentiment that he had indeed died. The ensuing silence only confirmed it. In a tense voice Onze finally announced: "Egon is dead." We were silent, numbed. Egon dead... But what had happened? We all stared at Onze. I had never seen him look so serious. He seemed to have aged right there before our eyes. "Egon is dead," he said again in a monotone, and played nervously with his cap. "Listen," he paused, "I will tell you the whole sad story. I was nearly killed along with him." He cleared his throat...

"It was the beginning of July. For several days we found ourselves in a desperate situation in the mountains of Roquefixade. We were encircled by German troops, but they themselves did not dare enter the *Maquis* or directly attack us. Instead they sent in the notorious, deeply hated *Miliciens*—the much-feared French Gestapo founded by General Durand. The FFI [the French Forces of the Interior] groups coded 'Gaby' and 'Oskar' had suffered heavy losses, while we had managed to break through the surrounding German line. In a rocky valley by Armentière, not far from Pamiers, we made camp late that night. Beneath a high rock I stood watch.

Because of a full moon, the night was so bright that I could see the whole valley. I watched our enemy camp for the night far beneath me, so I thought we were safe for the time being. I held my rifle ready and took note of every noise.—Then suddenly a barrage of gunfire! From fear my heart nearly stopped, and I fell to the ground. Shells whistled over my head and ricocheted off the rocks. Before I could even fire in retaliation, I was hit and lost consciousness. It was a miracle they didn't kill me.

Undoubtedly they wanted me alive to extort information!"

"For me things went better," Ruedi continued the account. "I was asleep next to Egon Berlin. When I heard the shooting, I threw myself into the nearest bush.

Egon wanted to do the same thing, but unfortunately stood up and got hit once or twice in the shoulder. He crumpled, and the *Miliciens* were on him. Some of them cried 'shoot him.' The night was so clear I could see everything. What happened right there before my very eyes in just a few seconds was atrocious. I saw Egon on his knees with his hands in the air. 'Don't kill me,' he pleaded. But the *Miliciens* mercilessly beat him with the butt of their rifles. They didn't notice me, for I had moved back deeply into the thickets. But I could see everything. As things quieted down and the shots came few and far between, right in front of me I saw Onze being carried off. Just for a second I saw his bloody face in the moonlight. He must be dead, I thought. And then, just as suddenly, it became totally still, as if it had been only a dream, a nightmare. I crawled out of my hiding place over to Egon. He lay on the ground, his broken arms stretched out. He was dead. There was nothing I could do for him."

We sat there in silence, speechless. One of our own was gone, his life taken in a most gruesome way.

Today, Egon Berlin's name is on a war monument in Pamiers. His parents survived and inscribed on the monument: "Dearest Egon, we will never forget you! Your loving parents."

Chapter 86

The Summer Months

The summer went by quickly. We no longer suffered under that oppressive worry: our Jewish children, little and big, were no longer in danger. The Germans were vanquished. Like criminals—which they were—they were chased by the Allies across all of France toward the Rhine. From the east the Russians were approaching Berlin.

At the Château we were enjoying the beautiful, warm summer days, taking excursions, and organizing afternoons of play and swimming at the New Mill. The evenings were long, staying light until 10pm. Often, in the evening after dinner and the kitchen was cleaned up, we would climb the hill very close by on the way to Borda Blanca, sit on the grass and under Heiri's direction sing all the songs that came to mind, learning some new ones as well.

One evening on our way back to the Château as it was already getting dark, Heiri unsettled me with some surprising news. He confided in me that he and Annelies would be returning to Switzerland as soon as possible. Instead of just six months, they had already stayed in France for close to a year. I was dumbfounded and couldn't respond. I climbed up to my little room, dismayed and depressed. The thought of Heiri's leaving us was hard to take. I felt the floor being pulled out from under my feet.

Eugen also wanted to leave the Château. He went to Toulouse, and returned angry and upset. "Unbelievable!" he said. "The Swiss border is still hermetically closed. It's impossible to go home! One needs a visa! What nonsense!"

We remembered the time when Miss Tobler was endlessly waiting for her visa that never did come. Eugen's news was a shock for Heiri as well. As for me, however, it was a relief. Heiri couldn't believe this old visa shenanigans. For France the war was over! Heiri soon went to Toulouse himself to check at the Red Cross office in Taur Street. The nasty Mr. Parera gave him the same information that Eugen had received. "Without a visa, one cannot cross the border," Mr. Parera said complacently. No doubt he was glad that his Red Cross co-workers would not be able to leave their posts and return home.

Infuriated, Heiri said angrily: "A Swiss citizen doesn't need a visa to return home!"

"But the French are demanding that every foreigner secure an exit visa," Mr. Parera responded. "Nonsense!" Heirie shouted. "Surely not for the Swiss who work for the Red Cross!"

Parera shrugged his shoulders. Heiri calmed down a bit and after a pause asked: "Why haven't we received any mail for the last several months? Couldn't the Red Cross do something about that for us?" Irritated, Parera answered that the borders were closed for the mail also. He did not say that every week an employee of the Red Cross left from Annecy for Geneva, to pick up the Swiss mail. That would mean that we could have written to Annecy, and our parents to Geneva!

Like Eugen, Heiri returned to the Château terribly angry. Clearly the Red Cross was playing games with us. What to do? Heiri didn't see any solution. To whom could one even go to secure an exit visa?

We needed a diversion. The weather was gorgeous, and so we decided to go on a three-day excursion with the Middles. Anne-Marie was no longer with us. She would never dare to come back because the tyrannical Mr. Parera in Toulouse would no doubt have humiliated her and sent her home. Annelies couldn't come on the excursion because she had to stay in the kitchen. Eugen didn't feel like coming and volunteered to take charge of my Mickeys. So Heiri and I with the young teenaged boys and girls set off over the mountain—where Walter had been hiding—in the direction of Tambouret—where Egon and Edgar used to work on the farm.

Toward evening we stopped by at the Schmutz family. They spoiled us with bread and butter and a glass of milk. It was an extraordinary treat for all of us who were constantly hungry! We happily slept on hay in the barn, and the whole next day we spent at the Ariège River, roughly ten kilometers from Tambouret. On the river we swam and played, returning that evening to Tambouret tired, hungry and content.

The next day we hiked home. All in all, it was a wonderful excursion, not to even mention the grand hospitality of the Schmutz family that genuinely touched our hearts. We vowed to repeat this excursion in the future, but sadly it turned out to be impossible.

Shortly after our hiking trip it was August 1, a Swiss National holiday. We began the holiday on our own little hill, and Heiri gave an August 1 speech. After having spent three years of service at the Château de La Hille, Eugen Lyrer departed on his (illegal) trip back to Switzerland two or three weeks later.

Heiri again went to Toulouse to find a replacement for himself, but had no luck. Nevertheless, Mrs. Pedrini, the mother of Jean Pedrini, one of our newer Middles, soon came to help out. Her husband was deported on the last train, the so- called "Ghost Train" that had left for Germany. That train trip lasted for weeks, since the resistance fighters constantly forced the train to take detours. Mrs. Pedrini was a great help to Annelies and was lined up to be her replacement.

The idea of Heiri's leaving truly made me ill. I could not imagine my life at the Château without him. In addition, Heiri and Annelies wanted to go home to Switzerland by way of Nice in order to bring Monique back to her parents who were still living there. The reader may recall that during their wedding trip Heiri and Annelies stopped in Nice to pick up Monique Evrard and bring her to the Château.

This pretty young woman had won over the hearts of everyone at the Château, including mine, and her departure from La Hille would have been unbearable for me. So I decided that I would leave the Château with Heiri, Annelies and Monique. I wrote a letter stating my intentions to the Red Cross on Taur Street, but received no answer. The people in Toulouse would not lift a finger for us! Miss Groth took steps to find a replacement for me and was successful. One day at the beginning of October, a French teacher came to visit. She was prepared to take over my classes that had already begun in September.

Technically, as a foreigner in France, I had no right to be teaching. One time a "Director of Primary Schools" came by and made us aware of this prohibition. But before leaving, he told us with a wink of the eye that he was not aware of anything amiss and would keep his eyes (and mouth) shut.

Heiri returned to Toulouse for the third or fourth time. It was already the end of October. He spoke again with the men at the Red Cross office on Taur Street and explained that because of his sick mother-in-law, he and his wife would be leaving the Château de La

Hille to return to Switzerland. The thick-set Parera, who obviously never suffered from hunger, was very annoyed by Heiri's stubbornness and repeated what he had already said: it was pointless to travel to the Swiss border because it was closed. Parera could easily have drafted some sort of "pass" on his stationery with the Red Cross letterhead, and stamped it with the "Children's Aid Society" and other such organizations. But that was not in his own interest, so he didn't lift a finger to help.

Heiri returned with a certain Marcel Gontier. I don't know how he managed to find this French teacher, but in any case Heiri had his replacement!

Chapter 87
Farewell to the Château

S o we had three replacements: for Annelies, Heiri and myself. Heiri was in a hurry to leave, but the departure kept getting pushed back. On the one hand, I was very happy to be traveling with Heiri, Annelies and Monique to Nice, but on the other hand, it was very painful for me to leave the Château and especially the children. I felt tired and rundown, and suffered from the boils on my leg, though they were not nearly as bad as the jaundice. But the longer they lasted, the more depressed I became. I tried to console myself by saying that I must go home because my health was shot.

Without paying attention to time's passing, we somehow found ourselves at the end of October, and then on our last day at the Château. I almost couldn't dare to look at the children, and felt I had betrayed them. Heiri apparently felt the same way. To assuage our guilty consciences we organized a festive afternoon. In the dining hall we pushed the tables aside and made a circle with the benches. We played one game after another: races, guessing games, songs, charades and so on.

We did our best to give the children a happy last day.

After supper—Mrs. Pedrini had taken over the kitchen—we all met up in the big classroom. On tables and benches, footstools and on the floor, all the children found a place to sit down for our last sing-along with Heiri. At first the songs sounded lively and up-beat, but then became slower and more muted, as if a black cloud hung over the children's heads. Gradually the singing faded out, and a strange stillness filled the room. The few older ones that were still at the Château—Irma Seelenfreund, Rita and Fanny Kuhlberg, Trude Dessauer and Martha Storosom—got up and left the room. The Middles and the Mickeys didn't budge but looked silently at Heiri, Annelies and me with seemingly reproachful glances. They all knew what was going on. They all understood. After a long, oppressive silence, Heiri spoke softly, with great difficulty, just four words: "Tomorrow we are leaving!"

For a while, nothing happened. Then twelve-year-old Jeanine Jacquet, always disheveled with her red hair in little braids, put her head down on her arms and broke out in heart-rending sobs. That worked like a signal: all the children began crying and weeping unabatedly. I had never experienced anything like it. I sat there, helpless on my stool. My heart felt pinched, and I silently sent Heiri some bitter reproaches: Why couldn't we simply have stayed here? What do I have to do in Switzerland anyway?

I could have stayed, alone so to speak, with the director. Anne-Marie, as already mentioned, was not coming back here after she successfully guided Walter Kammerer, Mrs. Schlesinger and her son Pauli into Switzerland. Eugen's illegal entry into Switzerland seemed to have been a success. In any case, he didn't keep in touch with us. No, I couldn't let Heiri and Annelies leave just like that. In our work together we had become so close, so bound up with one another.

Deeply moved, sad and depressed I sat there looking at my weeping children from the Château de La Hille. Heiri finally pulled himself together, clapped his hands and called out: "It's time for everyone to go to bed." Not one child moved. They sat there crying. How could we console them?

On this last night at the Château I didn't go to bed. I was too upset to sleep. I kept busy in my little room, packed one of my two suitcases, but decided to take along only the most necessary items. All the clothes that I could spare I would leave behind. My suitcase remained half empty.

Around midnight I wandered through the Château—like that time more than a year ago when I was plagued with jaundice and wandered deliriously through the hallways and up and down the stairs. For the last time I went to see the Mickeys in their dormitory. I walked quietly along the rows of beds, looking at the sleeping children who had become so familiar, but would no longer be "my" children: Conchita, Guy, André and François, Josette, René and Violette. In the little room next door I threw a final glance at Jeanne who had caused me so much trouble once upon a time, but she hadn't wet her bed in a very long while. All of the former bed-wetters had been cured. Next to Jeanne lay

Peggy and Friedel. I caressed Friedel's hair and said softly: "Goodbye, my children, your teacher is leaving you."

Near the big classroom I bumped into Marcel Gontier, the new teacher. "Couldn't sleep," he said. "I couldn't stop thinking about your departure, so I wrote a poem for you!" He read me a long, touching poem about saying goodbye.

At four in the morning we left the Château in total darkness. Reaching the Lèze, I looked back at the Château for the last time. In the dark I could make out the familiar walls and towers that reached toward the sky. Sadly, I left the Château de La Hille and its children behind me and headed into the great unknown.

Chapter 88
The Illegal Trip Home

Our trip to the Swiss border was long, tiring and complicated. Most of the trains were not running, and many of the bridges had been blown up. Hitchhiking by truck, it took us six days to get to Nice. On the Cote d'Azur not a single tree remained standing. Instead of the beautiful Mediterranean coast, we saw masses of entangled barbed wire and bombed out areas. In Nice we delivered Monique to her overjoyed parents. Standing on the roadside trying to flag down a truck, it took us six more days to get to Annecy. There were hardly any automobiles.

When we finally arrived in Annecy, we went to the office of the Swiss Children's Aid Society and were told what we already knew: the Swiss borders were closed and leaving France without an exit visa was impossible. And here's the payoff: the Swiss who worked for years under difficult conditions for the Red Cross and were engaged in saving the children, many of whom were French, were not allowed to re-enter their home country of Switzerland!

We had no other choice but to find a position in a Red Cross colony close to the Swiss border. In Cruseilles we climbed to the Château des Avenières, where the director, Madame Hofer, wearing a white apron and smoking a cigarette hanging from the corner of her mouth, welcomed us.

At the end of December Heiri and Annelies illegally crossed the border back into Switzerland. They were not caught.

On February 14, 1945, I tried my luck. On a farmer's wagon I was driven along the border near Carouge, and I was firmly convinced that just behind the barbed wire fence, the entire Swiss army was waiting for me! Although I had practically no chance in getting across, late one night I managed to clamber, unseen, over the two formidable fences and then to drag my suitcase underneath. I was stopped en route to Geneva when I was unfortunate enough to have asked the way from a border patrol agent! I had to trek the long way back to the border. At the customs station I found the officer in charge to be most unfriendly. I showed him my pass and said quite unnecessarily that I was Swiss. That didn't interest him in the slightest. "All those who cross the border illegally are refugees," he explained coldly. A small van picked me up around midnight and transported me to Camp de Calparède in Geneva where I was interrogated until 1:30am. After a bath—and half starved as I was—they had the good will to offer me a snack. The next day I was again interrogated and finally released around noon.

Chapter 89

A Terrible Ending

In February 1945 Miss Groth finally left the Château. She was urgently needed elsewhere. A certain Mr. Claude and his fiancée came to take over. He knew very little about childhood education, and—with the exception of dealing once with a group of boy scouts—also had little practical experience with children. At the Château de La Hille he turned everything topsy-turvy, and once he had exhausted its supplies, he called for a truck from Toulouse.

This particular truck had a history. During the Spanish Civil War, the truck was put to good use by a group, led by Olgiati, working for civilian aid. After the war, the truck was taken over by the civil service on Taur Street in Toulouse. The truck was used to supply food to the hundred children living in Seyre who would later become the children of Château de La Hille. When the Toulouse branch of the Swiss Children's Aid Society was united with the Swiss Red Cross, the truck became the Red Cross Children's Aid truck. It was painted white, and on its doors was imprinted the insignia of "Children's Aid" with its two children's heads beneath the rays of the Swiss Red Cross.

The truck sometimes came to deliver food supplies to the Château de La Hille or to transport new children to the Château. The new director, Mr. Claude, ordered this truck from Toulouse to go shopping for supplies in Pamiers. This was something Miss Groth had never been able to arrange, but Mr. Claude succeeded. The Toulouse office sent the truck, but unfortunately not with the Spaniard Mr. Salvide who knew the engine's tricks very well, but with a newly hired Swiss driver who was quite unfamiliar with it. As we shall see, that led to a catastrophe.

At the Château, everyone was preparing for the shopping trip to Pamiers. Mr. Palau and Mr. Marimon went along to help with loading the supplies. Despite the Spaniards' objections, the director, Mr. Claude took along four or five boys whom he particularly liked. "You'll see, everything will be fine!" said Mr. Claude en route.

Later, when the truck was fully loaded with fruits, vegetables, potatoes and other items, things began to go less well. "You see, Mr. Director, this will not work!" warned Mr. Marimon. "We don't have enough room for the boys."

The director laughed. "Everything will be fine. I will sit with two boys on the roof of the driver's cabin." And that's exactly what he did. One boy sat on his left, the other on his right.

The Spaniards sat with their backs to the cabin, and the truck set off again. On the way, they picked up an old woman—after all, they had so much room! Mr. Palau offered the woman his seat and stood for the remainder of the trip—to his death.

They were driving fast and making good progress. Mr. Claude was satisfied.

They could already see the schoolhouse in Montégut. "We're almost there," he cried. And that's when it happened. The truck overturned and rested at the side of the road, its wheels in the air.

The two barely-injured boys ran to the Château to sound the alarm. Everyone at the Château set off for the site of the accident. Ahead of them all ran Mrs. Palau, overcome with foreboding. What a sight to behold, as they came into Montégut. She told me about it later: "It was terrible. My husband was screaming and howling in the middle of the street. I ran up to him, but I could barely recognize him. His face was covered with deep cuts, red with blood. All around was total chaos. Potatoes, tomatoes, shattered crates, and the wounded children screaming like my husband!" The director's fiancée found him dead, not far from Mr. Marimon who lay on the side of the street with broken shoulders.

"It was dreadful! I was with my husband three days and three nights in the hospital. He screamed and screamed. He was blinded. Then he died. It was dreadful," she repeated again and again, totally demoralized.

That was the end!

La Hille was closed. The children who still had a home were sent home. The others were sent to various Red Cross colonies. Especially deplorable was Mrs. Palau's situation after her husband's death. With her children—little Pepito, Conchita, Jacques and the little Monique—she was abandoned by the Red Cross. They offered her no help. Mr. Parera advised her to return to Spain.

Epilogue

E leven children from Château de La Hille did not survive. Four of them had reached Switzerland but were shortly thereafter expelled, arrested by the Germans, deported and killed.

A group of American Quakers took 22 children. The Swiss took none! Why? Because "the boat was too full"! The Swiss government always acted under the direction of Germany. A prime example was the Swiss installation of an immense barbed wire fence along its borders. Swiss General Henri Guisan's army was prepared to capture and send back any Jews that managed to cross the border. "Sending them back" often amounted to sending them to their death. With tremendous courage and fortitude, some children from Château de La Hille did manage to cross illegally into Switzerland despite many obstacles and heavy surveillance on the border. Their success was largely due to Anne-Marie Piguet's guidance over Mount Risoux and a bit of good luck near the Red Cross colony at St. Cergues.

As it turned out, the Switzerland that profited so opulently from the war, quite unintentionally and inadvertently did save 21 children from the Château de La Hille, but not one of them was admitted legally into Switzerland.

P.S. In the spring of 1946, I completed my Master's thesis on my "waking therapy" in connection with Pavlov's theory of the conditioned reflex. I had already completed the practical experience and data-collection while I was working in the infirmary at La Hille, so all that was left to do was the required theoretical aspect of my thesis. I carried out my research at the University of Zürich Library, where I consulted all the books and journal articles already published on the topic of enuresis, or "bed- wetting." In the course of my research, I came upon the work of a certain Mr. Ufensteiner. Unbelievably, this

Ufensteiner had already published all that I had theoretically worked out in my head during my duties at the Château de La Hille. So I wrote up my practical experience, went to my professor, and explained what I had found in Ufensteiner's work. My professor gave me credit for my research into the theoretical aspects of my thesis and was satisfied with the practical side of my work. And thus I earned my diploma!

Appendix 1: What happened to the Children

Overview of the Fate of the Original 100 Jewish Children from the Château de La Hille:

1. Before the attack on the Château de La Hille on August 26, 1942, the following 22 children and Jews were taken by a group of American Quakers to America and thus were saved. In parentheses are their birthdates. The capital letters G = Germany, A = Austria and P = Poland, indicate their country of origin:

   Blau Rosa (1931) G Eckann Gérard (1929) G

   Eisler Bernhard (1928) P

   Findling Joseph (1928) G

   Findling Martin (1932) G

   Findling Siegfried (1930) G

   Flanter Klara (1929) G

   Flanter Lore (1934) G

   Kammer Herbert (1931) A

   Kantor Arthur (1926) A

   Kantor Eva (1928) A Krolik

   Max (1928)P Krolik

   Rosette (1933) P

   Obersitsker Gert (1925) G

   Rinsberg Werner (1924) G

   Schlimmer Hanni (1926) G

   Steinhardt Jules (1930) G

   Steinhardt Kurt (1930) G

   Steuer Antoinette (1936) P

   Sostheim Klaus (1926) G

   Weinmann Rolf (1931) G

   Wolpert Willy (1930) G

2. The Exodus of the "Older" ones between December 20, 1942 and January 4, 1943

   a To Spain:

   Berlin Inge (1923)

   Coblenz G Luzian Wolfgang (1925) Vienna A

Mr. A. Frank, former director of the colony
Stückler Norbert (1925) Vienna A

b Illegal entry into Switzerland:
Garfunkel Hans (1924) Königsberg G
Klein Helga (1925)Mannheim G
Klonover Ruth (1924) Dortmund G
Klonover Margot, Dortmund G Lewin
Leo (1925) Falkenberg G Nussbaum
Lotte, Rheydt G
Schütz Betty, Berlin G

c The group of four:
Kern Margot (1926) Aschersleben G
Rosenblatt Regina (1927) Langendreer G
Salz Peter (1926) Berlin G

d The group of two:
Rosenblatt Else (1925) Langendreer G
Wulf Ilse (1925) Stettin P

3. In France, those who found positions or were officially declared missing:
   Grabkovicz Lixie (1924) Vienna A: Maid in Grenoble
   Herz Ruth (1922): Temporary help in Swiss colony Praz sur Arly
   Kuhlberg Fanny (1929) Hannover G: Farmworker, 12K from Cilly
   Landsmann Peter (1925) Vienna A
   Leistner Rita (1925) Vienna A
   Schütz Ruth (1925) Berlin G. Resistance member
   Steinberg Frieda (1924) Vienna A: Teacher in Mégève
   Stückler Cilly (1929) Vienna A: Farmworker in Caillac

4. The Group of Five who were arrested on the Swiss border on January 1-2, 1943:
   Helft Inge (1926) Wurzen G: deported
   Hochberger Adele (1926) Berlin G: deported
   Joseph Inge (1925) Darmstadt G: succeeded on third attempt to enter Switzerland.
   Strauss Walter (1925) Duisburg G: returned to Château
   Vos Manfred (1924) Cologne G: deported

5. Those sent back at the Swiss border who returned to the Château:
   Blumenfeld Karl (1924) Breslau P
   Elkan Bertrand (1922)
   Klein Kurt ("Onze") (1925) Maltersburg G
   Moser Kurt (1922) Hannover G; later deported
   Nussbaum Adolf ("Addi") (1925) Rheydt G
   Oelbaum Ruedi (1927) Berlin G
   Schragenheim Inge (1924) Cologne G
   Strauss Walter (1925) Duisburg G

6. Individual deportation:
   Dortort Emil: deported March 1, 1943

7. Arrested by the French Police at the Château de La Hille in 1943:
   Brünell Heinz (1925) Camp Gurs, returned to Château
   Elkan Bertrand (1922) Camp Gurs, deported
   Kammerer Manfred (1925) returned to Château
   Schlesinger Ernst, husband of Château's cook, deported
   Strauss Walter (1925) Camp Gurs, deported shortly after his return
   to the Château from the Swiss border

8. Those who found positions outside the Château:
   Blumenfeld Karl (1924) c/o E. Savignol, Lézat/Isère
   Brünell Ilse (1923): in service to Mrs. Authier in Foix
   Mrs. Authier was a very difficult woman who made Ilse suffer.
   She turned out to be an anti-Semitic, pro-Vichy collaborator who
   held a high position at the Police Prefecture in Foix. She had in
   her possession a list of foreigners and Jews to be arrested. She
   had promised the Director to spare those at Château de La Hille
   in exchange for a managerial assistant. She did not keep her
   promise. Ilse's brother Heinz Brünell was one of those arrested at
   La Hille by the Foix police.

   Chaim Edgar (1924): farmworker for Schmutz family in Tambouret
   Herz Georges (1928): farmworker
   Eppstein Werner (1923): farmworker for Schmutz family in
   Tambouret
   Grossmann Leo: agricultural school in La Rochade
   Grossmann Willi: agricultural school in La Rochade
   Kwaczkowski Gerard (1926): farmworker
   Moser Kurt (1925): c/o Milleret, le Conteret/Cérisols
   Stückler Norbert (1925): agricultural school at Le Rochade
   Wertheiner
   Fritz, Heidelberg G?

9. On the escape to Spain, betrayed and arrested:
   Blumenfeld Karl, deported
   Eppstein Werner, deported but survived
   Moser Kurt, deported
   Wertheimer Fritz, deported

10. The "Oder ones" who hid in the *Zwiebekeller* upon the arrival of the
    Gendarmes on September 8, 1943:
    Brünell Heinz and Storosum Heinz, both escaped into the
        underground Jewish organization called 'JOINT'
    Kammerer Manfred, stayed at the Château
    Nussbaum, Addi, fled to Switzerland with Anne-Marie Piguet

11. The illegal border crossing in December 1943 by Gret Tobler
    (Kindergarten teacher at the Château) with two children:
    Bernhard Inge (1928)
    Rosenblatt Toni (1931)

12. The following children successfully entered Switzerland with Anne-
    Marie Piguet (with the help of Victoria and Madeleine Cordier) on her
    way over Mount Risoux:
    Goldapper Edith (1924) Vienna A
    Kammerer Manfred (1925) Berlin G
    Kammerer Walter (1922) Berlin G
    Moser Edith (1924) Hannover G
    Nussbaum, Addi (1925) Rheydt G
    Schlesinger Flora, Cook at La Hille, Vienna A
    Schlesinger Pauli (1929) her son. Vienna A
    Schragenheim Inge (1924) Vienna A

13. Those who went to an Orphanage run by the Franciscan Sisters in
    Pamiers:
    Fernanbuk Eva
    Jankielewitz Edith (1931)
    Kokoyek Guita (1930) Chemnitz G
    Kokotek Irene (1930) Cheminitz G

14. Those who arrived in summer 1944 at the Cloister Lévignac near
    Toulouse:
    Bergmann Peter (Pierre) Vienna A
    Manasse Gustav (1931) Frankfurt G
    Manasse Mane (1935) Frankfurt G
    Peter and Gustav fled, were captured, and fled again.

15. In Toulouse the following met by chance at Mrs. Giselle's, a coworker with the American-Jewish organization known as 'JOINT':

    Bergmann Peter
    Fernanbuk Eva
    Jankielewicz Edith
    Manasse Gustav
    Manasse Mane

    > *With the help of 'JOINT,' Eva, Edith and Peter reached Spain and then Israel (at the time called Palestine); Gustav and Mane went to stay with an uncle in New York, where they eventually were taken in by two Jewish families.*

16. Also with the help of 'JOINT,' the following three reached Andorra after a very difficult three-day hike, and then Spain, and finally Palestine:

    Brünell Ilse
    Schütz Ruth
    Storosum Heinz

17. In Spring 1944 Rosa Goldmark died in the Psychiatric Clinic in Lannemezan F

18. On July 9, 1944 Egon Berlin died fighting in the *Maquis*.

19. In autumn 1944 the following "older ones" were still at Château de La Hille:

    Bravermann Isi, Brussels B
    Dessauer Trude, Bamberg G
    Kuhlberg Rita, Hannover G
    Kriegstein Friedel, Cologne G
    Lind Gerti (1927) Vienna A
    Riemann Renée, probably from Vienna
    Seelenfreund Irma (1921) Frankfurt G
    Storosum Martha (1927) Cologne G
    Vos Henri (1933) Gymnach G

    > *In 1943 most of the Jewish children at the Château de La Hille were between the ages of 15 and 18. The younger ones included: Friedel, Toni, Isi, Mane, Gustav, Henri (brother of Manfred Vos), Inge Bernhard, Peter Bergmann, Edith Jankielewitz, Guita and Irene Kokotek, and Eva Fernanbuk.*

20. Jewish children at the Château who were not among the original 100 children transported from Brussels:

Daniel and Josette Mendes, Besançon F (6 and 7 years old)

Daniel Reingold, St. Malo (12 years old)

Gonda and Samuel Weinberg, Amsterdam (12 and 14 years old)

Rachel Borensztain, France (10 years old)

René Baumgardt, France (8 years old)

Appendix 2: List of names

List of names of those cited in the Text (other than the children):

CORDIER, Madeleine and Victoria. Champagnole. Friends of Anne-Marie's who helped guide those escaping into Switzerland by way of the Jura Mountains.

DARNAND, Joseph. Traitor in the service of the Vichy Government. Founder of the "Milice," the much-feared French Gestapo serving Germany, principally in their struggle against the "Maquisards," the French Resistance fighters. In 1945 Darnand was sentenced to death and shot.

DUBOIS, Maurice. Director of the Swiss Red Cross, Children's Aid office in Toulouse. DUBOIS, Ellen. Mr. Dubois's wife and co-worker.

FRANK, Elka. Director of the General Bernheim Home for girls in Belgium.

FRANK, Alexander, Director of the colony in Seyre following Gaspard Deway, Elka's husband.

GASPARD, Deway. Director of the 100 Jewish children in Seyre.

GILG, Richard. Director of the Swiss Red Cross office following Mr. Dubois.

GROTH, Luise, Director of Château de La Hille during most of Steiger's tenure there.

HÄSLER, Alfred. Writer, and author of the bestseller The Boat Is Full.

KÄGI, Heinrich ("Heiri"). Teacher of the Middle-schoolers at Château de La Hille.

KÄGI, Annelies, his wife. Successor to Mrs. Schlesinger in the kitchen.

KASSER, Elizabeth. Worker at the Swiss Red Cross in Gurs.

LAVAL, Pierre. Prime Minister in Vichy.

LYRER, Eugen. Teacher at Château de La Hille, primarily of the older ones.

MARIMON, Joseph. Spaniard working as gardener at the Château.

MARIMON, Carmine, his wife. Worked in the laundry at the Château.

NADAL, Mr. Spaniard. Woodworker. Built tables, chairs, benches for the Château.

NADAL, Mrs. Worked in the laundry.

NÄF, Rösli, first Director of the Château de La Hille.

OLGIATI, Rodolfo, director of the Swiss Red Cross Children's Aid Society in Bern.

PALAU, Chaime. Spaniard. "Jack-of-all-trades" at the Château.

PALAU, Maria. Housekeeper at the Château.

PARERA, Mr. Spaniard. Worked for Director of Red Cross office in Toulouse.

PÉTAIN, Philippe. Head-of-State in Vichy, appointed by the Germans.

PIGUET, Anne-Marie. Teacher from Le Sentier, Switzerland. Guide.

ROTHMUND, Heinrich. Chief of the Federal Police in Bern, Switzerland. Responsible for the total closure of the Swiss borders, especially to the Jews.

SALVIDE. Chauffeur, coworker for the Swiss Red Cross in Toulouse.

SCHLESINGER, Flora. Cook at the Château.

SCHLESINGER, Ernst. Her husband. Helper at the Château, deported.

SCHMUTZ, Ruedi and Hans, sons of Mrs. Schmutz, farmers in Tambouret.

STUCKY, Walter. Minister in Vichy.

TOBLER, Gret. Kindergarten teacher at Château.

VON STEIGER. President of the Council of State in Bern, Switzerland.

Author's Note: To preserve desired anonymity certain names have been changed in this text.

Appendix 3: List of Places

List of Places mentioned in the text:

Agde	French Camp on the sea, near Bézier
Anderlecht	Belgian town near Brussels, colony for Jewish children
Annemasse	Town on the Swiss border near Geneva. Last train stop for those escaping into Switzerland
Borda Blanca	Hamlet on a hill near Château de La Hille
Champagnole	Small town in the Jura, starting-point for Anne-Marie Piguet's escape route into Switzerland
Cruseilles	Château des Avenières, Red Cross Colony on the Salève
Drancy	Principal transit camp, near Paris. The prisoners—mostly Jewish—were assembled here from other camps in France and sent to concentration camps.
Elnes	Near Perpignan. Home for very young children run by the Swiss Red Cross Children's Aid
Foix	City 20 kilometers from the Château, toward the Pyrénées
Gabre	Protestant village 8 kilometers from the Château. Most of the other villages and towns in the area were Catholic. Heinrich and Annelies Kägi were married here.
Gurs	The largest and worst of the transit camps, in the foothills of the Pyrénées.
La Coste	Remote farm about an hour-and-a-half walk from the Château; Walter Kammerer was hidden there.
Lannemezan	French city, two train stops from Lourdes. Site of Psychiatric Clinic where Rosa Goldmark was taken and where she died.
La Bastide	Small village in France about 7km west of St. Girons. Meeting place with the traitorous "smuggler"
Mas d'Azil	Last stop on the bus line Toulouse—Pailhès
Mazères	Small village about 12km west of St. Girons. Kurt Moser was taken in by a farmer in that area.
Montégut-Plantaurel	Tiny village in the Ariège 2km from the Château de La Hille, which officially belonged to that village.
New Mill	Swimming place set among the rocks, near La Hille

Pailhès	Larger town, with bus station 4 kilometers from the Château
Pamiers	City for getting supplies for the Château 30 kilometers away
Rivesaltes	French Camp on the sea by Perpignan
Route Blanche	Road to the New Mill, to Gabre and to Mas d'Azil
Seyre	Village near Toulouse, first "home" for the 100 Jewish children who had fled from Belgium
Spa	Belgian town near the German border
St. Cergues	Red Cross colony on the Swiss border near Annemasse
St. Cyprien	French Camp south of Perpignan
St. Girons	Town about 25km from the Château. Meeting point for the group hoping to escape to Spain
St. Jean de Vierges	Town on the line between Varilhes-Foix. Train station for those escaping to Switzerland
Toulouse	Capital of the Haute Garonne Department. The bus line Toulouse-Mas d'Azil passed by Pailhès
Tambouret	Farm belonging to the Schmutz family, near Écosse
Tarbes	Larger town, one stop from Lourdes
Varilhes	Town between Pamiers and Foix
Le Vernet	Notorious camp 9km from Pamiers, toward Toulouse
Zven	Belgian town, cite of General Bernheim Home for Jewish girls

Photographs

1. View of the northern façade of the Château de La Hille. At the end of the long mountain ridge, at the far right, is the "New Mill"

2. View of the eastern side of the Château de La Hille

3. The entrance to the Château by way of the tower on the right. The tower in the rear on the left houses a staircase.

4. View from the high boulders at the New Mill. In the center, in the upper third of the picture, is the Château. Near the fork in the White Road is the hamlet of Borda Blanca.

5. Israel "Isi" Bravermann, originally from Brussels, rescued from Camp Vernet (Chapter 13)

6. The workshop behind and to the right of the entrance tower, where water is drawn for the kitchen. Next to the tower: wood for the kitchen and the cistern dug by the older male teenagers in 1941.

7. In the workshop was Mr. Nadal's carpentry shop. In front of the right wing of the building one can see the wheel used to draw the water.

8. Henri Vos from Cologne, one of the Middles. His older brother Manfred was arrested on the Swiss border and deported (Chapter 44).

9. Georges Herz from Germany and Fernand from Toulouse are carrying the giant pail of water between two poles.

10. At the quarry. Our "little train." The Mickeys enjoy sitting in the trolley- cart. Standing: André, Guy and François. Sitting: Jojo, Rose and Josette (Chapter 11).

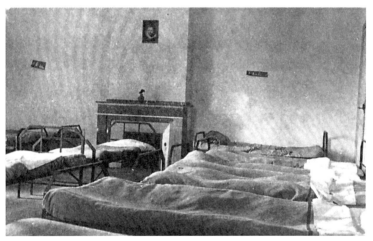

11. The Mickey's large dormitory. In the rear on the far right, next to Percy's bed, is the door where the night pail stands (Chapter 20).

12. Peeling vegetables in front of the kitchen. From left to right: Jojo, Pauli Schlesinger, Pierre, Friedel, Martha Storosom, Fanny Kuhlberg, Edith Moser.

13. Our classroom. The village school loaned us the blackboards. This is where I taught the six-to-ten-year olds, divided into four classes.

14. Edgar Chaim from Berlin, who was rescued by the Swiss farmer from Tambouret (Chapter 10).

15. Georges Costeseque from Pamiers and Mane Manasse, the youngest boy of our one hundred children at the Château at that time.

16. The giant boulders at the New Mill, seen from the rear. Around the bend was our swimming hole. The Maquisards were hiding below these rocks.

17. Anne-Marie Piguet sitting between the sisters Gerti and Cilly Stückler. Anne-Marie knew a safe and sure way into Switzerland.

18. At the end of January it was so warm that we could eat lunch in the Château courtyard!

19. On Taur Street in Toulouse was the Red Cross Aid to Children office. After Mr. Dubois retired because of ill heath, Mr. Gilg became the director.

20. Egon Berlin from Coblenz (in front) with Joseph Dortort on the high rocks at the New Mill. Egon lost his life fighting in the Maquis.

21. Friedel Kriegstein at the New Mill. She was a pupil in my fourth grade (Chapters 76 and 80).

22. Tug-of-war, one of our many activities on the lawn behind the Château.

23. An exception: we are wearing shoes! From left to right, front row: Jojo, Pierrette, Friedel, Marinette, Aurore, Violette, René. Back row: Josette, Guy, André, François, Percy.

24. Josette Mendes, also one of the first-graders with Conchita, on an all-day outing. We had some good soup!

25. Heinrich ("Heiri") Kägi, who arrived at Château La Hille one month after I did and took over teaching the Middles.

26. Conchita Palau, the daughter of the Palau family, refugees from Spain. Mr. and Mrs. Palau were housekeepers at the Château. Mr. Palau was the "jack-of-all-trades."

27. Pierre Costeseque from Pamiers playing marbles.

28. The hundred children who in 1940, after the German invasion of Belgium, fled on a week-long train trip from Brussels to France. They spent a cold, hard winter in Seyre near Toulouse. In spring they arrived at the Château La Hille.

29. Josette Mendes and Daniel Mendes from Besançon, and Lucien Cruc from Boulogne.

30. I am writing a letter and enjoying the sunshine in the courtyard of the Château!

31. Guy Perry from Foix, a first-grader, brother of little Mireille and of Raoul, one of the Middles. Guy is sitting on the running board of the Red Cross truck that bears the insignia of the "Aid to Children," the two children's heads beneath the rays of the Red Cross.

32. The Red Cross truck again, with the children on the loading ramp. In the middle is René Baumgart (Chaper 24).

33. All the Swiss from the Château La de Hille! From left to right: the Director Miss Groth, Sebastian Steiger, the bride and groom Annelies and Heinrich Kägi, Anne-Marie Piguet and Eugen Lyrer.

34. Heiri had the absolutely fabulous idea to rent these farm wagons for the wedding!

35. On the way to Gabre, a Protestant village, where the wedding took place in a small, unadorned room. A farmer from the neighborhood leads the horse.

36. Paulette and Maria on the rear platform of the Red Cross truck on the way home.

37. At the beginning of 1944, the Red Cross truck often came from Toulouse to deliver Swiss food supplies and sometimes newly-arriving children.

38. Mrs. Schlesinger from Vienna. Her husband was arrested at the Château and subsequently deported. Mrs. Schlesinger blamed herself for his arrest.

39. Kurt Klein ("Onze") and Joseph Dortort (right) in the courtyard. Joseph's older brother Emil was deported in March 1943.

40. Heinz ("Henri") Storosum from Cologne, our violinist. (Chaper 80 "Saved by the Violin!").

41. Every evening I would care for the children in the infirmary. One time we had an infestation of lice, which explains why Maria and Monique are wearing "turbans."

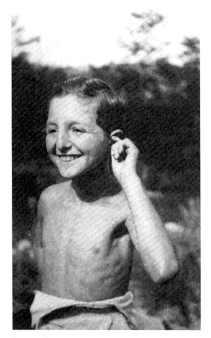

42. Pierre Bergmann from Vienna.

43. An all-day outing with the Middles and a few of the older ones. We watched the "charcoal-miners" at work extracting charcoal in a huge kettle-like container. In the foreground, from left to right: Monique Evrard, Gonda Weinberg, Eva Fernanbuk and Edith Jankielewitz.

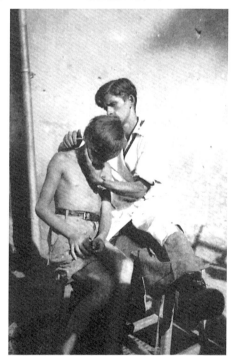

44. With a very painful boil on my leg, I could still cut the children's hair.

45. Mrs. Schlesinger with her girls. From left to right: Irene Kokotek, Irma Seelenfreund, Guita Kokotek, Mrs. Schlesinger, next to her a girl whose name I forget, and on the far right Fanny Kuhlberg.

46. A view of the Château courtyard with the entrance. Next to the entrance are the frequently used tables.

47. Addi Nussbaum (left) with our pianist Walter Kammerer—both from Germany.

48. The girls most in danger. In back, Eva Fernanbuk, Edith Jankielewitz and a girl whose name I no longer recall. Seated in the middle: Rita Kuhlberg, Renée Riemann, Martha Storosum and Trude Dessaur (on the right). I no longer recall the girl on the left.

49. War and terror in the surroundings of our idyllic Château.

50. In the cold of winter, an outing with the wooden clogs (chapter 35).

51. On the way to the Château. Maria Villas from Madrid, Monique Evrard from Nice, Gonda Weinberg from Amsterdam, and, holding my hand, François Clément from Toulouse.

52. On the Red Cross truck! Paulette Abramowitsch in the middle.